Advance Praise for *Future Search in School District Change: Connection, Community, and Results*

"It is my contention that public education in Canada and the United States is the primary vehicle by which democracy continues to enfold ever larger segments of both countries. In this exciting book, the authors provide practical examples of how tested social science principles are put to use in ways basic to human communication and problem solving. The authors provide rich examples of how future search principles guide participants to become the architects of their own future."

—Randall B. Lindsey, acting dean of the School of Education, Moorpark College, and the author of *Cultural Proficiency: A Manual for School Leaders*

"Describing how the future search process harnesses the wisdom and energy of diverse stakeholders to identify school district and community challenges, plan solutions, and move toward positive change, *Future Search in School District Change* covers a wide variety of settings and issues. The future search process transforms the often abstract exercise of planning into real cooperation and wide-ranging investment in school and community success. The clarity of the case studies, the voices of the participants, and the authentic recounting of the future search process in these communities will inspire others to realize that barriers to change are surmountable, even in the face of leadership change, funding challenges, and other obstacles. Educators yearning to transform their district and community environments to create lasting, positive change will experience these stories about how communities got clear, got on board, and made their visions happen as revelations."

—Jill Davidson, editor of *Horace* and the Coalition of Essential Schools

"I found the case studies to be an inspiration for engaging large groups of individuals to focus on acknowledging everyone's contribution and visioning what could be! System change can be an arduous effort, but the book reminds all of us that process is as important as the outcome, and

that systems can and do change when there is involvement and commitment from all stakeholders."

—Darline P. Robles, Ph.D., superintendent of the Los Angeles County Office of Education

"This book offers thoughtful guidance and specific examples of individual and group success for those who are serious about leading systemwide change in their organizations. The case studies illustrate 'strategic planning,' which is often misunderstood, in its highest and best use. As one who has both led and participated in such a process, I can attest to its effectiveness as a way to truly institutionalize meaningful change."

—Stuart E. Gothold, clinical professor at the USC Rossier School of Education

"Leaders seeking to engage their community in creating a positive vision for the future of their schools should read this book first. The future search case studies will guide any district leadership team in using this energizing, positive process to approach the challenges facing its public schools and produce needed results."

—Patricia A. All, Ed.D., deputy superintendent for the Olathe School District, Olathe, Kansas

Leading Systemic School Improvement Series

...helping change leaders transform entire school systems

This ScarecrowEducation series provides change leaders in school districts with a collection of books written by prominent authors with an interest in creating and sustaining whole-district school improvement. It features young, relatively unpublished authors with brilliant ideas, as well as authors who are cross-disciplinary thinkers.

Whether an author is prominent or relatively unpublished, the key criterion for a book's inclusion in this series is that it must address an aspect of creating and sustaining systemic school improvement. For example, books from members of the business world, developmental psychology, and organizational development are good candidates as long as they focus on creating and sustaining whole-system change in school district settings; books about building-level curriculum reform, instructional methodologies, and team communication, although interesting and helpful, are not appropriate for the series unless they discuss how these ideas can be used to create whole-district improvement.

Since the series is for practitioners, highly theoretical or research-reporting books aren't included. Instead, the series provides an artful blend of theory and practice—in other words, books based on theory and research but written in plain, easy-to-read language. Ideally, theory and research are artfully woven into practical descriptions of how to create and sustain systemic school improvement. The series is subdivided into three categories:

Why Systemic School Improvement Is Needed and Why It's Important. This is the *why*. Possible topics within this category include the history of systemic school improvement; the underlying philosophy of systemic school improvement; how systemic school improvement is different from school-based improvement; and the driving forces of standards, assessments, and accountability and why systemic improvement can respond effectively to these forces.

The Desirable Outcomes of Systemic School Improvement. This is the *what*. Possible topics within this category include comprehensive school reform models scaled up to create whole-district improvement; strategic alignment; creating a high-performance school system; redesigning a school system as a learning organization; unlearning and learning mental models; and creating an organization design flexible and agile enough to respond quickly to unanticipated events in the outside world.

How to Create and Sustain Systemic School Improvement. This is the *how*. Possible topics within this category include methods for redesigning entire school systems; tools for navigating complex change; ideas from the "new sciences" for creating systemic change; leadership methods for creating systemic change; evaluating the process and outcomes of systemic school improvement; and financing systemic school improvement.

The series editor, Dr. Francis M. Duffy, can be reached at 301-854-9800 or fmduffy@earthlink.net.

Leading Systemic School Improvement Series
Edited by Francis M. Duffy

Future Search in School District Change

Connection, Community, and Results

Leading Systemic School Improvement Series, No. 4

Rita Schweitz and Kim Martens
with Nancy Aronson

ScarecrowEducation
Lanham, Maryland • Toronto • Oxford
2005

Published in the United States of America
by ScarecrowEducation
An imprint of The Rowman & Littlefield Publishing Group, Inc.
4501 Forbes Boulevard, Suite 200, Lanham, Maryland 20706
www.scarecroweducation.com

PO Box 317
Oxford
OX2 9RU, UK

British Library Cataloguing in Publication Information Available

Library of Congress Cataloging-in-Publication Data

Future Search in School District Change : Connection, Community, and
   Results / edited by Rita Schweitz and Kim Martens with Nancy Aronson.
     p. cm. — (Leading systemic school improvement series ; no. 4)
   Includes bibliographical references and index.
   ISBN 1-57886-165-9 (pbk. : alk. paper)
   1. School improvement programs—Case studies. 2. School management
and organization—Case studies. 3. Educational change—Case studies.
   I. Schweitz, Rita, 1943– . II. Martens, Kim, 1959– . III. Aronson, Nancy.
   IV. Series: Leading systemic school improvement ; no. 4.
   LB2822.8.S43 2005
   379.73—dc22   2004018174

∞™ The paper used in this publication meets the minimum requirements of
American National Standard for Information Sciences—Permanence of Paper
for Printed Library Materials, ANSI/NISO Z39.48-1992.
Manufactured in the United States of America.

To all children who have joined the effort to make the best education possible available to everyone.

To leaders who have recognized the value of bringing future search to education.

To participants who use future search to make a difference in their communities.

To Marvin Weisbord and Sandra Janoff for developing future search and generously sharing their knowledge with the world.

To our colleagues who contribute to and believe in quality education for all.

To our families, a simple thanks for your support.

Contents

Contributors' Foreword

We wrote this book for all the people who truly want every child to have the best education possible—the students, parents, teachers, businesspeople, health and social service providers, police, and academics—the whole community! We have experienced what we have written about. Each case is a unique story set in its own local context; however, all of us have used future search to enable positive changes to occur in the school system in each of our very different situations. We hope you will be inspired to take a leadership role in making your education system the best it can be. These stories show that you need not sit at the top of your system's traditional hierarchy to make a difference. If you have the desire to lead in a way that encourages others to do their best, you should consider engaging your community in a future search. It will enable you to enlist many people in working together to create a better learning environment and a better system to educate students equally and individually. We hope that you will be inspired to apply the practices we describe. We believe that education is the great equalizer and that all citizens on our planet have the right to a high-quality education that will enable them to improve the quality of life in their communities.

—Nancy Aronson, Beverly Arsht, Emily Axelrod,
Rosemarie Barbeau, Mary Ann Bobosky, Claudia Chowaniec,
Sandee Crowther, Pat Deans, Michael Erwin, Karen Symms Gallagher,

Ray Gordezky, Jim Grieve, Sally Hilderbrand, Sandra Janoff,
Vera Jashni, Jean Katz, Chris Kloth, Rebecca Love, Kim Martens,
James Merritt, Sara Mullett, Kenoli Oleari, Jim Parry, Catherine Perme,
Alexa Posng, Sue Rowan, Rita Schweitz, Ken Seeley,
Shelley Sweet, and Marvin Weisbord

Preface

Both of us have experienced the power of future search in our work with school districts, individual schools, and other organizations. We have seen how bringing the whole system into the room and providing an opportunity for meaningful conversation has produced results not previously believed possible. We have heard from our clients that the energy and actions following their future searches are still producing positive results years later.

> The students in future searches are always memorable. Most begin unsure how they will relate to all of the adults in the room, especially educational and community leaders. Some are shy and some are cocky. As the meeting progresses, they find their voices. They speak out in the large group and add ideas in small groups. They are the reason for the future search. They are tomorrow's leaders taking a leadership role today.
>
> —Rita Schweitz

> One memory that stands out is when a judge participating at a district future search in Canada stood up and passionately declared, "I think it shows that we care, we have hope, and we're not dictated by polls. We are dictated by *children* and by love. This is not a political agenda. We are people who care deeply about children. And I think that's important."
>
> —Kim Martens

We agreed to take the lead on this book because we knew that other Future Search Network members had had experiences similar to ours and would also contribute their stories. There were articles about school-district future searches in the Future Search Network's newsletter, *FutureSearching: Exploring Common Ground for Community Action*. Reports were on the future search listserv and website, www.futuresearch.net. We also knew many of us would enlist school-district leaders to help tell these stories from their unique, insider points of view. Their words would express the reality of what it means to lead and live this change. What we hadn't imagined was how powerful these stories would be.

We are eager to share these stories with school administrators, school boards, parents, teachers, and government officials—everyone interested in making improvements in education. Future search is a method to find common ground and make wide-scale, positive change within the education system, even in difficult situations.

HOW THIS BOOK IS ORGANIZED

This book contains 16 compelling case studies arranged in five parts, with an epilogue. Together they illustrate how future search creates a lasting, whole-system change based on a radical principle: getting in the same room those who have authority, resources, information, expertise, and need. These cases document innovative initiatives in rural, suburban, and urban schools in both Canada and the United States on such key issues as districtwide strategic plans, racial divisions, curriculum reform, community partnerships, and district amalgamation. The original drafts of these cases contained more examples and details.

Each part is based on an underlying theme that runs through its cases. It was not easy settling on these themes because of the rich and detailed nature of the chapters. Many chapters could have fit into more than one part. To help you peruse the book, we have included table P.1, which lists themes and the chapters in which they are presented.

We hope that this organization will help you see the patterns and lessons illustrated in the case studies. Here's what you will find in each part:

Part 1: Demographic Variety. This part opens with a table that outlines the demographics of the 12 school districts discussed. The two future searches described later in the part involve school districts of vastly dif-

Table P.1.   Themes and Chapters

Theme	Chapters
Inclusion, equity, and equality	Chapter 1: Lawrence, Kansas Chapter 4: Ottawa–Carleton, Ontario Chapter 10: Santa Monica, California Chapter 11: Novato, California Chapter 14: Franklin County, Ohio
Schools as centers/hubs	Chapter 1: Lawrence, Kansas Chapter 2: Toronto, Ontario Chapter 4: Ottawa–Carleton, Ontario Chapter 6: North Platte, Nebraska
Engaging the frontline and supporting operational leaders	Chapter 1: Lawrence, Kansas Chapter 3: Carson City, Nevada Chapter 4: Ottawa–Carleton, Ontario Chapter 5: Perkiomen Valley, Pennsylvania Chapter 12: Montreal, Quebec Chapter 15: University of Southern California's Rossier School of Education
Opportunities for people to choose leadership roles and responsibilities, take initiative, and take risks	Chapter 1: Lawrence, Kansas Chapter 2: Toronto, Ontario Chapter 7: Naperville, Illinois Chapter 8: San Gabriel, California Chapter 13: North Montgomery Technical Career Center, Pennsylvania Chapter 16: Kansas State Department of Education
Creating processes or structures that respond to changes and providing stability while allowing for flexibility	Chapter 1: Lawrence, Kansas Chapter 3: Carson City, Nevada Chapter 5: Perkiomen Valley, Pennsylvania Chapter 9: Minneapolis, Minnesota Chapter 12: Montreal, Quebec Chapter 14: Franklin County, Ohio
Descriptions of process champion, community coordinator, and organizational weaver	Chapter 5: Perkiomen Valley, Pennsylvania Chapter 6: North Platte, Nebraska Chapter 7: Naperville, Illinois Chapter 12: Montreal, Quebec Chapter 14: Franklin County, Ohio Chapter 15: University of Southern California's Rossier School of Education
Future search as part of a strategic planning process	Chapter 3: Carson City, Nevada Chapter 4: Ottawa-Carleton, Ontario Chapter 5: Perkiomen Valley, Pennsylvania Chapter 10: Santa Monica, California Chapter 12: Montreal, Quebec Chapter 13: North Montgomery Technical Career Center, Pennsylvania

(continued)

Table P.1. Themes and Chapters (*continued*)

Theme	Chapters
	Chapter 15: University of Southern California's Rossier School of Education
	Chapter 16: Kansas State Department of Education
Setting boundaries and establishing non-negotiability to facilitate appropriate contributions	Chapter 5: Perkiomen Valley, Pennsylvania
	Chapter 15: University of Southern California's Rossier School of Education
	Chapter 16: Kansas State Department of Education
Standardization and centralization to meet local needs	Chapter 3: Carson City, Nevada
	Chapter 10: Santa Monica, California
Providing for health and mental health needs of students so they will be able to learn	Chapter 4: Ottawa-Carleton, Ontario
	Chapter 6: North Platte, Nebraska
	Chapter 8: San Gabriel, California
	Chapter 9: Minneapolis, Minnesota
Labor management	Chapter 2: Toronto, Ontario
	Chapter 7: Naperville, Illinois
	Chapter 9: Minneapolis, Minnesota
	Chapter 12: Montreal, Quebec
Synchronicity	Chapter 9: Minneapolis, Minnesota
	Chapter 12: Montreal, Quebec
	Chapter 14: Franklin County, Ohio
Social capital	Chapter 6: North Platte, Nebraska
Moving the system from fragmentation to coherence	Chapter 5: Perkiomen Valley, Pennsylvania
	Chapter 10: Santa Monica, California
	Chapter 11: Novato, California
	Chapter 15: University of Southern California's Rossier School of Education
Trust building	Chapter 3: Carson City, Nevada
	Chapter 7: Naperville, Illinois
Achievement	Chapter 10: Santa Monica, California
	Chapter 13: North Montgomery Technical Career Center, Pennsylvania
Sustaining momentum	Chapter 1: Lawrence, Kansas
	Chapter 5: Perkiomen Valley, Pennsylvania
	Chapter 6: North Platte, Nebraska
	Chapter 9: Minneapolis, Minnesota
	Chapter 14: Franklin County, Ohio
	Chapter 13: North Montgomery Technical Career Center, Pennsylvania

Table P.1. Themes and Chapters (*continued*)

Theme	Chapters
Return on expectations	Chapter 1: Lawrence, Kansas
	Chapter 2: Toronto, Ontario
	Chapter 5: Perkiomen Valley, Pennsylvania
Bond issue and procuring funds	Chapter 3: Carson City, Nevada
	Chapter 6: North Platte, Nebraska
	Chapter 7: Naperville, Illinois
Amalgamation and mergers	Chapter 2: Toronto, Ontario
	Chapter 4: Ottawa–Carleton, Ontario
	Chapter 12: Montreal, Quebec
Establishing and augmenting the professional learning community	Chapter 2: Toronto, Ontario
	Chapter 14: Franklin County, Ohio
	Chapter 16: Kansas State Department of Education

ferent sizes. The Lawrence Public School District in chapter 1 was interested in finding a strategic planning method to help it institutionalize its long-term goals. Lawrence has 10,000 students in 22 schools. The Toronto District School Board in chapter 2 wanted to explore how its seven merged school boards could come together on their most important task—educating their children. TDSB has 300,000 students in 558 schools.

Part 2: Leadership Perspectives and Tools. This part includes accounts of whole-district transformation in three districts, related from the leadership point of view. In chapter 3, Jim Parry, retired superintendent of Carson City, NV, schools, sponsored 14 future searches across the entire district to launch a districtwide strategic plan. In chapter 4, Jim Grieve, former superintendent of the Ottawa–Carleton District School Board in Ontario, describes how future search and the voice of community have changed the nature of his work, guided his actions, and redefined his role. In chapter 5, Director of Curriculum Sally Hilderbrand and former Superintendent Carole Spahr, of the Perkiomen Valley School District, PA, exemplify specific leadership roles that influenced strong, positive, and lasting change.

Part 3: Growing Community Partnerships. This part offers four examples of how future search can lead to strong community partnerships. In chapter 6, during a future search in North Platte, NE, the community agreed to focus on "schools as centers." Future search participants mobilized the community, established the program, and received over $1.5 million in federal and foundation grants. In chapter 7, Naperville, IL, stakeholders built community collaborations to support quality education and succeeded in passing a school referendum that had previously failed. Both the San Gabriel, CA, School District in chapter 8 and the Minneapolis, MN, School District in chapter 9 focused on health care with a belief that healthy students make good learners. These systems built coalitions with the local government, healthcare professionals, and local hospitals to increase health services to students and their families.

Part 4: Including Student Voices. The chapters in this part illustrate how influential student voices become when they are invited to participate. In chapter 10, during the future search in Santa Monica, CA, a number of disenfranchised students spoke up for inclusion, equity, equality, and closing the achievement gap. In chapter 11, the Novato, CA, future search focused on creating and sustaining a safe, just, and respectful learning environment after racial incidents tore at the school community. In chapter 12, following the Lester B. Pearson School District future search, students formed a council that has become an official consultative group to the board while another group is busy helping create flexible timetabling for the high school.

Part 5: Beyond the District. The concluding part of this book offers four examples of future search in nondistrict educational contexts with relevance to school districts. The North Montgomery County (PA) Technical Career Center in chapter 13 was on the brink of closing its doors when it held the system's first future search, which transformed its program and image. A biotechnical summit using future search principles and a second future search charting a course for new growth further accelerated its progress. In Franklin County, OH, in chapter 14, three future searches over 10 years led to a statewide policy on the access, quality, and affordability of child-care and early education that ultimately was written into law. The University of Southern California's Rossier School of Education in chapter 15 involved the whole faculty and its stakeholders in transforming its academic program. The faculty redesigned the curriculum and engaged in coordinated planning across all divisions of the organization. Lastly, in chapter 16, the Kansas State Department of Education's future search allowed stakeholders to reenvision the leadership role of this agency and deepen the partnerships among levels of the education system in the state.

Following the case studies, the epilogue summarizes some of the key points from the chapters, answers practical questions about implementing a future search, and suggests some ideas to get you started.

ACKNOWLEDGMENTS

This book has been a learning experience for both of us. We've been educated by our fellow authors as well as by others who have coached and mentored us during this adventure. We would like to acknowledge the hard work of everyone connected to this book and recognize the spirit of cooperation and colleagueship that was developed during the project. We would especially like to thank Nancy Aronson, Ray Gordezky, Beverly Arsht, and Jim Parry for their assistance in the overall organization of the book and their moral support throughout. We would also like to thank Yael S. Zofi, CEO, and Nita St. Hilaire, associate, both of AIM Strategies Applied Innovative Management, for illustrating the roadmap in chapter 15. We are indebted to Kyle Martens (Kim's son) for his assistance in the production of the graphics.

—Rita Schweitz and Kim Martens

Introduction:
Future Search in Education

Marvin Weisbord and Sandra Janoff

When we started Future Search Network in 1993, we had no idea that this planning process would make its way around the world. Least of all did we anticipate that network members soon would be helping school administrators to revolutionize their districts' capabilities for action and gain significant community support. The chapters in this book testify to some remarkable adaptations of future search by leaders and ordinary citizens in school systems across Canada and the United States. The cases include districts as small as North Platte, NE, with 11 schools and 3,870 students, and as massive as Toronto, ON, with 558 schools and 300,000 students.

The use of future search in schools was initially driven by amalgamation of school districts in Canada and by mandates in many states to include multiple stakeholders in strategic planning. Several districts that had used traditional planning methods discovered they could go farther, faster by involving diverse stakeholders than with expert-driven strategic planning exercises. Future search proved to be a flexible method that could be used at any level from single schools to whole districts.

In each case presented here a community faced new educational dilemmas: draconian funding cuts, school board mergers, racial and ethnic tensions, massive overhauls, school closings, and government mandates. Those who chose future search often had to confront their own and others' considerable skepticism about the wisdom of widespread community involvement in school planning. Those who acted on future search principles, involving students, parents, and diverse citizens, were rewarded with remarkable community consensus on educational goals and widely supported strategic plans.

FUTURE SEARCH PRINCIPLES

The keys to success with this method are a set of principles derived from research, theory, and practice going back 65 years:

- Getting the "whole system" in the room. By whole system we mean diverse stakeholders who have the authority, resources, expertise, information, and need to act right away if they choose.
- Exploring the whole before seeking to fix any part. When people put in what they know, all will gain an understanding of the whole that none had coming in, making possible actions built on a shared frame of reference.
- Putting the future and common ground front and center. Problems and conflicts become *information* to be shared, not action items. The agenda is a search for shared goals and mutually supported plans.
- Inviting self-management and responsibility for action. Groups can do much more than what is customarily asked of them. Each time leaders or consultants do something for a group they deprive everyone else of ownership.

Over several years we created a simple meeting plan to actualize these principles that is now used in Africa, Asia, Australia, Europe, and the Americas. We think of future search in three related dimensions, all illustrated in this book. First, future search refers to a planning meeting design based on the above principles. Second, it embodies a theory and philosophy of facilitating that might be characterized as "doing less so that participants can do more." Finally, future search enables a whole system change strategy requiring no special training or vocabulary. It is grounded in people's firsthand experiences and values of inclusion, discovery, wholeness, and hope.

FUTURE SEARCH ROOTS

To enhance your appreciation of the cases, we want to tell you of this method's origins. It derives from theory and research going back many decades. Future search is neither a fad nor a panacea. It is the result of intense, serious work on human capabilities and aspirations. In 1938, the late Ronald Lippitt arrived at the State University of Iowa to study social psychology with Kurt Lewin, a German refugee. In groundbreaking controlled experiments, they showed dramatic differences in the behavior of 10-year-old boys engaged in crafts projects under authoritarian, laissez-faire, and democratic leaders. They noted how the boys tended to exhibit task focus and mutual support or aggression and apathy in response to a leader's behavior. The same person could lead a group to productivity or alienation, depending on whether the boys were involved in setting goals and making decisions. Lewin and Lippitt coined a term for their discovery: *group dynamics.*

They soon joined with others (including Margaret Mead) in experiments leading to the development of participative management, human relations training, group problem solving, and, in 1947, to the founding of NTL Institute in Bethel, Maine. In the 1950s Lippitt, studying strategic planning groups using methods he helped to invent, concluded that problem solving often depressed people. He began working with "images of potential," developing a method for envisioning preferred futures that energized all who used it. In the 1970s Lippitt and Eva Schindler-Rainman, a community development consultant, teamed up to work with dozens of North American cities and towns on planning desirable futures. In each they got together a demographic cross-section of local residents to create action plans in future-oriented meetings that they called "Collaborative Communities." From this stream of work came our principles of "whole system in the room" and future focus.

Across the Atlantic, parallel developments were taking place. In 1939, for example, the late Eric Trist, a Cambridge-trained psychologist who was also a Lewin disciple, teamed up with psychiatrist Wilfred Bion to select field officers for the British Army. They put candidates into leaderless groups to solve field problems, and soon found the best leaders were those who could balance self-interest and group interest. After the war, they too devised new group dynamics methods, setting up the Tavistock Institute of Human Relations in London, England. They integrated principles of self-management into a group planning method in which people began by studying a system's history and external relations, discovering that this way of working greatly reduced "fight or flight." They dubbed this new form of group planning the "Search Conference." From their work came our principles of having everyone discover the whole and self-managing their work.

When 120 of us got together in 1993 to found the Future Search Network, we organized around this shared legacy. From these social science pioneers we derived principles and techniques that enabled whole systems, within a few days, to do planning that many people previously had thought impossible. We called our process *future search*, honoring the future-oriented conferences of Schindler-Rainman and Lippitt and the Search Conferences invented by Emery and Trist.

ORIENTATION TO FUTURE SEARCH

A typical future search involves 60 to 70 people, though hundreds can meet in parallel or sequential conferences. Most future searches take four half days. The agenda consists of five explorations: past, present, future, common ground, and action. In each segment, people work in small groups, present their deliberations to the whole, engage in dialogue on what they learn, and consider the implications for action. See the following for an example:

Day 1 (half day)—People explore the **PAST** from personal, global, and local (school, district, or issue) perspectives by noting milestones on long strips of paper (time lines) on the wall. They establish their history, differences, and shared values. Next, the whole group diagrams **PRESENT** external trends that are shaping their lives. This large visual map (mind map) reflects each person's observations. Before the end of the day, people affix colored dots to trends they feel passionate about.

Day 2 (full day)—Stakeholder groups review key trends and tell what they are doing now and what they want to do about them in the future. People describe what they are proudest of and sorriest about in their own efforts related to the task (prouds and sorries). Mixed groups develop scenarios of their desired **FUTURE** and enact them in creative ways. They also tell how they overcame barriers along the way (future scenarios). Before closing for the day, the whole conference notes **COMMON GROUND** among all stakeholders.

Day 3 (half day)—Common ground is confirmed by the whole group in an extended dialogue where people also note issues that are not agreed (reality dialogue). They make **ACTION PLANS** for projects and programs that will make the common ground themes live and decide how they will follow up.

Future search enables action on many fronts at once. One common thread in the cases presented in this book is the way educational leaders used their future search outputs to create an umbrella of support for new policies and procedures. Most got a great deal more implementation of action plans from future searches than had been accomplished previously in months or years of struggle. While these are just a few of the hundreds of education future searches in systems around the world, they show the power of dialogue, discovery, and hope. We are sure you will be as enlightened and stimulated as we were in reviewing these inspiring accounts. We hope that the stories here will enhance your appreciation of the rich educational planning legacy that can be yours if you choose to claim it.

Part 1

DEMOGRAPHIC VARIETY

One of the first things we are asked when discussing the possibility of a future search within a school district is whether another district of similar size and demographics successfully has used future search to achieve similar results that the current district is hoping for. Our response is that demographic differences have little impact on the kinds of results that can be achieved. Having said this, we have put together a school district demographic table (see table P1.1) to illustrate the range of populations in the systems discussed in this book to assure readers that future search has been used successfully in a district similar to their own. The chapters themselves delineate other similarities and differences with respect to desired outcomes and current challenges.

The two chapters in this section illustrate how future search can be used in a small district as well as in a very large one. Both districts share a strong desire to make education the best it can be for all children.

Lawrence, KS (chapter 1), is a district with 10,000 students. Its future search unfolded in a fairly typical way. People across the community and within the education system came together around a shared goal of improving education. The district continues to use the outcomes from the future search as a framework for districtwide decision making.

In contrast, Toronto, ON (chapter 2), is one of the largest school districts in North America, and the largest educational system in which future search has been used. Here the future search was anything but

Table P1.1.   School District Demographics

Name	Population	Student Population	Number of Schools	Area sq. miles
Chapter 6				
North Platte, NE	24,000	3,870	11	10.8
Chapter 5				
Perkiomen Valley, PA	29,000	5,000	7	30
Chapter 8				
San Gabriel, CA	39,804	6,000+	9	4.1
Chapter 11				
Novato, CA	47,630	7,794	17	28
Chapter 3				
Carson City, NV	54,000	8,400	9	30
Chapter 1				
Lawrence, KS	80,000	10,000	22	28
Chapter 10				
Santa Monica and Malibu, CA	102,000	12,500	16	79
Chapter 7				
Naperville, IL	130,000	19,000	23	36.5
Chapter 12				
Montreal, QC	450,380	33,000+	59	359
Chapter 9				
Minneapolis, MN	382,700	47,661	133	58.72
Chapter 4				
Ottawa–Carleton, ON	710,000	~ 80,000	145	1,715
Chapter 2				
Toronto, ON	2.5 million	~ 300,000	558	393

straightforward. Despite unanticipated disruptions and changes imposed upon the system, Toronto continues to make headway on some of the goals established during its future search. This chapter gives the reader a good idea of the challenges and realities of making systemic change in a large school district.

1

Lawrence Public Schools: Institutionalized Goals

Nancy Aronson, Emily Axelrod, and Sandee Crowther

When the idea for this book was in its early stages of development, we called Dr. Sandee Crowther, the executive director of planning and program improvement, to understand what significance, if any, the future search conference in January 1999 had in the life of the Lawrence Public Schools. We knew that the superintendent who initiated the process had left within the following year and wondered if the momentum for the initiative had gone with her. We had our doubts about what would be learned from this case. Nonetheless, we asked if the future search had led to meaningful, systemic change.

"Well," Sandee said, "The goals from the conference are alive and institutionalized."

"What does that mean?" we asked.

She replied, "We use the goals to guide all district decision making."

"Oh! Perhaps there *is* a story here!"

INSTITUTIONALIZED GOALS

As we asked more questions, we came to understand the significance of this seemingly simple statement. As we write this in the summer of 2003, it has been a time of compressed resources in education, particularly financial. The impact is being felt on a local, state, and national level. School districts are facing severe funding constraints. As one board member described,

3

"There is a state and local financial crisis. We're dismantling some things—and it is disappointing." Given this economic environment, we were interested in understanding how the goals were being used as a framework for decision making. Here are some examples we were given:

- The goals guide where the district commits resources. They serve as a common frame of reference. A budget and program evaluation committee was formed by the board to determine the best use of resources. It uses a rubric that was developed based on the goals. This rubric is analyzed and refined every year.
- One of the goals, recruiting and retaining a high-quality staff, has remained an important focus for the district. The leadership has found ways to maintain competitive teacher salaries, even in the midst of budget shortfalls. The district and board continue to maintain very favorable class sizes. Recognition for teachers and staff has been expanded. Principals have increased their efforts to support all teachers in their accountability for improved student performance.
- The goals are a living document. As one board member noted, "The goals did not get put on a shelf. The future search gave a different kind of start and sense of accountability. The goals are institutionalized into the annual strategic plan." Administrators update the board by describing what's happening with respect to goal areas. Even as the board changes, the goals provide a frame of reference for discussion and decision making.
- The goals are part of every community presentation by district leadership.
- When the district works on standards, three questions are asked: What do we want? What did the community say they wanted? How can we work toward that desired future?
- Funding decisions feel less arbitrary. One veteran board member described, "In the past, there was a perception that resources went to whomever begged better." Because the framework and decision-making rubrics are transparent, trust has increased.

As the current superintendent, Randy Weseman, notes, "During a time of minimal resources, you better know what you believe. The goals that were developed at the future search conference reflect what the community envisioned for its school district. It was an important starting point—a solid foundation. If you don't have this, you're always starting over."

THE IMPACT OF INSTITUTIONALIZED GOALS

As school district and community members talked about the goals, they identified what has been accomplished. This is summarized in a subsequent section of this chapter. They also talked about some shifts in system dynamics that are worth noting, specifically less fragmentation and more trust and less divisiveness.

Less Fragmentation

"Instead of the popcorn effect, the actions being taken are within a framework." This quotation from a building administrator captures a certain sentiment that we heard as we met with different groups to understand the impact of the future search conference. People described feeling less fragmented and more aligned. As a teacher noted, "The district pulled together and we're aligned around goals." Given that Lawrence is a community of 80,000 people with 10,000 students attending 22 schools and with many programs including local, state, and federal initiatives to meet a broad spectrum of student needs, this is a remarkable accomplishment. As one district office person said, "We are able to tell 'why' when questioned about a decision or program."

District office and building-level administrators credited the fact that ideas and initiatives are clearly tied to a larger picture for people feeling less *dumped on* (participant words) by those above them in the hierarchy.

More Trust and Less Divisiveness

The Lawrence community has always had strong opinions about education. In the past, the discussions could be very divisive, with people taking positions rather than seeking understanding. This has shifted and communication has improved. One of the contributing factors is being able to reference the future search conference and asking, "What did the community say?" The experience of the conference and the goals that were created serve as a powerful, positive reference point. As a parent who is a member of the district curriculum committee stated, "When issues come up, memories of the future search conference get triggered. We go back to the goals, instead of a knee jerk reaction."

The goals have been an anchor for this district and this community. They have provided a focus and a foundation as the district navigates the waters of continuous educational improvement during difficult economic times. The superintendent who initiated the future search conference, Dr. Kathleen Williams, had specific reasons for holding the conference and saw the potential of what could be accomplished. Let's take a step back in time.

THE DECISION TO HAVE A FUTURE SEARCH CONFERENCE

In August 1998 Kathleen Williams took over the leadership of the district. The importance of having a community conversation about the future of education became clear to her. As she said in January 1999, in her opening remarks at the future search conference:

> When I arrived in Lawrence . . . I was trying to glean a sense of exactly where this community, internal and external, wanted me to lead the district. . . . I have been made aware of what seems like hundreds of do's and don'ts through a variety of formal and informal lobbying efforts. . . . I have been unable to get a handle on what it is that this community can agree upon with regard to its children and their schooling. . . . We needed an opportunity for members of this community to . . . confirm their mutual values, and commit to action grounded in reality—an opportunity for everyone to share leadership and participate as peers. A future search conference is one vehicle to accomplish that and thus, the purpose for your being here is to set priorities and goals for the education of our community's students and to chart a course to the future.

Maley Wilkins, then president of the Lawrence Board of Education, invited 100-plus members of the Lawrence School District and community to give the district direction and answer the question, "Where should we take our schools in the future?" This diverse group of parents, teachers, administrators, board members, students, community partners, postsecondary educators, government officials, and support staff studied their past and present and found common ground for their desired future. They agreed upon six goals and identified key initiatives for exploration under each goal.

Student-centered schools. Schools will be student-centered environments that ensure that all students learn academic and life skills to reach their maximum potential. Key initiatives: design and deliver curriculum and instruction that are responsive to students' individualized needs; offer challenging, rigorous, and comprehensive curriculum; and build on the successes of early childhood and alternative programs.

High-quality staff. The district will recruit, develop, and retain only high-quality staff to educate and support all students and demonstrate the staff's value to our community. Key initiatives: reduce class size; offer serious, continuous districtwide training and education of staff; work to enhance salaries; and build on partnerships with universities.

Comprehensive schools. The Lawrence Public Schools will be comprehensive centers for accessible community services. Key initiatives: revisit and expand school designs; assess existing information to determine needs; explore existing facilities and resources; and build on collaboration with all community stakeholders.

Technology. The district will expand and integrate technology into all phases of the educational process. Key initiatives: develop a comprehensive technology funding plan; have equity in access to technology; create a curriculum-driven plan for instructional technology; and create a technology-based maintenance budget.

Resources. The district will evaluate existing resources and identify additional educational support. Key initiatives: assess existing and potential funding and grants; increase lobbying efforts; consolidate and coordinate resources; and build on city/county school district coordination.

Collaboration and teamwork. The district will implement effective collaboration and teamwork and continuously involve our community in setting, refining, and implementing goals and initiatives. Key initiatives: form an interagency council; establish city/county board of education regular meetings; develop a districtwide student council; and build on relationships with University of Kansas (KU) and Haskell for professional development.

NEW LEVEL OF SYSTEM AWARENESS

There is a story underlying the Lawrence future search. It is the journey from the district being what a member of the superintendent's advisory team described as a *confederation* to seeing the district as one system. One of the key results of the future search was that participants had the opportunity to see the big picture. They saw the school system in relation to the community and saw how the parts fit together. One of the Lawrence School Board members said, "The pieces of the puzzle came together and began to fall into place." As a result of institutionalized goals and an emphasis on system awareness, Bruce Passman, executive director of student services, who is new to the district, says, "One of the reasons I came here is it is a school system not a system of schools."

What Is Meant by *System?*

A school district is a complex, dynamic system with many interrelated parts. People assume a variety of roles such as teacher, support staff, student, administrator, etc. There are the schools themselves across different levels and different curricula. People are most familiar with their part of the system and rarely know what happens in other parts. They rarely have a chance to get a view of the whole district. They seldom take the time to reflect on the district's relationship to its larger environment. As Randy Weseman, the superintendent, said, "The personality of the future search is you get to know all of the system—get to know it as a whole."

The Future Search Conference and System Awareness

The concept of system awareness was created in three ways at the conference. One was getting the parts of the system together to talk, another was mapping the district's relationship to its environment, and the third was creating shared goals.

   Getting the parts together to talk. The first element of creating system awareness was literally getting the variety of stakeholders in the room together. People from different parts of the school system and the community shared information, dreams, and different perspectives. They connected with each other. A county commissioner remarked, "After spending three days with all these people you got to know them as whole human beings—not just their roles."

Mapping the district's relationship to its environment. Another way to understand the system was to visually map the external environment. All 100 participants were encouraged to share ideas about what was currently impacting the system. In doing so, people saw the relationship between the district and the larger educational and societal trends. Often the stakeholder groups saw things differently. As one parent said, "There were many different points of view and some conflictual ones." However, seeing the different views in their entirety gave everyone an expanded view of the current capabilities in the system and what was desired for the future.

Creating shared goals. As superintendent Randy Weseman said, "The future search conference showed our interdependence and where we could come to agreement." Participants could see parts of their ideas in the goals that were being created.

The future search established a model of many different stakeholders coming together to share information openly, form relationships, and acknowledge their identity as a school system. This type of system awareness is important because it enables people to have a greater sense of where they fit in the whole and where they can take aligned action. We would assert that using a systems lens and reinforcing that lens through activities and structures over time is at the heart of how goals get institutionalized. This district was, and is, tenacious in keeping the goals alive through focus and follow-up.

Using a System Lens

There were several activities and structures that reinforced and nurtured this system lens. Three major initiatives and events took place in the 18 months following the future search conference that reinforced the goals and nurtured the values that the future search conference had laid in place.

The curriculum management audit. The curriculum management audit was a comprehensive study of curriculum, instruction, and assessment in the district. The 11 recommendations from the audit were complementary and added depth to the district goals. As one school board member said, "This audit was an opportunity for the board and staff to reinforce the goals.

We did this by linking the recommendations to the goals." A key result of this audit was a major change to school board policy development. The format and procedures that had been in place were inconsistent and not in support of curriculum alignment. A totally revamped format and set of procedures has now been institutionalized. Other recommendations from the June 1999 audit have been integrated throughout the district strategic plan.

Junior high scheduling summit. Ninety stakeholders including parents, teachers, school board members, students, administrators, and representatives from higher education came together for a three-day summit to develop recommendations for new ways to organize time across the four junior high schools. A year and a half later, administrators and teachers discussed the impact of the restructuring to a block-type schedule. A sample of their responses follows:

- It convinces teachers to think more about outcomes. We have to move from thinking about *pages* to thinking about *concepts*.
- In the block, students are able to use more class time for understanding the material.
- There is more time for writing. Writing scores have improved on state writing assessments. We even have time to do writing in math!
- The increased time block (plus inclusion) has had a positive impact on students with developmental disabilities. They've made greater strides academically and socially and have more of a place in the school community.

Back to the future search meeting. This meeting was designed to reconvene participants from the original future search conference and gather ideas for moving forward, reinforce the process, and update people on the system. Information was shared, more relationships were built, and creative ideas were implemented. The meeting was organized to balance the presenting of information with gathering input and providing time for joint planning, with the benefit of diverse stakeholders in the room.

Information Flow—The Lifeblood of a System

Members of the school district used a variety of structures and practices to keep information visible and circulating in the system. Some of the communication structures were already in place; others were newly created. Meetings are structured to ensure that many perspectives are heard and valued. The intent is for all parts of the system to get a better understanding of what's happening across the district.

The future search goals progress committee. This committee was active in communicating the goals to the Lawrence school/community and in keeping the spirit of the conference alive. Julie Boyle, director of communications, helped this group formulate and implement their ideas. The group kept the goals visible during the first year following the future search conference through presentations at various district and community forums; regular updates in the local newspaper, in school newsletters, and on the district website; and a presentation and video on the public access channel.

School liaisons. Each school's site council has a central office and a school board member liaison. Information flows down as these liaisons connect the school to the larger system picture. At the same time, the activities and ideas at each school flow up and shape and inform the whole system picture. This flow allows each entity—site councils, board members, and central office administrators—to be more supportive and understanding of each other.

District meetings. Meetings involving district office personnel have been designed to foster broader involvement and increased information flow and connection across the various departments and groups within the district. For example, the educational programming team meetings are held one day a week. Two structures are used. First, all district office administrators involved in educational programming meet for an hour. The purpose of this meeting is problem solving and planning. Next the executive directors have a series of 30-minute meetings with the various departments to review accomplishments and address specific needs and concerns. Meeting notes are circulated to group members and the superintendent.

The superintendent also runs a series of meetings designed to keep members of the system aware of what's happening and connected to the larger picture. Each meeting has a different purpose:

- The district administrative meeting involves district office administrators and key support staff. The meeting has three purposes: for people to get to know each other better, to keep each other apprised about what's happening, and to set the school board agenda.

- The district management team meets monthly. The purpose of this meeting is for the district office administrators who are school liaisons to share information about their assigned schools and for all to get a snapshot of what's happening across the district.
- The superintendent's advisory team includes the executive directors, the department heads, and two principals—one elementary and one secondary. The purpose of this meeting is to address districtwide issues.

Practices from the future search. Some of the practices from the future search conference have been adopted as a way of life in the district. At meetings, flip charts keep information visible, and self-management distributes responsibility for good outcomes among all participants.

Raising system awareness and utilizing and creating vehicles for open, visible communication have nurtured the goals and helped to institutionalize them so they are living in the system today.

ACCOMPLISHMENTS SINCE THE CONFERENCE

The leaders of the district, including the board of education and administrative team, have kept these goals alive and at the forefront of decision making in the district. As one parent observed, "The board and the superintendent took the outcomes of the conference seriously." The continued focus on these goals has enabled the district to move ahead steadily and systematically during extremely challenging times. Examples of what has been accomplished are discussed below.

Student-Centered Schools

- Report cards have been totally redesigned. As Tom Christie, the executive director of educational programming, described, "They are standards based and reflect what we're doing."
- K–6 instructional resource guides have been developed. They include benchmarks and standards.

- Some conversations have shifted. The talk now is about all kids being successful, not just some kids. There is a consciousness about equity among schools and providing for all.
- Early childhood professionals are now at the table as pre-K–12 planning occurs.
- All-day kindergarten is on the drawing board for the future.

High-Quality Staff

- In partnership with KU, the district has two professional development schools.
- District curriculum staffs have met with the methods professors from KU and Haskell, two institutions that do teacher preparation, to ensure better alignment among the three organizations.
- Legacy Awards are presented monthly to outstanding educators who work tirelessly to ensure student success. Class Act Awards are presented monthly to educational support staff to recognize their value to the system.
- A peer assistance model has been developed and implemented for new teachers.
- Collaboration time is a part of the master agreement for elementary and junior highs, with early dismissal on Wednesdays. The junior high schools have created opportunities for teacher dialogue, school improvement, and professional development. For example, in one of the junior high schools SAM (structure a month) meetings are held during collaboration time. They are run by teachers for teachers. During the session, an instructional idea that can be used across content areas is presented. Since high schools felt a need for similar time, they worked with their site councils and the board of education to gain support for a late arrival time once a month.

Comprehensive Schools

- Some community services, such as community-based after-school programs, have been incorporated into the school building. The district's nursing facilitator works with Health Care Access to have services available to students who need them.

- An expanded gym was built into the Langston Hughes School for community recreational use.
- Lawrence Free State High School shared their site with a new community swimming pool.

Technology

- The district is at the early stages of creating data banks for formative assessments.
- The board allocated money for R&D for technology.
- Every teacher now has a computer on his or her desk that is used as a vehicle for getting information out and back. E-mail is the norm for communication.
- Six prototype technology-rich classrooms are in operation across the district, which provide opportunities for web-based research and teaching.

Adequate Resources

- A decision was made to bring instruction, assessment, and curriculum under the broader umbrella of educational programming. There is now one pot of money instead of three separate ones. This allows for much better use of limited resources as well as better coordination of programs and initiatives.
- The district has partnered with the community to secure grants. For example, the school district partnered with external groups to support students outside of school with The Safe Schools/Healthy Students Grant.

Collaboration and Teamwork/Community Involvement

- With community support to the Lawrence Schools Foundation, the Lawrence Public Schools provide several full-day preschool classes.
- The Success by Six Coalition covers the fields of mental and physical health, parent education, and safety. Services start at birth and involve partnerships between the school district and community organizations.

- The city, county, and board of education are engaged in joint capital planning. They meet quarterly to find ways they can work together, share limited resources, etc. Two of the original 100 people at the future search conference serve in elected positions—one on the city council and one on the county commission. Both are leaders in looking at ways to explore funding sources for the schools.
- Community involvement has helped with athletics and the arts. For example, the Lied Center at KU sponsors educational residencies for visiting authors. Following budget cuts in athletics, Sport 2 Sport, a local business, is offering intramurals at the junior highs. Citizens for Students raised $85,000 to support the "Pay to Play" program so students would only have to pay for one sport. This alleviates some of the financial pressure on low-income families.
- Business partnerships have expanded and are reciprocal. Businesses provide resources to the schools and create learning opportunities for students. The district has more than 100 business partners. Last year the state recognized the partnership of Hillcrest School and Free State Credit Union for its student-run credit union and finance education for elementary students. The district provides skill development to employees of businesses in areas such as test taking and reading to their children.
- A Lawrence School Board liaison is assigned to the Lawrence/ Douglas County Planning Commission, the Lawrence Tax Abatement Committee, and the Lawrence Parks and Recreation Board. This liaison keeps the district voice in the larger government and policy-making system of the community.
- Parent groups are stronger. During Project Graduation at the high school, parents worked to keep the postgraduation festivities safe. Parents are more likely to ask, "What can we do?" when a problem comes up.
- The district has incorporated community services into the building. WRAP (Working to Recognize Alternative Possibilities) workers are available in all schools to assist targeted students and families. They are employees of Bert Nash, a community mental health agency.

Work on the six goals continues in Lawrence. They are part of the annual planning at the board, district, and building level. During a time of limited financial resources coupled with sweeping federal mandates that require compliance—this is the era of No Child Left Behind—the district has held its focus and keeps making progress toward improving the educational experience of all students.

The leadership of the district has clearly been instrumental in making the goals become part of the culture of the school district. The future search conference provided the foundation, the launching pad for this effort. This methodology was different from two previous strategic planning processes that did not have staying power. As Sandee Crowther says, "One was too top down. The other just involved the administration. This one had much broader involvement and much deeper ownership. We came out with a product that people were proud of."

ADVICE

During on-site meetings with various groups to gather the information for this chapter, we asked for advice that we might give to others considering a future search. Their advice is summarized below.

Perspective of the Person with
District Planning Responsibility—Sandee Crowther

- Start thinking about follow-up as you begin planning the conference.
- Honor the planning—it's critical. You'll build a cross-stakeholder core of people who stick with you. This ownership at the front end is critical for success down the road.
- Get a broad representation of stakeholders and have a good mix at the tables.
- The devil is in the details—particularly around the logistics.
- Be ready for whatever comes out. What you expect may not happen, so be ready to go with what unfolds.

Perspective of the Leader—Randy Weseman

- People behave differently eye-to-eye than to a reporter or through letters. The face-to-face nature of the conference (in contrast to surveys, etc.) enables people to see each other and have contact with other human beings.

- Entertain a diversity of opinions.
- Don't tie yourself to a specific outcome. Let the process work. *Wiring* the results becomes obvious and you lose integrity as the leader, and so does the process.

Perspective of the Board and Community Members

- Involve a broad range of the community. Invite your skeptics. You'll have active discussions and hear different perspectives—and you'll find where you can agree.
- As a board member, understand the process.
- Leadership must be invested in the process—really out there in front.
- Know the staff people who are going to follow it through so roles and expectations are clear.
- Keep bringing the goals into people's mind-set.
- Get help (facilitation) from outside.
- Develop a plan for communicating to others. Remember: They don't have the context of the conference.
- Issues are complex. It takes time. It takes a group sitting around a table together. As one parent said, "I was invited into a very professional discussion. This was a window into more strategic issues. I learned a lot."

CLOSING THOUGHTS

Setting the Intention

In looking through our files, we discovered a memo to Kathleen Williams and Sandee Crowther summarizing the initial conversation we had about the possibility of doing a future search conference. It was dated November 4, 1998. One of the topics we had discussed was why they wanted to do a conference. What was their initial thinking about hoped-for outcomes? They listed the following:

- Set a shared direction for the future of the school district by setting priority goals and initiatives.

- Reinstill trust.
- Hear and acknowledge *all* voices of the school community.
- Have these priorities be the umbrella for decision making (i.e., drive the budget process and guide building level site plans).

In revisiting the impact of the future search four and a half years later, it is clear that these aspirations were met. Interestingly, during that initial conversation Sandee Crowther emphasized the importance of follow-up. This was on the radar screen from day one of the effort. The intentions that were set from the beginning, coupled with a robust tool like future search, combined with the commitment of leadership to keep it alive, have led to institutionalized goals in the Lawrence Public Schools. These goals are anchoring the district even as the larger environment shifts. They are informing the decisions that impact teaching and learning.

Costs and Benefits

A final thought is offered as you reflect on this case and consider the implications for your own setting. During a time of limited resources, it may be tempting to scale down planning. In addition to the budget considerations there is also the time factor. The members of the planning group committed time to get clear on purpose and make sure that they got a cross-section of the district and the community to the table. Time was spent up front orienting the board of education to the process and making sure board members were clear that the goals were going to be cocreated at the conference. Time was spent with the superintendent's advisory team to discuss how the outcomes of the conference would be used for district decision making.

People's plates are full. Three days at a future search conference is a substantial time commitment. It may be tempting instead to get a few people around the table to expedite the process. What we ask you to consider are the costs of not including all the stakeholders. What is the cost to the system of having certain perspectives missing? What is the cost to the system of having people make decisions with only partial or self-oriented views of the district and what is needed? As one community member said, "Even during a time of scarcity, we trust each other."

2

Influencing Systemwide Change at the Toronto District School Board

Ray Gordezky, Kim Martens, and Sue Rowan

INTRODUCTION

Changing a large, complex school system is messy business. Results from change efforts are often unpredictable, show up in ways that are difficult to quantify, and can lead to counterintuitive and undesirable consequences. Visible change frequently unfolds at a pace that frustrates sponsors and stakeholders and can lead to abandoning the change effort altogether. This chapter tells how the Toronto District School Board (TDSB), one of the largest school systems in North America, attempted to influence systemwide change.

We want to show how future search, a multistakeholder, collaborative planning process, moved the TDSB toward a set of desired future scenarios even in the face of significant and unexpected demands placed on the school board. Most important, we believe that the TDSB's "Shaping the Future for Tomorrow's Schools" future search demonstrates how the principles of personal responsibility and self-organization that are embedded in the future search process are the cornerstone of successful change in a large, complex system.

ABOUT THE TORONTO DISTRICT SCHOOL BOARD

The current Toronto District School Board was created on January 1, 1998, following the amalgamation of seven individual boards of education. Each of the boards had a unique culture and provided a broad range of services and innovative programming.

The TDSB serves almost 2.5 million people in the Toronto metropolitan area. It covers 632 square kilometers and is located on the northwest shore of Lake Ontario. One-third of Canada's population lives within a 160-kilometer radius of Toronto, and one-half of the population of the United States lives within one day's drive of Toronto.

TDSB is the largest school board in Canada. This board serves over 300,000 students, employs 26,000 people, and operates over 550 schools. The school system operates in a very culturally and linguistically diverse community. Only 53 percent of TDSB secondary and 59 percent of elementary students speak English as their first language. More than 47,000 (24 percent) elementary students were born outside of Canada, and just above 11,500 (12 percent) secondary students have been in Canada for three years or less.

The board has a large number of magnet and alternative schools. Students can take an international baccalaureate program and advanced placement courses. There are programs for students who enjoy hands-on learning and want to go straight to work, including apprenticeship programs. There are schools for the arts, science and technology, international business, and elite athletics and many different alternative schools for elementary and secondary students. Links with universities and community colleges in the city and with other school boards create many opportunities to talk about teaching, learning, and how to advance classroom practice in order to improve learning.

CONTEXTUAL OVERVIEW

In 1999, the director of education gave Superintendent Sue Rowan a portfolio called "Successful Schools." The director hoped that a shared vision of successful schools would act as a magnet to facilitate the integration of the seven boards into a unified whole.

The Challenge

> I think the toughest problems; the "wicked" problems . . . are the ones that somebody dumps on you from right out of the blue. That's what

happened to us. What I wanted to address was how we, as a system, could come together on the most important thing that we do: educating our children. I believed that focusing on the child and what we can do to create a successful schooling experience was one strand that could pull the seven disparate school boards together.

—Sue Rowan, TDSB superintendent

Decreased Government Funding

In 1995 the newly elected provincial government committed to a 30 percent tax rebate. To do this, the government had to cut spending. Education was hit hard. The government's new funding formula, meant to equalize funding for all of the province's school boards, was based on (among other things) usable teaching space. With its large stock of older buildings that were not as efficient in space utilization as newer buildings, the TDSB received less funding than would another board of equal size.

Amalgamating Seven School Boards

In addition to the decrease in government funding, the seven different and outstanding school boards operating in Toronto were forced to combine their operations into one large school board. This meant, for example, unifying staff and policies, renegotiating contracts, closing schools, and letting staff go.

New Curriculum and Classroom Time

In addition to amalgamation and cost cutting, the provincial government's education agenda included revising the curriculum, compressing five years of high school into four, and increasing the time teachers spend in the classroom.

Why Future Search

The impacts of these actions were enormous. Our 26,000 employees were dealing with amalgamation issues, major budget cutbacks, and significant redesigns with the curriculum and its delivery in the classroom.

We needed to look well into the future and imagine what life will look like when today's kindergarten students are tomorrow's high school graduates.

—Sue Rowan, TDSB superintendent

Sue did not want to create another correlate list of factors that make schools successful. There were many of them already, and all were based on what has been successful in the past. Instead, Sue wanted to find a way to look at the global forces that were impacting the school board and the lives of people living in its communities, and what people desired for their future.

PLANNING

Planning for "Shaping the Future for Tomorrow's Schools" began in April 2000 and was carried out by a team that included superintendents, principals, teachers, program staff, community liaison personnel, and a student. They identified the desired outcomes, the stakeholders who needed to be included, and the individuals to invite. And they were beset by a number of challenges and dilemmas, some of which are typical of most future searches, others that were unique to the TDSB:

- **Diversity of the school board and its communities.** The mix had to include a large geographic area; ethnic, linguistic, religious, cultural, and economic differences; a cross-section of students and programs from across the TDSB; and a broad diversity of community stakeholders. After much discussion, the planners decided to run two conferences simultaneously. Each conference would have the same mix of people. All participants would meet together for the opening, and then both groups would work independently in two separate rooms. On the third day, all participants would gather again to build consensus around a shared vision of the future and to establish areas for action. The planning team also decided to invite 30 students so that each conference room would include two groups of young people instead of the typical single group for each stakeholder.
- **Selection criteria.** As mentioned previously, the planning team decided it was important to include representatives of the TDSB's mul-

ticultural community. Yet there was discomfort about identifying people by income, as well as by cultural and ethnic origin. Racial profiling by police was a contentious issue in Toronto, and some members of the group felt there needed to be other ways to ensure diversity of perspectives.

- **Contract negotiations and labor disputes.** The amalgamation resulted in multiple, ongoing contract negotiations that included integrating benefits, pay scales, pensions, etc. This resulted in significant labor disputes and strikes and concerned the planning team enough to delay the conference by six months.

- **Follow-up and sustainability.** The planning team realized that it faced a daunting challenge for ensuring follow-up and sustainability in a system as large as Toronto's. It decided to convene a training session on managing a future search for a cross-section of staff a few months after the initial future search conference. The team believed that there would be a number of opportunities within the TDSB to use future search, and they knew that they could not continue to pay for outside consultants. When the future search conference was postponed because of labor disputes, the planning team decided to run the training on the original dates (i.e., pre– rather than post–future search conference).

- **Involvement of elected officials.** Board trustees were facing difficult decisions with the decreased education budget, labor disputes, and the costs associated with amalgamation. They found it impossible— not only from a financial but also from an ethical perspective—to balance the budget being set by the government. Closing schools and their facilities angered parents and communities across the municipality. In addition, a trustee election during the planning process preoccupied those trustees interested in returning to office.

- **Involvement of provincial government officials.** The planning team knew that the provincial government's perspective was important since the province establishes funding and curriculum direction for all public schools. Unfortunately, when personally approached early in the planning, officials from the Ministry of Education were quite clear they could not be available for three whole days, no matter what the reason. In the end, an MPP (member of the provincial parliament) was contacted and agreed to come to the future search.

However, on the day of the future search, the room sadly lacked government representation. The planners put a tremendous amount of effort into attracting government stakeholders but were unsuccessful in getting them to the conference.

- **Involvement of the business community.** The planning team also sought significant participation of leaders from the business community. A few highly visible business leaders agreed to attend; however, similar to the government representatives, many did not see the value of giving up three days to participate.
- **The pending change of board leadership.** When the planning team postponed the conference, it knew that the director of education would be nearing the end of her tenure with the TDSB. When the future search dates were changed, the planning team wrestled with whether the timing was right for the conference. "Might it be better," some asked, "to wait for the new director to take over?" On the other hand, the arrival of a new director would likely come with new priorities; priorities that might not see the value of a future search. So the planners decided to go ahead.

THE FUTURE SEARCH CONFERENCE

The two parallel future search conferences were held October 21–23, 2001. Approximately 160 people came together to determine what was needed to ensure that all children born in the millennium year can declare, at graduation in 2017, that they have had a successful schooling experience. Stakeholder groups included students, parents, teachers, support staff, trustees, businesses, community groups, senior staff, and school administrators. A follow-up reunion, held on May 29, 2002, reviewed what had happened since the future search conference, streamlined the original 18 action groups into 11 action areas, and then identified next steps. Table 2.1 describes each of the action areas.

The possibilities for centrally supported, coordinated, and sustained action on many of the action plans described in table 2.1 were limited by provincial government intervention in the board's governance, the demands of the new provincial funding formula, and harsh budget cutting. The TDSB provided some resources to support communication be-

Table 2.1. Summary of Action Areas

Action Areas	Objectives
Whole child through the whole curriculum	Developing and supporting a balanced, inclusive pedagogy for all students that emphasizes multiple intelligences, differentiated instruction relevant to the student and neighborhood contexts, and school-to-work programs.
Strengthen school and community linkages	Developing schools as a hub in the community and pursuing political action to develop a ministry within the provincial government focused on children.
Strengthen readiness to learn for ages 1–5 years	Working with community groups, teachers, and parents to help prepare students with the skills required to be ready to learn at school.
Develop a leaderful organization	Helping students to excel by supporting development of teachers, staff, and leaders within the system.
Joy of learning	Building appreciative approaches to support staff and students in their learning activities and raise morale.
Teacher recruitment and support	Supporting new and newly recruited teachers through mentoring programs and strategic placement of experienced staff.
Safe schools	Encouraging positive student behavior, engaging students in making schools safe, developing violence prevention activities, and building community awareness.
Children with special needs and learning disabilities	Developing protocols to identify and disseminate best practices and to promote differentiated instruction.
Environmental and experiential education	Building broader involvement of schools and teachers in environmental and experiential education activities.
Student leadership	Promoting student leadership, encouraging students to speak out on issues that affect their education, and honoring student involvement and leadership.
Technology tools and sharing resources across jurisdictions	Improving the use of technology for learning and teaching, and creating an online trading post for the exchange of services between schools and districts.

tween action groups and convened meetings a couple of times for chairs to exchange ideas and report on progress. Competing priorities and distance to travel to these meetings may have contributed to the low turnout. As a result, direct support for these meetings was discontinued. Sue decided to put into operation the self-management principle from future search and to trust that groups would continue their work for as long as they could.

Despite the province's intervention in the board's governance and the disappointing turnout at meetings, common-ground directions and action plans have been moving forward. A few were incorporated into the mandates of senior staff; others have been carried forward by individuals including board staff, principals, students, and parents.

RESULTS

Future search action areas continue to operate and are having an impact across the system. We have selected six of these areas to describe further. Since future search also enables action that isn't predictable, we'll also look at unintended outcomes—the opportunities and dilemmas that occurred as a result of future search. Finally, we will ask to what extent the results achieved the stated expectations of the planning team.

Whole Child Through Whole Curriculum

The TDSB student population is arguably one of the most diverse in the world. Yet secondary school curriculum has not adequately addressed the needs of students not bound for college or university. TDSB research estimates that over 55 percent of students do not go on to university or college, yet the curriculum and the orientation of teachers and principals have been primarily attuned to students bound for higher education. Consequently, many students who would not otherwise be at risk of school failure are finding it difficult to be successful in school. How to serve students at risk of failure in school was a theme that cut across a number of groups at the future search. While the future search process didn't initiate action and systemwide change in this area, it certainly confirmed that it was a critical priority.

"Pathways for success" for secondary school students has become one of the five systemwide priorities for the TDSB. It looks at what can be done for students who go straight from school to work, and what it will take for all students to see for themselves a successful pathway through school. For example, high school principals must create school improvement plans that consider how best to support students who will not continue their schooling after high school. Focusing on students not continuing on to university or college will require a major shift across the system. Principals and vice principals will need strategies to support teachers as they make this shift.

Strengthen Readiness to Learn for Ages 1–5

Readiness to learn has been identified as a key component of student success. But this doesn't happen by accident. Students need the proper supports to be ready to learn. With its large population of non-English-speaking families, the TDSB has many entering students unprepared for school.

The work in this area focuses on screening kindergarten children to provide teachers and parents with knowledge to help them better prepare children for school success. At the time of the future search, this work had not reached across the system, and few people knew what could be done with the research on children's readiness to learn. Now the concept of readiness to learn appears to be better known across the system. There is greater TDSB involvement with community agencies in support of students and their families. A curriculum connection has been established between kindergarten, child-care, and parenting centers programs. The TDSB has established partnerships with the provincial and federal governments, as well as with the Early Years Centers and Parenting Centers, to better screen and prepare entering students.

Develop a "Leaderful" Organization

> Having a leaderful organization was one of the main action areas from the future search. It confirmed what I needed to do and gave me permission and direction to move forward. Future search gave me the depth and the breadth that I didn't have and the permission to influence those areas that I believed needed to be influenced.
>
> —Sue Rowan, TDSB superintendent

In a time of severe financial difficulties the board has still set increased dollars aside for leadership development and has identified support for beginning school administrators as one of its key system priorities. Actions taken by the board include promotion of two coordinating principals to create and implement a systemwide plan to develop future leaders through an Aspiring Leaders Program; support to potential vice principals, principals, and superintendents through a Growth Track Program; support for current school leaders with a comprehensive staff development plan; and support for beginning administrators with induction and mentoring programs.

Teacher Recruitment and Support

From 1999 to 2002 the TDSB hired in excess of 1,500 new teachers each year, leveling off in 2003 with just over 700 new teachers. Since the future search, the board has established support for beginning teachers as another of its five system priorities. It has formed a central project manager's position to manage a comprehensive mentoring program for new teachers. Significant budget dollars have been allocated to mentoring and support of new teachers. The TDSB has become a board of choice for new teachers in College of Education programs throughout Ontario because of its support programs.

Safe Schools

> I was determined to take on a leadership role around the prevention piece and I did. The Empowering Student Partnership Programs (ESP), which were run in collaboration with the Toronto Police Services, were a great success.
>
> —Bill Byrd, TDSB health and safety staff

Many students at the May reunion had started safe school initiatives as a result of their involvement in the future search. For example, Crime Stoppers programs now exist in many schools, and antibullying programs and resources have been produced for school administrators. Schools now have access to extensive Safe Schools data for use in their school improvement planning process. The TDSB continues to be committed to the safe schools actions through improved police protocols, emphasis on prevention programs, increased programs for at-risk youth, and required Safe Schools plans in every school.

Technology Tools and Expanding Resources by
Sharing Resources across Jurisdictions

> I feel that the work we wanted to do—a collaborative learning culture
> where teachers would be energized in their schools—has been vali-
> dated by the future search. Having the days together at the future
> search, we didn't have to seek permission; we already had the support.
> What we are doing meets partnership, mentoring, and use of innova-
> tive technology criteria that the action group established.
>
> —Anne Kerr, TDSB principal

The Ursula Franklin Academy became the pilot site in the TDSB for
ABEL (Assisted Broadband Enabled Learning project) in the summer of
2002. Funding for this project is being provided through CANARIE Inc.
(Canada's advanced internet development organization, funded by partners and the federal government). A summer institute was held in 2002.
Half of the Ursula Franklin Academy school staff met with colleagues
from Alberta and other Ontario schools to immerse themselves in learning
to use new broadband tools to develop inquiry-based units. Collaborative
learning spaces have been created that span geographic and institutional
boundaries: Students in more than one location learn together and challenge one another with problems.

Participating teachers get advanced degree credit through York University for what they are doing in the classroom; some teachers are working
on master's degrees through the University of Alberta. This is the first
time that teachers, creating lessons and knowledge in the classroom, are
getting university credit for their work without having to leave their
schools to do so.

UNINTENDED CONSEQUENCES

Any time you bring together a large number of people from a broad range
of positions and perspectives, you open the door to expectations and consequences that are unpredictable. People who participate bring with them
a set of expectations that are unique to their experiences and stakeholder
perspective. Some unintended consequences build momentum toward the

outcomes desired by the sponsor. Other consequences produce dilemmas that challenge the sponsors to examine what they can and will support.

Individual Change—Building Momentum Toward the Desired Outcomes

Some of the changes that have happened are difficult to track and articulate because they take place at the individual level. In conversations and correspondence we've had with participants, there was a common theme that individuals did take action as a result of their attendance at the future search conference and May reunion. Following are some examples:

- One student said his experience at the future search led him to run for and win the leadership of the TDSB Super Council (boardwide student council).
- Several senior staff and a former board member highlighted the importance of involving multiple stakeholders in a process of consensus building.
- Some staff members said that the future search affirmed directions they personally believed in and were already working on. Some of the initiatives mentioned were safe schools, readiness to learn, technological innovations to improve learning, teacher mentoring, student empowerment programs, and staff development.

> My practice has been enhanced due to the fact that I met a variety of stakeholder groups at the future search conference who have transferred knowledge of programs/ideas that have assisted my work.
>
> —Valerie Sterling, coordinator, Readiness to Learn Project, TDSB

Dilemmas That Challenge the School System

The idea of having the school as a hub to support vitality and health in the community is one example of an action area that has produced some challenging questions for the TDSB school system, the governments that fund the board, and parents:

- What purposes beyond educating our children in curriculum areas should our schools serve?
- Are schools supposed to be the hubs for families and communities?
- If schools are to act as community hubs, who is responsible for setting direction?
- Does the purpose of a school system include the provision of recreational services for the community?

RETURN ON EXPECTATIONS

Future search brings together a diverse group of stakeholders, some of which have a history of conflict, to create a shared plan for the future. This is a noble goal in and of itself, but how do you measure the value of such an initiative? Did the future search do what the TDSB wanted it to do? Did it provide a satisfactory return on investment? How do you separate the effects of the future search from all other factors? These are questions that arise for every sponsor of a planned systemwide change initiative.

To answer these questions, many sponsors use return on investment (ROI) analysis to determine if expenditures are worthwhile. This kind of analysis, while desired by funders, is often expensive. It is difficult to identify what to measure and even more difficult to measure the elements identified. We prefer to focus instead on return on expectations (ROE). ROE starts by identifying the expectations of the planning group and sponsor and then comparing the current practice to original expectations.

The planning group worked hard to describe what it wanted the future search to do for the TDSB, its students, and its communities. Its work began with one key question: "What do we want children born in the first year of the new millennium, and later enrolled in our schools, to say about their school experiences?" From this question, the planning group arrived at a consensus on five expected outcomes:

- Build commitment among key stakeholders in the education of all students.
- Create a vision of the preferred future for students.

- Be as open as possible to creative thinking about tomorrow's schooling.
- Demonstrate a commitment to address the needs of every student.
- Acknowledge the diversity that is the reality of our public education.

Reflecting on our report of where the system is today, we would say that commitment was built among many of the participants who attended the future search toward a shared vision that moved them to action. A number of the outcomes from the future search have been incorporated into board priorities, and participants who came from the TDSB leadership are moving these ideas forward. New forms of learning, as exemplified by the ABEL project at the Ursula Franklin Academy, show the promise of using creative thinking for tomorrow's schooling. Work on successful pathways, leaderful organization, and teacher mentorship are examples of a commitment to address the needs of every student, as well as teachers.

But the following factors adversely affected the ROE. Some of the key stakeholders (government representatives, board trustees, senior administrators, and business partners) were not present or were present in small numbers. The number of participants (150 of the 326,000 from the TDSB system) does not appear to have been sufficient for generating a shared vision for the system as a whole. The TDSB was unable to undertake additional future searches at the local or school levels to help build momentum toward a shared vision due to financial and systemic challenges.

Two years after the conference, Sue Rowan spoke on how future search has met her initial expectations:

> Even though some of the things we had hoped would happen here didn't, the future search has influenced our direction. I had bigger dreams than what I've seen transpire. I had hoped there would be committees that continued to work after the conference. The change-over in our system leadership and the massive reorganization had something to do with things not happening. But for me it is the themes that came out of the future search that matter. I feel some responsibility to forge ahead on these. For example, support for new teachers is now one of the five school board priorities, and this was a future search action priority. The long-term staff development plan I've been working on also came up at the future search. The future search gave me the confidence to believe that the community supports the actions I'm taking.

LEARNINGS: SYSTEMWIDE CHANGE AND FUTURE SEARCH

Determining the success of a future search only by measuring achievement of the plans declared at the end of a conference can blind us to the subtle, enriching changes that occur at the individual and small group levels. After reflecting on the entire process, from planning to the present, we've drawn a few conclusions about systemwide change and future search.

Systemwide Change is Preceded by Change at the Individual and Local Levels

We have described changes in behavior and attitudes, and have given examples about ways action is being initiated by a number of individuals—principals, superintendents, teachers, students, and community partners—who participated in the future search. Several senior board staff members who were involved with the future search have become key persons on important board committees. Others have been asked specifically to represent their area when system feedback or committee representation is needed.

> I really enjoyed the future search. I loved the experience and I loved the interaction. I marveled at the students who were there and having the chance to meet the different stakeholders. As well, many people that I talked to who were in the school system said to me that this was the first time since the TDSB had gone through the huge transformation that we have come together in a meaningful way that was positive.
>
> —Rhonda Singer, business representative at the future search

Scientists working in the fields of chaos and complexity call these chance encounters *emergence*. Change emerges from local interactions that can grow into a network of interactions that suddenly becomes a new emerging order. A number of recent changes witnessed in our world are changes that took place seemingly suddenly, from out of nowhere, but are better described as resulting from emergence. Think of the dismantling of the Berlin Wall, municipalities passing bylaws restricting homeowners' use of pesticides, or Canada's support for lowering the cost of AIDS medications in Africa. In their beginnings, these changes were small and slow in developing, taking place as isolated incidents or unseen by any but those closest to them. Each of these picked up momentum as individuals in one area linked to similar initiatives elsewhere, then became widespread, visible phenomena.

Future search provides an opportunity for these chance encounters to occur around questions and issues that matter—issues that are usually complex and messy. Initiatives taking place around readiness to learn, safe schools, use of technology tools and sharing of resources, and support for new teachers are making an impact across the system without a top-down, centrally controlled change program.

Organizational Leadership and Supportive Infrastructure Matters—but Only Up to a Point

Leadership is a primary factor in most discussions about successful, systemwide change. Usually leadership is addressed from the top-down perspective: Formal power structures and supportive infrastructures are needed to ensure cooperation and alignment of initiatives. The assumption behind this assertion is that it is possible for people in positions of authority and control to implement specific actions that produce desired outcomes. We believe that the formal systems of authority and control can and do support change. However, they are often overly cumbersome and too plagued by political considerations to initiate or sustain change without the spontaneous, self-organizing behavior that occurs in informal networks.

To accomplish systemwide change, we needed involvement of senior board staff and alignment of infrastructure. Accordingly, the future search planning team involved a number of superintendents and principals, the director of education, as well as stakeholders from outside the board.

Some people who were trained in the future search process are applying future search principles and practices in their work. We've seen this influence in their work and hear it in the language they are using—in meeting minutes and reports they write, in how they run and participate in meetings, in how they consult and collaborate. For example, the kindergarten registration now includes community fairs where people from different agencies and services that support young children and young families come to connect with parents as they register their children for school.

Throughout the process, information was openly shared. Results of the future search were posted on the TDSB website; proceedings were recorded on video for use across the school system and outside to inform and inspire others. While these were important undertakings, extreme pressure on the board's budget has interrupted final production and interfered with this process.

At one point in our conversations in preparation for this chapter, Sue asked: "Can you still make significant change in a huge system like ours if someone several layers down in the organization, like me, leads it?" Our answer is, yes, someone a few layers from the top can lead a significant, systemwide change. A number of factors, however, militated against broad systemwide change rippling out from this future search.

As Michael Fullan (2001) suggests, change requires both support and pressure. This comes from the senior leaders within a system and from structures that are created to support and align all policies and initiatives. We suspect that greater support and pressure from the formal structures and leadership hierarchy might have further enabled Sue to lead a broader systemwide change effort. The imminent departure of the director of education created more uncertainty in an already uncertain system. In addition, the wounds from amalgamation and the lack of a coherent corporate culture made many of the board's senior staff insecure. Thus, the needed pressure and support for the systemwide changes proposed at the future search were either absent or too weak to create a coordinated, whole-system shift.

Perhaps what is most important is that in order to get change in a large, complex system, conditions to nurture and support self-management and self-organization must be created. These conditions include inviting a cross-section of the whole system into dialogue about questions that matter, giving people opportunities to meet informally, encouraging budding seeds of change by providing support but not managing their work, and creating other opportunities for cross-stakeholder learning and planning.

It is not enough to say you want to change. A supportive infrastructure matters. People need to understand how change happens within their system, what to expect along the way, how decisions will be made, and how they can get support.

Knowing how change happens helps people manage the transition from the current state to the desired future. It also sets norms for what people may feel and experience along the way, including unanticipated obstacles. Helping people manage the transition to the proposed changes can take a number of forms. Most important are providing people time to make meaning of the issues affecting them, helping everyone place their work within the framework of the desired future, making knowledge sharing easy and a priority, and aligning organizational processes and initiatives to build coherence.

CLOSING THOUGHTS

TDSB offers a good example of how change started in small steps between individuals who met informally when their separate paths converged in a chance encounter.

> Future search really does empower people and enables them to take some control and action around what they feel is important. Future search brings the structure for allowing voices to emerge and choices to be made. People can then work on things they believe are important and for which they know they have system support.
>
> —Sue Rowan, TDSB superintendent

Part 2

LEADERSHIP PERSPECTIVES AND TOOLS

Future search is not a substitute for strong leadership. However, future search does strengthen leadership by bringing together vision, reality, service, and courage to act. When leaders follow future search principles, they will find success with future search. This section describes connections between leadership and future search. The leaders in these three chapters chose to use future search as part of their strategic planning effort.

In chapter 3, the superintendent of schools in Carson City, NV, describes how his community utilized future search at all of its schools to identify building-level as well as districtwide measures. The superintendent used innovative reporting processes and tools to keep the whole community informed about progress.

After the future search for the Ottawa–Carleton School Board in Ontario (chapter 4), action-planning groups refined their plans, set priorities, and added measurable objectives. The director of education became the champion of the entire effort and appointed school superintendents as champions for each action team initiative. To support implementation, the system used tools related to an accountability framework.

Chapter 5, on Perkiomen Valley, PA, delineates the new superintendent's approach to refinement and implementation of plans. She enlisted the assistance of the board of directors, gave strong backing to everyone responsible for implementation, and appointed the director of curriculum and instruction as process champion. These top leaders built capacity within the system by selecting, training, and supporting teachers and community members in their new leadership roles. Tools in this chapter include a step-by-step roadmap of the process, a detailed time line, and a process map tracking faculty and community involvement.

Converting Outsiders to Insiders: A Grassroots Approach Using Future Searches at Each School to Design the Districtwide Educational Strategy

Jim Parry

Schools start process of fixing their problems

—Headline of story by Dick Murray,
newspaper columnist and school future search participant

This is the best thing the district could have done. I'll tell the board that. We've put the bond behind us, and the people here have done a lot of hard work. It's very positive. If this kind of consensus-building had been used before the bond campaign, the bond likely would have passed.

—Karl Neathammer, a leading opponent of $48.5 million
school construction bond defeated by voters in 1996

This is the first time the board has sought such broad communication from the public in a workshop format, asking residents how they would like schools run.

—John Sammon, *Nevada Appeal* reporter,
reporting on the Fremont School future search

The students participating here were well accepted. I think one of the biggest concerns from the students is that we kind of realized some of the problems are our own, and we have to find solutions for them.

—Ethan Cleveland, Carson High School student

CONTEXT

The comments above symbolize the rebirth of the Carson City School District in Carson City, NV, after a five-month ordeal during which the previous superintendent resigned under pressure due to a significant personal issue. In August 1997 I was named district superintendent after 10 years as associate superintendent for educational services.

I was responsible for planning. I had conducted planning sessions with the proverbial "superordinate" group, composed of the board, too many administrators, too few teachers, some districtwide consultants, and virtually no other stakeholders. Lacking any precedents, I used the traditional "40 anointed ones go to the mountain top and bring back the smoldering tablets with the deeply etched words of wisdom" approach. It was guaranteed to win us little local support.

Our planning sessions, however, had surfaced six focus areas needing attention: 1) increasing reading achievement in the first two grades, 2) increasing core instruction time, 3) improving kindergarten student readiness, 4) improving teacher performance through staff development, 5) increasing systematic collection of achievement data, and 6) improving the language skills of limited-English-speaking children.

In 1996–1997 we rolled out these focus areas to school staffs and a 25 percent sample of parents. Since we had roughly 8,000 students, I sent surveys to about 2,000 homes. After getting the usual 20 percent return, I ended up with feedback from about 5 percent of our parents. Both staff members and parents had prioritized the six focus areas in similar ways.

We entered the summer of 1997 with almost $1 million of action plans to advance the goals behind the six focus areas. We were at best a loose confederation: six elementary schools, two middle schools, and one high school. There was no unifying philosophy, structures, or K–12 plan, and no plan for the departments that traditionally offered support to the schools. Thus, only Educational Services had any close connection to the district focus plans. Human Resources, Operations, and Fiscal Services, all key areas, had none.

Senge, Weisbord, Hamel, and Greenleaf

The district had (and has) a wonderful group of pragmatic "line-leaders" who kept our schools running effectively and efficiently. They had local passions along with local interests. However, their commitment to districtwide issues, like cohesive planning and close articulation of policies, procedures, curriculum, and materials, was latent at best. I was embarrassed by a history in which the central office did not create conditions for close unity among departments that needed to work together.

I found myself frustrated by my inability and lack of skill in helping to create the conditions that would have fostered the sense that the district was truly a system. My frustration increased as I read such books as *The Fifth Discipline* (1990) and *The Fifth Discipline Fieldbook* (1994). Yet Peter Senge and his coauthors gave me hope and ideas regarding the tools needed to help lead this loosely coupled district to a more unified vision of the future.

I began to see ways to foster systems thinking and team learning and to understand the nature of the mental models around and within me. Thankfully, through Senge's writings I met Marvin Weisbord and Sandra Janoff. Future search gave me a sense of how to do participative planning and inspired me to learn more about it. In *Competing for the Future* (Hamel and Prahalad, 1994), Gary Hamel advised that "senior managers must seek to identify and exploit the inter-linkages across units that could potentially add value to the corporate whole" (p. 317). He asked questions like, "How often has the monarchy led the revolution?" (p. xiii). He added, "Front-line employees and middle managers today, inclined to regard themselves as victims, have lost confidence in their ability to shape the future of their organizations" (p. xii). Hamel suggested that there is value in "enlightened collective strategy and . . . cross-unit opportunities" (p. 318). Robert Greenleaf, in *Servant Leadership* (1977), demanded that administrators "disturb, stretch and goad" (p. 99) the people who worked in the district in their efforts to create outstanding results. These authors and their words both unsettled me and inspired me to find different ways to unify the district.

Stakeholder Discontent

In 1990, the voters approved a $29 million bond to build two new elementary schools, to remodel and expand the high school, and to do a variety of mechanical updates. Although the two elementary schools came in on budget, the high school remodel/expansion was a nightmare of asbestos abatement cost overruns. Because of those overruns other schools had fewer resources to accomplish needed improvements. Our reputation and our self-image both suffered greatly. The public perception of our management was very negative. It certainly contributed to the defeat of the next bond issue in 1996. We were a closed system in which parents were held at bay, unless we needed something (funds) from them. District leadership had no desire to empower them or the larger community to be serious players in the conduct of our affairs. It showed.

THE MOHONK MOUNTAIN HOUSE AFFAIR

The school board named me superintendent in late August. Shortly after, I learned about a future search training scheduled for October 18–21, 1997, at the Mohonk Mountain House in New Paltz, NY. I made plans to attend.

I wanted a mechanism to open the system to all stakeholders, get wide-spread involvement, help emphasize systemic behavior, make insiders of outsiders, have those closest to the work provide key planning input, and transmit strategic educational direction "upward." I wanted to add an education/achievement stream of priorities to several other sources of strategy: board achievement initiatives, conclusions about voter preferences (gleaned from our polling efforts) about new school construction and multitrack year-round schedules, our previous facility-planning efforts, and administrative leadership team priorities. I thought that I could combine these streams of priorities into a strategic management plan.

As I prepared to participate in the future search training, I had one huge question. How could I overcome the superordinate group idea? I wanted groups from each of our nine schools to be involved. I wanted a mechanism to get wide involvement from the stakeholders in our two large middle schools (800 and 1,100 students, respectively) and the high school, which contained 2,400 students. I decided I would no longer take the anointed 40 people to the mountaintop. I wanted a way to involve hundreds of people in a unified approach in which the schools designed their initiatives and in which the large themes that surfaced at each school could be unified into a cohesive strategy for the educational future of the district. Thus, I wanted a way to diverge in the school planning and then converge common themes into a district educational strategy component.

During the future search training, I talked over my goals with Marvin Weisbord and Sandra Janoff. They assured me we could have parallel planning sessions in the larger schools and that we could integrate the work of multiple sessions. Thus we conceived the idea of having one future search (50 to 70 stakeholders each) at each of the six elementary schools, two parallel sessions each for the two middle schools, and four parallel sessions for the high school. This idea of integrating multiple parallel conferences gave me the capability of involving at least 800 people in planning for the future of the district. I knew this process would concern the principals. Those respected pragmatists were about to have their collective worlds turned upside down. I left the training conference with an agreement to work with Dano Weisbord, Marv's son, on the use of the Future Search Network facilitator group to give me the expertise to plan and facilitate a total of 14 future search sessions in four months.

A second (but still important) question I had was how to add structure and substance in the implementation of the future search action plans. A fellow participant helped me with that issue. He described his company's project management approach to give structure and add accountability to the action plans. Another participant briefed me on simple, easy-to-use project management software called Project Quickstart. Its simplicity made it possible for neophytes to turn action plans into project plans, including simple Gantt charts.

Now I had the answers to the key questions. Paradoxically, I had been to the mountaintop (alone) and I returned with the precious tablets relating to our districtwide future search process and my recommendation (read top-down mandate) about a grassroots planning process that would involve all schools. I also had (and still have) an entrepreneurial spirit and somewhat of a risk-taker personality. While I was proud of the schools individually, it offended me that we weren't acting as a system. I returned to the district with the intention of "selling" this whole process to the principals, the staffs, and the board.

I projected the cost of this project to be at least $80,000. This included facilitator fees, their travel expenses, workshop materials, lunches, and some overtime for classified staff who would be involved in set-up/tear-down activities. Needless to say, I was the first Carson City superintendent to expend these kinds of dollars on planning. Our planning costs had heretofore involved some flipcharts and markers. As a new (or an old) superintendent, this project was not for the faint of heart.

Breaking William Bridges's Rules

Upon my return to Carson City, I unveiled my top-down recommendation (read mandate) to implement a bottom-up planning process. Yes, I did entertain thoughts of that paradox in a leadership team meeting. I owned the contradictory nature of what I was asking and asked the team of principals and central office administrators to help bring this process off successfully. Even though I had previously read *Managing Transitions* (1991), I forgot several of William Bridges's key recommendations. I failed to "think through who will have to let go of what when change occurs" (p. 4). Against one of Bridges's key dicta, I "overwhelmed people with a picture that was so hard" for these hard-working, dedicated pragmatists "to identify with that many of them became intimidated rather than excited" (p. 57) by the thoughts of the future search process. I underestimated how much they needed a transition management plan, how much of a stretch this was, and how much of a shock to our system it would be.

I, the risk-taker, knew we could pull it off, and I was comfortable with the stretch it was causing. I was still in a honeymoon period with the board, and they wanted to support the idea of massive community/staff involvement in our planning process. Maybe not to the tune of $80,000, but they went along with it. Yet, while I had no problem leaving the past behind, I spent too little time and consideration on the needs of those who were being asked to help implement (and abide by the results of) this audacious planning process. I was also naive enough to think that every principal wanted to learn what information the future search would provide for that school. At least one had nothing to learn from the process and had to be told to attend.

Four Feverish Months

In November and December 1997, I worked with Dano Weisbord and a fabulously talented group of facilitators who had gotten wind of the crazy guy in Carson City who was planning to have 14 future search conferences and then integrate the common themes from these conferences into a unified educational segment of the strategic management plan for the district. These wonderfully inventive, talented people pitched in to help me with all the details and helped ensure the project's success. They simply agreed with the intent and the philosophy of the process. Without them, and their professionalism, I know that the process would have failed.

In January and February 1998 we held the conferences. At each school we formed stakeholder groups that included teachers, classified staff (secretaries, cooks, custodians, bus drivers, etc.), parents, administrators, communitywide activists, and board members. Students were included at both the middle-school and high-school levels. We decided not to include them at the elementary level.

Needless to say, the student participants made a reputation for themselves in terms of the depth of their thoughts, their candor, and their grasp of the issues. Their contributions to the process were nothing less than outstanding. They took on the adults respectfully, candidly, and thoughtfully during the whole process. Sadly lacking in our conferences, however, were both student and adult representatives of our community's subcultures and their advocates. For example, we did not include the Hispanic students who were illiterate in their own languages yet were asked to carry armloads of books through the hallways of our schools.

At a time when we were growing in diversity, the conferences, I'm sorry to say, didn't reflect it. Were I doing this again, I would surely include a true cross-section of our community. We did a much better job of methodically including most of the fairly well-known school critics, bond opponents, ultraconservatives, and those who simply did not trust the district. Including them was well worth our efforts. Many became our allies in the marketing of the 2000 school bond. They became more trusting of us and more supportive of our solutions to the problems we were facing. We made insiders of them, and it paid real dividends.

For each conference we had a secretary who kept a written record of all activities. Each principal and I got a copy of this conference summary. I also had a videotape record of each conference. We published conference pamphlets summarizing the activities for all participants. All staff members and parents got a pamphlet for their particular school.

The Immediate Aftermath

Reactions from participants ran the gamut from euphoria to hostility:

> Jim, you have caused me to lose my school and you have caused me
> to have to be the one to bring these people back down to earth after all
> this "pie-in-the-sky" dreaming. They dreamed up action plans that are
> not in keeping with my own concept of the future of my school and
> they think that I am the "bad guy" who has to tell them that we won't
> be able to afford most of the action plans.
>
> —One of the principals angrily in a closed-door session
> a few days after that school's future search

> Jim, I am still on a high from the great feelings, thoughts, and the en-
> tire two and a half day process I just experienced. Our school com-
> munity came together to effectively conceive of the steps we will take
> together to create the best school in the world. Parents and teachers
> have built new relationships and ways to work together in a non-
> threatening way for the future of the children and the school. I can't
> thank you enough for this process. I know it was long overdue in our
> school and our district. Thanks for having the courage to support this
> kind of change in the district.
>
> —a principal during a post–future search phone call

These are just a few of the hundreds of comments that ran the gamut from
total elation about a rebirth of the district to cynical complaints that the
district was slipping into a chasm of site-based decision making, nonpro-
ductive "outsider" meddling, and handing over the reins of the district to
parents. Thank goodness that the overwhelming tone of the feedback was
very positive and that the board was very much behind this progressive
project. The media coverage was positive and the parent feedback was ex-
ceedingly indicative of new beginnings and hope. On March 8, 1998, I
published a full-page ad in the *Nevada Appeal* (Carson City's daily newspaper) including the names of the 800 participants and thanking them for
coming together to conceive of the future of the district. I included comments about the integration process that would bring forth the key themes
and action plans as unifying elements of the districtwide strategic management plan. I knew that the future searches were only the first step.

Now I had to pull all the elements of the plans, our past initiatives, community polling information about school capacity and growth, board priorities, and the central office/building administrator focus points into a cohesive, yet relatively simple, five-year districtwide plan.

AGGREGATING THE INFORMATION

During March and April 1998, I worked feverishly to chart the common themes that had surfaced at the nine schools. There were certainly no huge surprises. The key themes were improving K–12 achievement, increasing student accountability for achievement, upholding appropriate class-size standards, increased parent/community involvement, improvement of our facilities, increased use of alternative education, and increased use of technology as a teacher/student productivity tool. Additionally there were 52 education processes pertinent to the elementary, middle, and high school levels mentioned in action plans that were uniquely "local" issues and were not included in my aggregation process.

The seven themes served as the unifying educational areas that would be the subjects of schoolwide and districtwide action plans. The school board, central office leadership team, and principals all confirmed and supported these themes.

A STRATEGIC MANAGEMENT PLAN UNFOLDS

That spring and summer I pulled our information from the following sources:

- The future search themes: mostly achievement-related issues.
- Our voter polling information and previous facility master plan recommendations to provide more school capacity in the face of our continuing 4 percent annual growth pattern.
- Previous board mandates regarding achievement.
- Administrative (principals and central office) leadership team priorities.
- Previous facility master plan recommendations about developing additional school capacity.

My intention was to combine the new information with the more endur-
ing, important concepts from our immediate past. I could not build a comprehensive plan without a view that extended past the future searches to
important topics that had not surfaced in them. I also failed to anticipate
the national events of the spring and the following year.

Jonesborough, Springfield, and Columbine

In March 1998, two middle school students in Jonesboro, AR, ambushed
their fellow students and their teachers from a knoll outside the school
grounds. In May, young Mr. Kip Kinkel opened fire in his Springfield,
OR, high school and also killed his parents. These actions brought the
concept of "emergent strategy" (Mintzberg, Ahstrand, and Lampel, 1998)
into consideration. School safety "emerged" as the theme that would over-
take achievement, facilities, and zoning in the minds of our community
members. Yet nowhere in the future searches did school safety manifest
itself in any way. It was not on our radar screen. It should have been. The
events at Columbine High in Littleton, CO, on April 20, 1999, would
move the theme of school safety to the front of the list.

A Shared Strategic Agenda

The previously mentioned sources gave us a strategy development package.
Education system goals included optimum safety, breakthrough student
achievement, maximizing instructional delivery in each school, maintaining
effective class size, emphasizing student accountability for achievement,
increasing staff satisfaction, and others. Support system goals included safe
school environment/operation, internal/external customer focus, maintain-
ing/enhancing the educational environment, alignment of department goals
to support school goals, business process improvement, and others.

Key Performance Indicators

The support departments were asked to align their goals to support educational goals, wherever possible. When that was not possible, I concen-
trated on process improvement as a way of doing business in each department, with an emphasis on both internal and external customer

satisfaction. Each school was to implement key projects related to the education system goals. For instance, all schools had to have a school safety plan that was put into an accountability-based format (either a Gantt chart or a three-year strategy staircase). Each support system department was to have goals that either supported the education goals or improved the processes of that department. Again, these goals were supported by initiatives (projects), which were put into either a Gantt chart or a three-year strategy staircase.

All projects had to have key performance indicators, which became metrics by which progress could be noted and published. For instance, each school safety plan was related to key performance indicators such as fights in school, arrests for weapons or drugs, the structural and physical safety of the school grounds, and the level of safety-related training of the staff. Because of the differences in leadership and management styles, I gave district leaders the choice of using the project management software (Gantt charts) or designing a three-year strategy staircase with key action plan steps, regarding a specific strategic theme, over a three-year period. For the very task-oriented managers, the project management software worked well. The others appreciated the less structured staircase approach.

The Dashboards

Thanks to a *Harvard Business Review* article (Meyer, 1994), I got the idea of using dashboards, with colorful graphic indicators and easy-to-read gauges, to help us all monitor progress on the key performance indicators. This article referenced the Quantum Corporation in Milpitas, CA, and its development of a 2.5-inch disc drive. They used the project dashboard to "show current results vs. target performance."

According to Larry Wilson, operations team leader (personal communication, February 22, 1999), they wanted "a critical understanding of where we were relative to our goals. We also used the dashboard to trigger immediate action in our team meetings, much as you would act if your 'check engine' light came on in your car while driving."

Thus, as our strategic management plan unfolded, it included two main categories: education and support. Education included typical learning issues. Support included all departments and employees not directly associated with learning. For each category we devised goals, projects, and initiatives to reach the goals. To judge performance we included indicators of project completion and the metrics to show the progress. Last, we used dashboards to offer graphic depictions of the level of completion of projects and student performance. This process operationalized the future search action plans.

Although many of the future search projects did not live on in the strategic management plan, the most important ones did. The principals had the money and resources to keep major projects going in a functional way and wanted to concentrate on those achievement-related projects that helped them to show student progress on the high-profile, accountability-based academic results. The state of Nevada had gotten into the public school accountability business, and individual school academic results had to be published yearly. Thus, school achievement in basic skills and subjects (the prime action plans of the future searches) was also the principle feature of the state accountability plan. These plans and projects received extensive focus and resources.

Leading and Managing

We know that the issues facing education are not "one-year problems." All of the themes that surfaced in the future searches were big-picture, long-term sorts of issues. They, along with the communitywide growth issues and our internal customer focus and process-improvement efforts, became the leadership issues that had to dominate our future and receive the needed resources. Once those were clarified, I believed that we had to have a solid management plan to help us to sustain the efforts over at least three-year periods. Thus, I included the project management, three-year strategy staircases, and dashboards. Examples of a dashboard, a Gantt chart, and a three-year staircase can be found in figures 3.1, 3.2, and 3.3.

The three-year staircases caused managers (principals and department heads) to publicly set forth three-year action plans to manage our way to progress on the goals. Without the themes and goals we have no aspirations. Without the management section, we simply keep the doors open and hope those lofty goals will just happen.

Semiannual, face-to-face updates on all management plans were necessary to keep me abreast of the progress being made on the management plans. We opened each school year with a yearly, up-to-date version of the

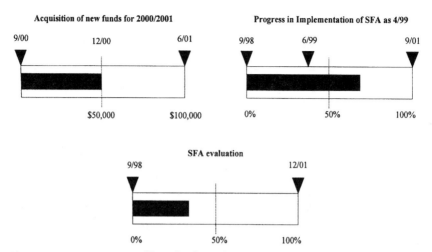

Figure 3.1. Most Recent Dashboard Information: Success for All (Data from Carson City School System document, 2000–2001)

management plan. My next step, had I continued on as superintendent, would have been to run this whole system through enterprise management software that would give all of us real-time knowledge of the status of all action plans and steps. Thus, the goal would have been to have everything in the strategic management plan online and available to the public to facilitate knowledge of progress. My retirement in 2001 obviated the need for this expensive step, which would have been controversial. I would have liked to have seen that step implemented, but it would have possibly been simply too difficult.

THE IMPACT

I wanted the management plan to give us the image of a forward-looking business with an emphasis on planned improvement and stakeholder involvement. I wanted the residents to trust us and believe in our intentions and capabilities. After the cost overruns of the 1990 bond and the failed 1996 bond, we passed our next bond in 2000. The town trusted us to spend $18 million to modernize and remodel the schools. Our image in the media was much improved. (Also, thanks to the efforts of Dr. Mary Piercynski, the current superintendent, the district passed a 2002 bond issue to

1. Reduction in "Fault" accidents. This will continue to be focus to be measured against. Zero target is applicable on the Dashboard.

2. Building and Grounds improvement. As is outlined in this chart, we are currently in the beginning stages of this project, Dashboard should reflect a 20% completion for this new project.

3. Improve budget process and understanding. We have applied ourselves to this project but seems the farther we go into it the more questions arise. It is still a viable goal and the Dashboard should still reflect 60%.

Task Name	Start	Finish	Days
Define Needs	3/28/99	4/1/99	5
Write specification	4/1/99	5/1/99	31
Bid Units	7/22/99	8/13/99	23
Evaluate Bids	8/13/99	8/13/99	1
Let order	8/13/99	8/17/99	5
Vehicle pre-inspection	7/1/00	7/10/00	10
Delivery	7/10/00	7/15/00	6
NHP Inspection	7/15/00	7/20/00	6
Route Assignment	7/20/00	7/25/00	6
Long Term Cost Control	7/20/00	8/15/01	392
BUILDING & GROUNDS IMPROVEMENT			
Survey Employees	1/12/00	1/14/00	3
Define Needs	1/14/00	1/24/00	11
Create Committee	1/14/00	1/24/00	11
Formalize Data and Report	1/24/00	1/24/00	1
Define Short Term Line Items	1/24/00	6/1/00	130
Define Long Term Line Items	1/24/00	6/1/00	130
Create Timelines	6/1/00	6/15/00	15
Implementation	1/12/00	9/15/02	947

The Gantt chart portion spans quarters: 1998 (4th Quarter); 2000 (1st, 2nd, 3rd, 4th Quarter); 2001 (1st, 2nd, 3rd, 4th Quarter); 2002 (1st, 2nd, 3rd Quarter).

Figure 3.2. Dashboard and Gantt chart for a Transportation Department. (Data from Carson City School System document, 2000–2001)

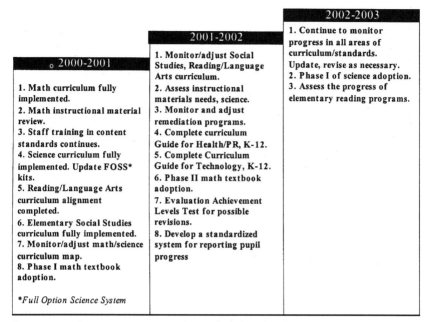

Figure 3.3. Three-Year Strategy Staircase for Educational Services, with Goal of Curriculum Mapping and Alignment to State Standards (Data from a Carson City School System document, 2000–2001)

renovate one of the schools.) We slowly made progress on the academic goals in the midst of major changes in our demographics. We took a tough stand in rezoning the district and equalizing the demographics in the schools. While it was a daunting challenge, our efforts to create options and room for as many people as possible to get what they needed caused parents to believe in our intentions and the community to respect us for taking on the unpleasant issues that demanded attention.

THE KEY LEARNINGS

Here is the advice I would give myself if I were doing this process again:

- Forget Nike; don't "just do it!" Have a solid, well-thought-out planning and implementation design. Make sure that design is both elegant and simple. Consider the impact you want to make on the organization and proceed from your values to the steps involved in your planning process. I agree with Terry Pearce, who says, "Do not try to gradually discover it through trial and error. Your lack of ability to paint an authentic picture of the whole process will result in an inconsistent message and a lack of commitment in those you are leading" (2003, 18–21).

- Understand the nature of the managers in the organization and think hard about the sort of planning style and procedures you are considering and how these fit the management team. In this situation, my ego got in the way of realities. Prepare the management team with the tools, theories, and vocabulary to understand and accept major changes in how you plan and how you implement the plan. Yes, sincere buy-in and support are helpful.
- Use William Bridges's ideas to build a change-management plan.
- Remember the words of Peter Senge in *Leading Learning Organizations*:

Nothing can start without committed local line leaders (principals). Local line leaders are individuals with significant business responsibilities and bottom-line focus. . . . However, engaging local line leaders may be difficult. As pragmatists, they often find ideas like systems thinking, mental models, and dialogue intangible and "hard to get my hands around." If they can find new approaches to enhance results, they will commit time and energy to them. Such people have more staying power than the "fans" who get excited about new ideas but whose excitement wanes once the newness wears off (quoted in Hesselbein, 1996, pp. 46–49).

- Read Senge's comments again and again. Heed them.
- Student involvement in the future searches was a huge asset and must not be discounted. We should have included our fifth graders at the elementary level.
- Our stakeholder groups should have been much more diverse in order to have more representative numbers (regarding our ethnic makeup) "in the room."
- Our size (8,000 students in nine schools in a relatively small geographic area) was ideal to undertake the future searches. Yet it might be hard for me to justify the $80,000 expenditure (in these times) to lead us to the themes and initiatives. At the time, I knew that the proj-

ect would only be successful with the use of the facilitators of the Future Search Network. They were the major (even at their much-reduced rates) component in the costs, and I am absolutely convinced of their contribution to the positive outcomes.

- I stretched the comfort zone of the district way past where there may have been a more suitable middle ground. I settled for a kind of compliance in which all my requests were honored, but some key players' hearts weren't in it. Try to get the hearts and the minds involved.
- I created a fairly complex, hard-to-duplicate process that took a lot of effort to renew and keep updated. Go for simplicity.
- In your own self-evaluation, assess the degree to which you are liable to jump on bandwagons and ascribe to "programs du jour." Force yourself to understand your tendencies in terms of how comfortable you are with change. Try to put yourself in the shoes of those who are your opposites in terms of their comfort with change. For instance, an entrepreneurial change agent should look through the eyes of an ardent pragmatist.

4

Supporting the Merger of Two School Boards in Ottawa, Ontario, Canada: The Ottawa–Carleton Community and Public Education to 2015

Claudia Chowaniec, Ray Gordezky, and Jim Grieve

INTRODUCTION

"The involvement of the whole community in public education is vital for student learning," remarked Jim Grieve, director of education, as he thanked participants at the conclusion of the future search conference. "The challenge is to set achievable goals and find the commitment and community support to make them happen. Educators know they cannot succeed on their own."

The Ottawa–Carleton District School Board's long-range planning conference, held on May 13–15, 1999, brought together not only senior staff and trustees, as is traditional in strategic planning, but also principals and vice principals, teachers, union and non-union teaching and support staff, students, and parents. In addition, there was representation from the wider community, including the government of Canada, the Ontario Ministry of Education, postsecondary institutions, businesses, health and social service providers, police, and members of the local media. The future search conference generated ideas for future directions in public education in Ottawa–Carleton, looking forward to when the current group of junior kindergarten students would graduate in 2015.

This chapter describes the major areas of focus, how the wider community became involved in implementing the actions, the coordinating function played by the steering committee, and how the action plans became part of the board's strategic plan. The chapter concludes with a description of the progress achieved by the action groups to the end of the school year in the spring of 2002 and the community's hopes for the future.

BACKGROUND

In 1995, the government of the Province of Ontario, which has responsibility for education, undertook a massive overhaul of the school system in the entire province. Reforms were initiated in many areas, including equalization of funding provided to all of the province's schools, reduction of administrative costs by amalgamating school boards and closing underutilized schools, and revision of the curriculum to delete the fifth and final year of high school to bring Ontario in line with the other provinces. In what was then called the Regional Municipality of Ottawa–Carleton, two large public school boards—the Ottawa Board of Education and the Carleton Board of Education—were merged on January 1, 1998. With the merger of these two boards, the Ottawa–Carleton District School Board (OCDSB) became the largest school board in Eastern Ontario, serving students within a 2,760-square-kilometer area (1,715 square miles). The OCDSB is the seventh largest school board by student population in Ontario. It serves approximately 80,000 students across 118 elementary and 27 secondary schools. In all, the board owns 11 million square feet of building space worth approximately $1.1 billion.

The newly appointed board of trustees selected a new director of education, Jim Grieve, formerly a superintendent with the Toronto District School Board (see chapter 2) and coauthor of this chapter. His first task was to lead the integration of the two school boards and undertake other challenges set before the board by Ontario's Ministry of Education. When the two boards amalgamated in 1998, there were huge differences between them that had to be accommodated. Differences between the Ottawa Board and the Carleton Board included

- Mainly urban versus largely suburban and rural populations to be served.
- Older, often early twentieth-century infrastructure versus newly built schools.

- Stable, in some areas declining, school-age populations versus rapidly growing communities of young families.
- Schools that were not fully utilized versus schools with dozens of portable classrooms. The Ministry of Education claimed it would not fund new schools unless those that were not 100 percent utilized were closed.

The Ontario Ministry of Education had dramatically shifted the funding formula for education, along with ordering the amalgamation of these two vast school districts. Traditionally, education money had come from the municipal property tax base. Communities could decide, within a preset range, what percentage of local taxes would go to education. The goal of this new approach to education funding by the province was that all schools would be funded equally, based on their population, eliminating the disparity between wealthier and poorer communities. At the same time, the new funding formula essentially froze and, in the case of wealthy boards such as Ottawa, reduced the amount of overall funding available. All decisions on local education were taken away from the municipalities, since they no longer controlled the funding allocation. The local school boards were now required to report to the Ontario Ministry of Education rather than to their board of trustees.

WHY FUTURE SEARCH

Jim Grieve, the new director of education, knew the challenges he faced when he accepted the position in 1998. With all of the immediate differences to be faced, Jim decided that the only way to bring all these people together with their diverse backgrounds, interests, and concerns was to appeal to the passion they all shared—excellent education. His decision to conduct a future search in the spring of 1999 was, therefore, one of his first steps. In Jim's own words:

> I chose future search to present to the trustees as a process, a conceptual process, because I felt that Ottawa–Carleton in its amalgamated new version was already highly interested in community involvement. The school board had a history of having strategic planning over the years that was more clas-

sical and more management and senior trustee-oriented. I felt I wanted to hear from the whole community.

Two boards with two very distinct cultures had to be brought together. This doesn't just happen on its own. Nothing was done in advance of amalgamation to bring the cultures together. There was no long-term plan in place; the two boards were just fused. There needed to be a grassroots, community based review of what the new board should look like.

The inherent risk of the future search process is that what comes out of the process may not be all that senior staff and trustees want. When we started in Ottawa–Carleton we were unsure of the result at the end of the process. This was a big leap of faith for politicians (trustees) and senior staff. I'd done enough reading and talking with the former director of the Toronto District School Board to know that the future search process looked sound. I believe when you put the right people in the room, it has to work. Our future search consolidated the will of not just a few, but of many, many voices. You can't easily abandon these notions that represent the common voice of the community.

THE FUTURE SEARCH

The steering committee first met in January 1999, in the midst of one of Ottawa's worst snowstorms. Five years later, looking back on all those various issues and decisions the steering committee had to make in planning the future search, one aspect continues to stand out: the commitment of all the community leaders from so many different walks of life. Their attendance attests to the leadership and the passion that Jim, the steering committee, and the very supportive administrative team were able to communicate.

The future search conference itself turned out to be just about textbook perfect, but we all knew this was just the first step. About 80 people attended the conference, including students and parents, senior staff and trustees, principals and vice principals, teachers, union members, and affiliated and nonaffiliated support staff. In addition, there was representation from the wider community, including the government of Canada (Learning and Literacy Directorate), the Ontario Ministry of Education, postsecondary institutions (Carleton University, University of Ottawa, and Algonquin College), business (Nortel, Ottawa Centre for Research and Innovation), health and social service providers (the Children's Hospital of Eastern Ontario, the Children's Aid Society, the municipal government's Child Care Division), and the Ottawa–Carleton Regional Police.

THE ACTION AREAS

Seven action-planning groups were active following the conference. Some were later merged; others saw their work incorporated into activities already being undertaken by board staff. Following the conference, plans were made for organizing the work, and reports of the action groups were circulated to all participants. The seven action areas are summarized in table 4.1.

In the six weeks following the future search, each of the seven groups named a chair, developed a clear statement of mandate and goals, and set out an action plan. A postconference steering committee was established to support the groups with the resources they required, including meeting space, secretarial help, and the resources of additional experts who had not been part of the future search conference. This committee also maintained the long-range view and ensured ongoing communication among the groups.

In January 2000, the school board held a one-day workshop that brought the original future search participants together with many others who had become actively involved in the work of the seven groups. They discussed their progress, challenges, and next steps.

ACTION GROUP PROGRESS 2000–2002

1. Expectations for Learning/Accountability

1.1 Set Achievement Targets for All OCDSB Graduates

Secondary school and grade 1 teachers working on "Student Knowledge and Skills" profiles developed target profiles for OCDSB graduates and for grade 1 students. Teachers used these profiles as a reference point to develop achievement targets for all levels from grade 1 to high school graduation.

Table 4.1. Summary of Action Areas

Action Areas	Objectives
Expectations for learning and accountability	Objectives include establishing expectations for the skills and knowledge that an OCDSB graduate in 2015 should have when entering the workplace and going on to postsecondary studies. Primary focus areas are literacy, mathematics, and social/life skills (communication/interaction and problem solving). After defining expectations, the group will turn to accountability issues: How do we know our students have reached these expectations? What measures should be used to ensure expectations have been met?
Staff training and support	The goals are to develop a plan to provide time for creative ways of providing staff training, including the use of community resources and new strategies for supporting and valuing teachers and staff.
Student-tailored learning, technology, and programming	This group will develop plans for action in three linked areas identified during the conference: student-tailored (individualized) learning/ability to learn at one's own pace, technology as an enabler, and programming to include more variety and choice.
The school as hub in the community	While it might not be realistic to expect increased financial resources, increased efficiencies through cooperation are hoped for. The objective is to see one or more pilot projects that make the campus concept a reality. To achieve this vision, help will be needed from many agencies as well as local communities.
Safe schools	Objectives include ensuring a continuum from junior kindergarten to grade 12 of programs that address "kids caring for kids" on a daily basis and a support model for students at high risk for recidivism. This action group will work through the board's existing Safe Schools Committee.
Volunteerism	The focus will be on parents' involvement in their children's education, ranging from at-home activities such as reading with each child to at-school activities such as meeting with teachers for interviews, helping in the classroom, and becoming involved through school councils in a wide range of activities in support of students.
Board structures and processes	This group will work to facilitate increased interaction among the many players in our system (trustees, staff, parents, students, and business and service providers) with a view to improving decision making. Objectives include gathering information on alternative models and identifying goals/time lines for possible structural and procedural changes in the short, medium, and long term. Development of a policy on consultation with the community is to be a priority.

These profiles were to serve as achievement targets for specific grade levels. A "fridge checklist" version for monitoring of progress, and a "student friendly" electronic version were planned for students to build their own "portfolios" of knowledge and skills development. Care was taken to include skills that could be achieved by students who are workplace-bound, as well as for those who are college- or university-bound.

1.2 Audit Program Variability

A number of initiatives were undertaken, including a plan and draft questions developed by multiple stakeholders for use in the 2001–2002 Review of Education in the Arts. This work was used by staff in their Arts Education Review Process in 2002.

2. Staff Training, Development, and Support

2.1 Create an Inventory of
Existing Available Technology Resources

Several projects were undertaken to enhance teachers' resources for teaching. For example, one initiative identified and obtained consensus on a common set of software applications needed to support the curriculum. Another initiative evaluated computer-based tools that would assist teachers with their administrative activities and improve access to information for teachers, communication with parents, attendance record keeping, access to report cards from home, class lists, standard marks keeping, and secure remote access to board resources.

2.2 Employee Recognition Policy and Morale

Development work in this area began with an Organizational Effectiveness Survey and subsequent work plan. Based on the survey results, the board's Employee Support Services Division of Human Resources worked with the Quality Assurance Division to assess what would be required to improve employee morale. Union presidents met with staff to discuss issues and possible approaches for improving morale.

Progress was made on revising the board's Employee Recognition Policy to include recognition of individuals and groups from all sectors of the OCDSB community. This included recognition of long service, outstanding achievement, and contributions to further the aims and objectives of the board by community organizations, community volunteers, parents, students, and staff.

3. Individualized Student Learning Opportunities

New technologies explored for classroom uses include assessing possible uses of videoconferencing; creating an inventory of best practices for student-tailored learning, including web- and computer-based software applications; upgrading student systems and exploring data transfer for potential administrative uses of PDA technology for schedules, class lists, and emergency information; and exploring e-learning course development with local colleges and other partners.

4. School as Hub of the Community

A community dialogue session took place in November 2001 with representation from school principals, Children's Hospital of Eastern Ontario, the Youth Services Bureau, the University of Ottawa, City of Ottawa People Services Department, school councils, and a variety of other organizations. The group reached consensus on the essential characteristics of the hub, its values, and its implications. Participants agreed that hubs share certain key features wherever they may be located (in a school, community agency, church, etc.), including family focus, continuum of services, reduction of duplication and gaps in services, collaborative funding and planning, staff training and development, and community capacity building. Following the community dialogue, the school board supported the establishment of hubs in the school system.

The board's website (www.ocdsb.edu.on.ca) provides information on resources and potential funding to schools and school councils. It is the intent of the Hub Action Group to continue working with community groups to assist all schools in their community development and partnership strategies.

5. Safe, Caring Schools

*5.1 Ensure Continuous Updating and Consistent
Application of Safe Schools Policies*

Following additional consultation with stakeholder groups in the fall of
2001, the board approved a series of Safe Schools policies. These policies
have recently been revised to meet the new Ontario Ministry of Education
regulations, particularly with respect to suspensions and expulsions, as well
as hearing and appeals panels.

*5.2 Alternatives for Students Experiencing Repeated or
Long-term Suspension or Expulsion*

Under a provincially funded partnership with the Ottawa–Carleton
Catholic School Board (OCCSB), and with assistance form the Youth Services Bureau, plans were completed in January 2002 for a boardwide,
strict discipline program located at St. Elizabeth's Elementary School.
This program provides alternative measures for students on full expulsion,
with a specialized educational service and a therapeutic component. It
also provides specific services on an as-needed basis through community
mental health providers.

6. Volunteers

6.1 Increase Number of Volunteers

As of February 2002, in addition to parent volunteers, there were 751
nonparent volunteers in the schools providing 2,124 volunteer hours per
week. This is almost double the number of volunteers and hours recorded
the previous year. Most schools (98 percent elementary and 50 percent secondary) reported having enough volunteers to support school activities. Areas identified for increased support were remedial and special education and
tutoring (elementary and secondary), mentoring and cocurricular activities
(elementary), and library assistance and office assistance (secondary).

6.2 Training Sessions for Volunteers and Volunteer Co-coordinators

Volunteer training sessions cosponsored with the Ottawa Centre for Research and Innovation were held November 2001 and January 2002, with

120 and 105 volunteers in attendance. Two training sessions were provided for volunteer coordinators in September and October 2001. In December 2001, 117 schools or sites reported the names of their volunteer coordinators. A celebration and recognition event was held for volunteer coordinators during National Volunteer Week in April 2002.

7. Board Structures and Processes

This group worked to facilitate increased interaction among the many players in the education system: trustees, staff, parents, students, businesses, and service providers, with a view to improving decision making. Objectives included gathering information on alternative models and identifying goals and time lines for possible structural and process changes in the short, medium, and long term.

NEXT STEPS: DEVELOPING A STRATEGIC PLAN: 2000–2003

The development of a strategic plan was one of the most important goals that Jim Grieve had set for himself and his executive team. The strategic plan would include specific areas of focus, as well as a formal process for setting performance measures and reporting on progress achieved. The school superintendents and the trustees developed the strategic plan framework for 2000–2003 in a series of meetings. They agreed that the themes from the future search action groups would serve as the backbone of the plan. Corporate management and fiscal planning were added to round out the administrative requirements for regular reporting.

Once the trustees agreed to develop a strategic plan, the director undertook a systemwide evaluation that was to provide a snapshot of what existed at the beginning of the new planning cycle and a baseline against which progress could be measured. By September 2001, system improvement plans had been developed based on the systemwide evaluation and were starting to be implemented. Jim appointed school superintendents as champions for each action team initiative. The individual action teams met nearly every month. A number of the original future search participants were actively engaged on these teams. Every six months the group of superintendents came back together again to report on progress. Each group set a target date for action and advancement of ideas, with a date to report back on their work. One year later, senior staff and members of action teams gave a report to the board of trustees. This report set high expectations for the planning and review process to achieve real gains for the students.

The future search initiatives served as the basis for the performance objectives for all senior board staff, including the director, school superintendents, and the principals. All were responsible to the board of trustees to complete the actions they had committed to. Jim spoke of the process in this way:

> I believed in what we produced that day. I believed that each of the seven areas was going to improve the lives of children in Ottawa–Carleton. I was the champion over all. Each of our senior staff was given one of the directions to champion. In any sector, the leader sets the tone. Once the action started, I had to get out of the way and let those who were prepared to lead take responsibility. I counted on them to lead in the best way possible.

Superintendents were asked to visit all the schools for which they were responsible and to prepare school reviews for improvement three times a year based on information they gathered in their schools. Superintendents remember these conversations with each of their schools with enthusiasm. In a recent interview, one superintendent said, "Although this process of setting priorities and establishing measurable objectives was at times very painful, it helped to build a stronger team with a better focus."

SUCCESS AND MAJOR ROADBLOCKS

By the start of the school year in September 2001, Jim Grieve had achieved his goal. The grassroots, community-based ideas and directions that had come out of the future search had been formally embedded in an effective strategic planning process that was to ensure their continuing relevance and evolution as requirements changed.

However, the past five years have been very difficult for Ontario education as a whole, and the OCDSB in particular. The budget freeze imposed by the Ministry of Education as part of the school reform program has reduced resources and increased pressures. After the new provincewide funding formula came into effect, school districts, especially Toronto and Ottawa, the largest urban school boards, found themselves with too little money to balance the expenses of maintaining their aging inner-city education infrastructure with the demands for new school construction in their rapidly growing suburbs.

The strategic plan had listed the following goal for the development of the board's budget for 2002–2003: partner with trustees to acquire additional funding from the provincial government to address the shortfall in areas such as salary and benefits, facilities maintenance, ESL (English as a Second Language), and special education. Public meetings were held in five locations across the OCDSB jurisdiction in January 2002 to obtain input on ways to cut the budget. The chair of the board of trustees and the director of education met with the Ontario minister of education in January 2002 to emphasize the urgency of the board's financial difficulties under the current funding model. The board and its staff continued to urge the provincial government to improve funding for the OCDSB for fiscal year 2002–2003. Regrettably, no settlement could be reached. The immediate budget shortfall began to take precedence over maintaining the rigor of the strategic planning process for some of the trustees.

Progress on the strategic plan was further slowed when, in July 2002, Jim Grieve accepted a new position as director of the Peel District School Board, in central Ontario near Toronto.

The strategic plan suffered another setback just a few months later when the municipally elected board of trustees of the Ottawa–Carleton District School Board decided not to present a balanced budget to their ministry of education, even though it was required to do so by law. The board was unable to balance the budget because it was woefully inadequate. It knew that it would be impossible to continue its many excellent programs: special education programs to mentally and physically challenged students; ESL training to its diverse, multicultural, and multilingual populations; distinctive performing and visual arts programs; and coaching support for a broad range of athletic teams. These varied and often expensive educational programs and services serve as a major economic lever in attracting people and their skills, education, and investment to this large urban center.

The Ministry of Education responded by replacing the board's trustees with an appointed supervisor. However, the board continued to meet in an unofficial capacity and has since returned to office. An independent auditor was eventually hired to evaluate the Ontario government's funding formula and to recommend action. The auditor's report, titled the *Rozanski Education Report*, was released in late spring 2003. It acknowledged that the schools, particularly in the large urban school districts, did need more money. Finally, in September 2003, the province gave additional funding to the OCDSB to cover the deficit and to provide some extra funds for the year ahead. Much damage had been done to the district and to the strategic planning process.

IMPACT OF THE FUTURE SEARCH ON STUDENTS, SCHOOLS, AND EDUCATION

The future search and priorities for actions had a major impact on the students, the individual schools, and the education system in Ottawa–Carleton. Following are Jim Grieve's reflections on the process.

Future search had a huge impact on students that can be demonstrated by some very specific and measurable outcomes. A fairly large number of students have traditionally been at risk of school failure. By developing the "school as a hub" concept, for example, we brought medical and mental health workers right into the school where they could help students and their families.

One idea behind the hub is to make a difference in how children feel about themselves, and how they engage with others at school. There was a significant impact on their readiness for school. This came up fairly dramatically on behaviour statistics, especially in terms of reduced absenteeism and suspension rates at school. These are proxy measures for how well children are relating to one another. Within two years you could see a difference in absenteeism and suspension rates. Given another five years, I am convinced we will see major positive results.

In terms of impact on the community, the future search really helped bring different communities together. For example, systems for delivering programs and services tend to be entrenched in their own activities. We asked them not so much to spend more money, but to come into the education system and deliver some of their programs right in the schools.

As a leader, future search directly impacted how I work. When I interviewed for my current job with the Peel District Board of Education, I committed to spend a full day every week in the schools, a good two hour visit to each school in our fast growing district to talk to students, principals, custodians, secretaries and parent volunteers. I now spend 20 percent of my time in schools because I value the advice I get from teachers, principals, and staff. I've added to my school visits monthly focus groups with teachers, monthly focus groups with support staff, and one with school council chairs. None of these meetings has an agenda. I just start with several questions: "What brings you joy?" and "What are your issues?" I also spend a lot more time meeting with leaders in the community—the police, Children's Aid Society, social services, and mayors. I've established a Community Education Council, inviting all organizations that provide services and funding for children to come together. This is a once a month breakfast meeting. I do the same with business leaders in our community. They give me an ongoing sense of what is going on in the community. I feed this back to the trustees, who appreciate it. The feedback from teachers, principals, superintendents, and parents is extremely valuable. Again, all of this is a direct result of seeing the power of the community coming together.

CONCLUSION: A WAY FORWARD

In October 2003, provincial elections brought a new political party to power. The new premier of Ontario has formed his cabinet and named a Torontonian, Gerard Kennedy, to the post of minister of education. We're awaiting news on what policy and program changes are likely from this new government. At the municipal level, elections in November 2003 brought a new slate of school board trustees to office. A new director has been hired. An important challenge for him is to reestablish the strategic planning process by working together with the trustees. The question is how to revitalize the process that had just begun to work effectively from 2000 to 2002. The trustees need to recommit to the long-range planning objectives and get the strategic plan back on track. While there are always new issues, the director and the trustees need to balance the short-term, often very political concerns with a focus on the future. One important objective is to ensure the public education system in Ottawa–Carleton continues to maintain and expand its market share of student enrollment in the face of growing competition from private schools. To stay fully aware, there is a requirement to be out in the community and to commit the time, effort, and funding needed to hold regular meetings with key stakeholder groups from teachers to businesspeople.

Now perhaps the conditions are right again to continue to build on the foundation of the future search action areas that were translated into clear-cut objectives in the board's strategic plan for 2000–2003. The hope is that these plans and the efforts they stimulated and encouraged will be revived by the new director and board of trustees of the OCDSB.

5

Perkiomen Valley School District: Creating a Collaborative Culture

Beverly Arsht, Nancy Aronson, and Sally Hilderbrand

The future search conference produced the broad goals for the district, but that's not what transformed the district. What transformed this district were the ongoing collaborative processes used. The potential power of future search is its philosophy and the way of working that comes with it. Engaging stakeholders and having them truly shape the future of education in the district was a precedent that was set in motion and has since become our way of working.

—Dr. Sally Hilderbrand, assistant to the superintendent for
curriculum, instruction, and assessment

INTRODUCTION

In this chapter we describe how the Perkiomen Valley School District (PVSD) overcame local cynicism and disappointment to make fundamental, long-lasting changes in the relationship between the schools and community. In addition, these changes greatly improved cooperation among members of the community as they worked with each other on behalf of their children.

It has been nine years since PVSD began its strategic planning process based on future search principles and methods. The specifics of what has been accomplished are now known. Institutionalized change has occurred. Conference goals and objectives have been achieved. The culture of the organization has shifted from blame to responsibility and from fragmentation to unity.

CONTEXT

In Pennsylvania, school district strategic planning that included multiple stakeholders was mandated starting in 1993. Understanding how the PVSD turned this mandate into a vehicle for communitywide cooperation offers useful insight into the conditions under which large group planning processes such as future search are most likely to be effective. The past strategic plan had sat on the proverbial shelf. The community felt that its input had not been used, resulting in a great deal of cynicism. District leadership felt accountable to the community and knew the process had to be different this time around.

Other realities were also having an impact. Demographic changes were beginning to occur at a faster rate. In 1993 the district had already grown to 2,700 students (now there are 5,000 students), four schools (the seventh school is now opening), and 250 professional staff (now there are 400). The changes in the community were impacting longtime residents. New housing developments were bringing in residents with different economic, sociologic, and educational experiences. Area residents saw themselves as having different lifestyles and different ideas about what they expected from the school district. The community was fragmented and tensions existed.

To add to the complexity, the position of superintendent had been unstable. Over a two-year period the district had hired five superintendents. An acting superintendent held the office while a search and interview process for the next candidate was underway. Despite these complications, Sally Hilderbrand, in her role as assistant to the superintendent, felt an immediate and pressing need for the district and community to begin working together on strategic planning. She hoped to start a planning process that was robust enough to constructively manage these realities.

Selection of the Future Search Approach

In the fall of 1993, Sally attended a one-day conference in a neighboring district on determining the skills and capabilities needed by high school graduates in the twenty-first century. This conference brought into dialogue 100 school and community members in a format that she had not experienced before. This conference, she learned, was built on the future search principles for effective planning: 1) having the "whole system" in the room, 2) exploring the global context before seeking to take local action, 3) focusing on the future and common ground rather than problems and conflicts, 4) having participants use self-management in their small groups, and 5) sharing responsibility for follow-up.

Sally liked this process for a number of reasons. It was a match with her own personal preferences for organizing and leading, and it fit with what she believed the district and community needed to move ahead in a constructive way. For example, conference participants were highly engaged and actively participating. There were no long lectures. During this conference, Sally experienced the kind of active learning that she valued and wanted to see in classrooms. Additionally, she noted that the design and facilitation of the activities were structured so that diverse stakeholders could find common ground, even in light of many differences. The group, large as it was, could still stay task focused and make decisions even when tensions were expressed along the way.

TWO LARGE GROUP PLANNING CONFERENCES

Given the unsteady state of the district's top leadership and the state-mandated process, Sally felt it was essential that the school district make decisions about how to proceed in a manner that communicated structure, enabled collaboration, and promoted stability. Sally believed that the district would benefit from having two large group planning conferences, since these two events would engage more stakeholders over a longer period of time. These conferences would serve as anchoring events, designed to bring the district and community together to chart a positive, realistic course for the future. The first meeting would be a one-day community convention—similar to the process Sally had experienced. The second would be a two-day future search conference.

The Community Convention

On March 12, 1994, the district convened A Community Convention: The Graduate of 2010. One hundred community members—students, parents, senior citizens, leaders from business, the trades, nonprofits, and higher education along with school administrators, faculty, staff, and board members—put their minds together to discover what skills and capabilities students graduating in 2010 would need to succeed.

A Turning Point for the District

Having a large, task-focused meeting was a bold move on the part of the district. A new, public way of working was being offered. Participants from three townships and three boroughs worked together constructively as they deepened their understanding of the past, present, and future in relation to student skills and capabilities. This group included long-term residents and newcomers, residents with no children in the schools, and young families wanting the district to be more responsive to their needs.

Tension was in the room. Personal and group agendas were evident. While the dialogue about needed skills and capabilities for students graduating in 2010 was in progress, a challenging issue surfaced. Participants soon began debating the extent to which they were treading on *values*. As people listened to each other—whatever their differences on wording—they discovered that they wanted the same basic skills and capabilities for students. Participants realized they needed a way to express their intentions so that they could all stand behind their desired message. A term soon emerged that everyone could support: *responsible citizenship*.

This was a breakthrough, a transformational experience. For the first time 100 local residents discovered what it meant to successfully develop *shared meaning*. In just a few hours they had shifted their relationships across and within the district and community—moving from individualism to connection. People were sharing their thinking and building on each other's ideas rather than having a hodgepodge of individual or group agendas. One stakeholder, the then-executive director of the Perkiomen Valley Chamber of Commerce, remarked with awe, "People today are taking responsibility for our community!"

Results of the Community Convention

This first conference launched a new way for the district and community to work together on behalf of children. It demonstrated that large groups of local citizens who had never worked together before could engage in healthy public discourse and achieve significant agreements. The conference participants discovered common ground on six skills and capabilities that they wanted the graduates of 2010 to possess for life in the twenty-first century. These identified skills and capabilities became the graduation goals and have served as a framework for guiding all curriculum revisions:

- *Effective communicators* who gather, process, and articulate information through reading, writing, speaking, active listening, and visual presentations.
- *Creative problem solvers and complex thinkers* who apply basic knowledge to assimilate, analyze, synthesize, and evaluate information in a variety of contexts.
- *Collaborative workers* who use effective interpersonal skills and work collaboratively to reach a common goal within diverse settings.
- *Responsible citizens* who understand and appreciate the diversity of others, demonstrate environmental responsibility, and make personal commitments to improve the quality of life in both the local and global communities.
- *Technoliterate processors* who use various forms of technology including those that access information.
- *Self-directed learners* who accept responsibility for their own physical, social, emotional, and mental well-being, make decisions independently, develop life skills, adapt to an ever-changing world, and are accountable for their actions.

By their senior year, students understand the graduation goals and what type of work is represented in each area. Students—and their families—can see the tangible evidence of development and feel the pride of accomplishment as they are given their portfolios at graduation. The items selected for the portfolio relate to the six skills and capabilities. By graduation, students understand the graduation goals and what type of work represents each area. At graduation all students and their families can see the tangible evidence of development and feel the pride of accomplishment as they are given their portfolios.

Having collaboratively created these specific graduation goals greatly boosted the system's stakeholders and their views of how they were making an authentic contribution. One parent enthusiastically said, "The graduate of 2010 will have a great advantage over the kids today. We are learning a lot more about what we need to do to prepare them." This spirit is described beautifully by Michael Fullan: "Shared meaning and organization connectedness are the long-term assets of high performing systems" (1999, p. 28). PVSD had begun its journey of collaboration with varied constituencies. This effort of working together signaled a new beginning for the district.

The Future Search Conference

The theme for the future search was "Perkiomen Valley Committing to a Shared Vision!" A diverse group of 15 people formed the future search steering committee and planned the conference. They also selected the state-mandated strategic planning committee of 35 community and district participants who served as a sounding board after the conference and before the final approval of the district strategic plan by the school board.

During planning, decisions had to be made about purpose, inviting other stakeholders, communications to stakeholders, and documentation of the conference. The overall roadmap for moving this change process forward was shared with the group, and there were opportunities for clarification and modification (see figure 5.1).

To provide a congruent experience for the future search steering committee and the strategic planning committee, the consultants designed their group work to model the format that would be used during the future search conference. As an example, for each task there was dialogue in small groups (five to eight people), report-outs to the whole room, and then large group dialogue to bring the thinking of all groups into the final agreements that were needed.

Engaging Others prior to the Future Search Conference

Building-level teams were instrumental in involving others in the strategic planning process. Even before the future search, faculty and staff members in all schools were engaged in dialogue. They were brought up-to-date about the activities of strategic planning and had an opportunity to explore and express their thinking. They learned about the work of the

STRATEGIC PLANNING PROCESS *

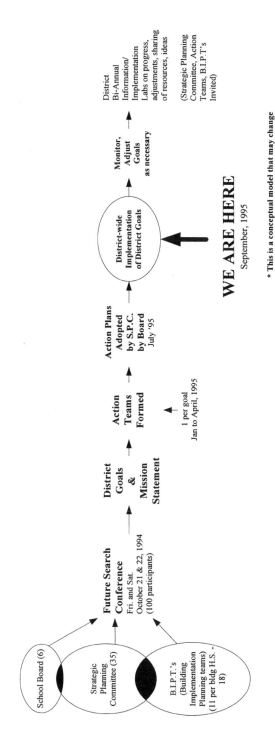

Figure 5.1. Overall Roadmap (Courtesy Beverly Arsht and Nancy Aronson)

School Board (6)

Strategic Planning Committee (35)

B.I.P.T.'s (Building Implementation Planning teams) (11 per bldg H.S. - 18)

Future Search Conference Fri. and Sat. October 21 & 22, 1994 (100 participants)

District Goals & Mission Statement

Action Teams Formed
1 per goal Jan to April, 1995

Action Plans Adopted by S.P.C. by Board July '95

District-wide Implementation of District Goals

WE ARE HERE September, 1995

* This is a conceptual model that may change as the process develops

Monitor, Adjust Goals as necessary

District Bi-Annual Information/ Implementation Labs on progress, adjustments, sharing of resources, ideas

(Strategic Planning Committee, Action Teams, B.I.P.T's Invited)

steering committee and came to understand that the district's future goals would be created as a product of the future search. They too engaged in small group dialogues and reported out their conclusions. These conclusions were documented and later brought into the future search as information to be considered in planning.

The Future Search

The future search conference was held in October 1994. Ninety diverse stakeholders met together for approximately 16 hours to determine the district goals. Although there was some overlap in participants from the community convention, most of the attendees were new to the process. Also participating at the conference was the newly appointed superintendent of schools, Dr. Carole Spahr.

Results of the Future Search Conference

While the community convention launched community participation, the future search conference reinforced that this was a viable way for a community to influence and work with a school district. Seven strategic goals for setting the broad directions for the future of the district were identified:

1. Increasing technology resources within the district
2. Effective communications with the entire community
3. Expansion of the school facilities beyond the scheduled school day
4. Partnerships: integration of businesses, colleges, the community, and education
5. Coordination of development and community resources
6. Ongoing curriculum development
7. Funding sources

These goals did not sit on a shelf. They were in front of people all the time. They were used as a framework for important district activities such as curriculum planning and revision; administrator planning, both at the district and building level; and biannual, open review meetings that were instituted to monitor progress.

As the actual work to achieve the goals and their more specific objectives proceeded, community participation at all district levels became institutionalized. For instance, the community curriculum advisory council (CCAC) has been meeting monthly for eight years. This group has a real voice in the education of students. When, for example, they came to believe that a foreign language program was needed at the elementary level, they were instrumental in making this happen.

THE GOALS WERE MET

The overwhelming majority of goals and their objectives were met. The impact of the future search was felt, as the dreams became plans and the plans led to actions and desired outcomes. A sense of pride and accomplishment was experienced within the district and in the community. Student test scores improved. The community committed time and participated in the changes. During the future search there was a point when participants discussed that they would recognize that change in the district had happened if they became a community of choice. What this meant to them was that Realtors would promote moving into the community because of the school district's reputation. At the time of the conference this was not the case. However, today PVSD has fulfilled this aspiration, and the school population continues to grow. Examples of the district's accomplishments relating to each of the goal areas follow.

Goal A: Technology

- Promoted integration of technology into all curriculum areas. Completed staff development program over a five-year span for *all* professional staff members. Held extensive summer workshops.
- Completed a district network for e-mail with all computers having Internet access.
- Installed video networks and TV studios in all buildings.
- Converted all school libraries to electronic research and information systems.
- Created a district website, as well as one for each building.
- Held computer and technology workshops for senior citizens.

Goal B: Effective Communication

- Established a full-time school and community relations coordinator position.
- Established building-level news release coordinators.
- Reinstituted, after many years, parent conferences at the high school.
- Established a CCAC "focus dinner" once a year for community, parents, and staff.
- Used the new middle school auditorium to host many community events.

Goal C: School Facilities

- Implemented library open hours one evening a week from 6:00 to 8:30 P.M. in the middle school and high school; this includes use of library computer facilities.
- Expanded the number of programs in community ed.

Goal D: Partnership Integration

- Began a high school job shadowing program for students into local businesses; this has expanded greatly in the years since.
- Increased steadily the number of students enrolled at the vocational-technical school.
- Formed a career education committee and implemented a K–12 career education program.

Goal E: Community Resources

- Established school volunteer coordinators in each school to handle parent and community volunteers.
- Began class and schoolwide service learning projects organized by school volunteer coordinators, such as collecting soda can tabs for Ronald McDonald House.

Goal F: Curriculum Development

- Began a community curriculum advisory committee (CCAC) in September 1995 that is still going strong.

- Accomplished a major high school course revision.
- Instituted monthly reading and math meetings by grade level in elementary buildings.
- Held a developmentally appropriate practices in-service for kindergarten teachers such as how to teach alphabet recognition at several different readiness levels.
- Articulated multicultural activities in all content areas, grades 1–5.
- Began an exploratory foreign language program in Spanish, German, and French for all grade 6 students at the middle school; level I study of one language is then taught to all middle school students in grades 7 and 8.
- Explored block scheduling at the high school level over a two-year period.
- Implemented peer mediation programs at both high school and middle school levels.
- Promoted character education via a "What Is a Responsible Citizen?" forum held over two evenings where five characteristics were agreed upon by stakeholder participants.
- Created an annual district assessment report in 1996 that has been continued ever since.

Goal G: Funding

- Participated as a district in a consortium of several nearby school districts to bid as a collective for health benefits to help reduce costs.
- Formulated new rental fees for use of district facilities to increase income into the district.
- Researched grant opportunities and subsequently applied for several.

A RETROSPECTIVE STUDY: FACTORS INFLUENCING SUSTAINED ACTION

In 1994, as we designed this intervention, we worked to deeply understand the question, "What will it take to institutionalize the changes that the system says it wants?" In 2003, nine years after the events just described, the authors of this chapter met to review what had been accomplished in

PVSD. As the three of us examined the significant events that helped shape how the intervention was implemented, we identified four important factors influencing sustained action. Although these factors are described separately, in reality there is a great deal of overlap among them.

Identification and Use of a Compelling Purpose

In 1993, it was more the norm for committees to set the *goals* for the district rather than set the *purpose* for the strategic planning process. Understanding the difference between developing the larger purpose for the future search and strategic planning versus creating the goals for the district's future helped clarify the core difference in this approach. Schlecty (1991) states this well: "Purpose does not refer to goals. Goals are targets; purposes have to do with values and commitments . . . purpose defines the kinds of goals the organization will pursue" (p. 30). An important role of the future search steering committee was to set the purpose of the district strategic planning.

Axelrod (2000) makes the connection between developing purpose and the building of relationships sensitively: "For a purpose to connect people, it must reach both their heads and hearts. In other words, they must perceive the purpose as meaningful" (p. 83). As a result of collaborating on purpose, steering committee participants were building connections, and their rhythm of working together developed further. The task of creating a shared purpose represented an important achievement in the life of this group and its increasing confidence in advocating for this approach to planning.

It was important to the planners that the district staff and the larger community understand the major issues discussed in the planning meetings and how those ideas were directly linked to the purposes. The purpose statement of the district strategic planning is described below. The notes in parentheses were used as a tool to assist in sending consistent messages across the district.

- To keep a focus on children and their preparation for life in the twenty-first century. (This serves as a bridge to the community convention of six months before.)

- To create broad-based support for the district by the various constituencies and communities. (This addresses the need to reduce fragmentation.)
- To develop a shared vision for the future of PVSD. (This represents the desire for collaborative work.)
- To build a bridge to the next stage of action planning. (The desired outcomes are imbedded within the goals, and they lead to action.)

The use of a collaboratively developed purpose to frame the context of the planning process helped with communication, inspiration, and focus. The purpose statement developed by a diverse group was more apt to resonate with others because it was conceived by understanding many different perspectives. The importance of discovering shared agreements regarding purpose is described below. This step of the process was

- A real task for members of the steering group to discover shared meaning and grasp the fundamental nature of how future search principles are realized in a work product.
- A tool for deciding who needed to be included in the future search conference.
- An anchor for communicating with others outside the steering committee.
- A guide for participants at the future search conference as they worked to discover the common-ground goals for the future.
- A frame of reference for checking progress over time.

Active, Committed Leadership and Capacity Building

It was critical to have active, committed leadership from the top leaders. As strategic planning was launched, Sally Hilderbrand understood the district's responsibility in providing opportunities for building capacity throughout the system. The original design for systemwide change was enabled by encouraging district employees and the community to take leadership roles as facilitators, active supporters, or responsible implementers. When Carole Spahr began her job as superintendent, she effectively joined in the collaboration. Central to the success of this leadership duo was their ongoing part in cultivating systemwide participation in planning and implementation. These two top leaders actively initiated and nurtured widespread involvement. As Fullan (2001) deftly captures, "The litmus test of all leadership is whether it mobilizes people's commitment to putting their energy into actions designed to improve things. It is individual commitment, but it is above all collective mobilization" (p. 9). Their clear roles, together and apart, did influence collective mobilization, as evidenced by the ongoing commitment of stakeholders giving their time and energy on behalf of improving the district. A closer look at each of the leaders' roles follows.

The Superintendent's Leadership Roles

As the fifth superintendent in two years, Dr. Carole Spahr was new to the district. Her first major introduction to the system was her participation in the future search conference. This was a terrific way for her to accelerate learning more about the district and community. In just a few hours she was able to work with a group of 90 people, hear about their experiences, and learn from their perspectives on the district's past, present, and future. From her involvement in the future search and her support for this approach to planning, Carole became a beacon of light for the community. Below are several aspects of the superintendent's role that had a strong, positive impact on lasting change:

- *Placing strategic planning front and center in the district.* Carole reinforced the importance of strategic planning when she spoke publicly. She continually grounded people in its purpose, ongoing progress, and upcoming actions.
- *Limiting the number of meetings for action planning work.* The superintendent put a five-meeting limit to the number of action-team sessions. Carole believed that, all too often, so much energy was expended in action planning that there was little energy left for implementation. The five-meeting limit helped action-team members keep their focus on higher-level ideas without micromanaging details.
- *Committing to an administrative process that would translate district goals to building-level implementation.* Annual administrator retreats were used to further connect operational goals with district goals and

objectives. This was a useful way to discuss and track overall district changes and also inform each other of projected changes for the up-coming year.

- *Maintaining the board of directors' connection to the plan, action items, and related budget.* During budget meetings the superintend-ent highlighted those items that were related to strategic planning. She discussed new initiatives in relation to how they fit with the goals.

- *Institutionalizing public strategic planning review meetings.* Ongo-ing annual public meetings continue to link district progress and plans with the larger community. The review meetings are structured for face-to-face interaction to allow for a two-way exchange of in-formation.

- *Supporting the efforts of the process champion.* Resources were allo-cated to support the district's highly collaborative approach to change.

The Process Champion's Leadership Roles

Sally Hilderbrand was responsible for seeing that strategic planning fit state requirements and met the needs of the district and community. Sally felt strongly that active engagement was needed. In 1994 this way of plan-ning was not the norm in the region; she was breaking new ground. In the description that follows, we captured the highlights of what she did so that others might benefit from seeing the tasks that made her role work so well. The tasks are organized into four main areas.

1. The process champion developed an overall roadmap. This roadmap (figure 5.1) illustrated the structures and activities for planning the conference and what would be put into place to sustain implementa-tion once the goals were established. The roadmap was also used to de-scribe the change process and reassure stakeholders, particularly those in the community, about how this planning would lead to action. This was especially important because of the cynicism surrounding the previous strategic planning efforts.

2. The process champion secured the resources to support the work over time. Sally played a central role in mobilizing essential resources. Her focus, energy, and strong relationships, within the district and community, combined to set the stage for success. As process champion, she saw that strategic planning items were included in the district budget. She planned in-service days for staff involvement in the process. Sally campaigned for active participation by influential stakeholders to form the 35-member strategic planning committee (required by the state mandate), and with help from the steering committee (15 members), recruited stakeholders for both conferences and for action planning. She enlisted a local corporation to provide a beautiful site for both conferences. Sally also designated a person responsible for writing newsletters.

3. The process champion built capacity in self and others. Sally felt that she was extending her own design and facilitation skills as she worked with the consultants to map out events, participate in collaborative planning, and facilitate large group processes. The leaders of the action planning teams and the teacher-leaders of the building-level teams took part in facilitator training that prepared them for their roles. Sally cofacilitated designing and leading these sessions. She also played the central role in supporting these team leaders between sessions.

Barth (1990) endorses the great potential of teachers: "Teachers harbor extraordinary leadership capabilities, and their leadership is a major untapped resource for improving our nation's schools" (p. 124). PVSD found innovative ways of tapping the resources of the system and provided the necessary support for individuals and groups to extend their skills and experiences.

4. The process champion continued to use future search principles and processes in the district. Most notably, in 2001 when a new superintendent arrived, it was time to do the next round of strategic planning. Large group process had become tradition in the community; the community held the expectation that a large group, high-engagement event would be the way to go. The district once again implemented strategic planning using a large group process.

As we look back to see how future search principles and practices have been institutionalized, it is clear that PVSD has continued to utilize diverse stakeholder groups when the situation calls for a collaborative perspective. The practice of using self-managed groups has also become a way of managing large group dialogue and discussion.

A Vigorous Two-Way Communication Plan: An Ever-Widening Circle of Involvement

PVSD's communication plan emphasized informing others, engaging stakeholders, and continually inviting in people who were ready to enter the process. The district kept the planning and implementation process open to stakeholders so that when people were ready to get involved there was opportunity to do so. PVSD often invited stakeholders for valuable purposes where their thinking was used to shape results. The communication strategies that kept the district staff and community well informed and continually contributing to the process follow. 1) At each school, faculty and staff were continually informed about how the process was going and the results. In addition, they had multiple opportunities to provide their perspectives to the district. 2) The larger community was kept up-to-date with newsletters and the public review meetings. Both venues had vehicles for feedback. 3) It became a norm at PVSD to send an information summary to all participants after any collaborative meetings with stakeholders. Participants saw their thinking in the meeting recorded and knew their voices were being considered. These summaries also helped the district administration keep track of what was happening.

A Clear Emphasis: Action Planning as a Bridge to Action

One of the most effective strategies of the entire strategic planning process was how PVSD went about action planning. It emphasized to action teams that their job was to create a bridge to action. This simple statement was critical. Each action team knew that its charge was to operationalize the initial intent from the future search regarding each goal. Its job was to give a more specific description of *how* each goal could be accomplished. The possibilities that were proposed at the conference were brought into this planning. The teams built on these ideas, modified what was proposed, and added new ideas that were true to the intent proposed at the future search. A significant guideline given to the action teams was that what was being developed by them would be examined in even greater detail and then implemented by other groups, committees, or individuals in the district. The intent was to clarify that those who would be implementing the goals would accomplish the more detailed planning.

As part of building the bridge to the next stage, action teams suggested stakeholder groups or specific titles of people who were needed in implementation planning. The action teams also identified the title of the person who would be responsible for this next stage. The actual flow of planning, decision making, and approval that occurred follows:

- Broad goals and the intent of each were developed at the future search conference.
- Action planning teams further developed objectives and next steps.
- Action plans were reviewed by the 35-member strategic planning committee.
- The school board approved the goals and action plans.
- There was public review of the entire strategic plan (30 days as mandated by the state).
- Further development and, ultimately, implementation of objectives began.

PVSD maintained supportive and positive connections with parents and the community throughout the planning process and beyond. The action planning phase helped frame clear boundaries. The explicit framing of this action planning helped avoid many of the struggles between the district and the community that others in Pennsylvania experienced. The action planning as a bridge to action emphasis kept a high-level focus so that micromanaging was avoided. The professional staff were able to effectively make the educational decisions that they needed to study, select, and implement.

CONCLUSION

Currently, in the Perkiomen Valley School District, the second round of strategic planning has just been completed. The district is in the midst of implementing an even more ambitious strategic plan as it continues its quest to improve its efforts to meet the needs of each and every one of its students. Parent and community involvement remains high.

Because of the future search conference and its related principles, Perkiomen Valley School District created a new way of working. The district and community saw that their input, time, and efforts were truly able to shape the future. Fragmentation shifted to unification. Cynicism shifted to increased trust and optimism. Personal agendas shifted to personal work on behalf of the greater good, the well-being of the children of the community. They witnessed the goals and objectives being not only planned but implemented. At PVSD education improved, attitudes changed, and stability emerged.

Sally Hilderbrand, who has led strategic planning efforts in the district since 1993, believes that the future search processes launched by the school district in 1994 have led to unity and collaboration far beyond the schools. The school district and community successfully developed the interest, skills, and structures for collaborating on an ongoing basis. PVSD leadership developed the know-how to hear the voice of the community, build positive connections, and take the necessary actions for implementing their shared dreams. As a result, confidence in and commitment to the district have increased. Stakeholders have given their time and energy over the years, because they see the results of their efforts. They have realized that they have common aspirations for the education and development of their children. This collaborative work continues to shape 1) the broad directions for the district, 2) the supporting action plans, 3) curriculum issues, and 4) other educational initiatives and issues as they arise. A by-product of this collaboration—task-focused work—is that the Perkiomen Valley School District and the community it serves are more unified.

Part 3

GROWING COMMUNITY PARTNERSHIPS

Those who consider future search may wonder about the wisdom of widespread community involvement in school planning at the outset. Often they fear that "outsiders" will have too high expectations of the school district or else overstep their role. What has been found is that by opening the system through a future search, people better understand their role and find ways to contribute more fully and appropriately. The four chapters in this section highlight some partnerships and collaborations that followed these future searches.

Community partnerships among the school system and agencies, organizations, and citizens have fueled the schools-as-centers program that followed the North Platte, NE (chapter 6), future search. A community organization that coordinates and celebrates these services has garnered state, federal, and private grants to support these programs.

In Naperville, IL (chapter 7), parents and citizens have become true partners in the school district. A foundation was able to procure more monies to support teachers' innovative ideas. Business mentorships for teachers have linked them to specialized knowledge and skills in their community. In addition to these and many other tangible outcomes, the intangibles of trust, empowerment, a network of stakeholders, increased leadership capacity, and ownership of outcomes have also been enhanced.

Both San Gabriel, CA (chapter 8), and Minneapolis, MN (chapter 9), used future search to develop ways to provide health services to students in response to research showing that students who are sick and hungry are unable to learn. San Gabriel's community collaborative worked hard to receive a state grant to launch its "one-stop shop" that meets the health, mental health, and social needs of students and families. Now a clinic provides services for uninsured sick students, administering general checkups, immunizations, and sports physicals. Their "one-stop shop" partners with other agencies to provide after-school programs, language instruction, emergency food supplies, tutoring, pregnancy prevention, and services to pregnant teens and teen mothers.

In Minneapolis, MN (chapter 9), a partnership among public health providers, private health providers, and the school system now provides equity and access to quality health care for students. By including the private sector despite initial objections from some public sector providers, this strong partnership is able to meet the health needs of students, including primary care, immunizations, asthma treatments, and sports physicals, with a focus on prevention and early intervention. The creative infrastructure of this partnership sustains the vision, focus, and energy of this community effort.

6

Activating Social Capital through Community Support and Interagency Cooperation: A Future Search Success Story in Education

Rita Schweitz, Ken Seeley, and James Merritt

Never doubt that a small group of thoughtful committed citizens can change the world; indeed, it's the only thing that ever has.

—Margaret Mead

This is the story of how a small group of thoughtful, committed citizens started an effort that changed their community. Their work mobilized citizens in North Platte, NE, a middle American city of 24,000, to provide better educational and support services for children, youth, and their families. Their endeavor emphasized and formalized the importance of social capital in the North Platte community. For its vision and work, the city has since received more than $1.5 million in grants and national recognition, including the 1998–1999 Award for Excellence in Community Collaboration for Children and Youth, sponsored by the National League of Cities and five other national organizations representing school systems and local governments.

FUTURE SEARCH AS A CATALYST OF SOCIAL CAPITAL

There is a good deal of debate about the exact definition of *social capital*. For our purposes, we agree with Ian Falk (2003) that social capital holds the promise of being a framework that can show us why and how common values, networks, and trust can help provide individuals, families, and communities, in partnership with governments, with the ability to change and improve their social and economic well-being. Future search can produce these same results, prompting the increase of social capital by bringing the system together to discover its common values and agree on desired actions.

BACKGROUND

In 1996 and 1997, Nebraska Lt. Governor Kim Robak led a major overhaul of the state health and human services agencies to develop a statewide system of care for Nebraska's most vulnerable families, children, and citizens. Not a believer in incremental change, Lt. Governor Robak set forth a rapid, radical format of planning and local implementation to occur within one year.

The pace of this state reform required fast community response. The state created local grants to promote collaborative planning. It granted funds to integrated services that produced systemic results for people rather than to departmentalized services that produced isolated process data like number of clients served or financial statements.

The North Platte region's many collaborative efforts fit into the state's integrated system of care. Future search appeared to be an excellent approach to addressing the urgency for local integrated planning when Lincoln County/North Platte decided to be a lead community in the new Nebraska Partnership Project.

THE STORY BEGINS WITH A FEW PROFESSIONALS

The path to this success began in the 1980s when regional Director of Special Education and Assistant Administrator Marge Beatty, Region II Human Services Program Director Kathy Seacrest, and Jan Spalding from the Department of Social Services began to work together to look at professional services for families and children in their community. These leaders knew that different community agencies worked with the same families and children but had little interagency communication. Professionals from these agencies were unaware of what the other agencies were doing. They frequently received partial or disjointed information from their mutual clients. No one ever saw the whole picture. Beatty, Seacrest, and Spalding realized that everyone involved was missing a chance to maximize their efforts.

The three invited other service providers to join them in exploring the services and activities of each agency. These early information-sharing gatherings grew to include representatives from the school district, human services, the health department, the mental health department, law enforcement, the juvenile justice system, recreational organizations, and others. All of the participants soon realized that by working as a network and opening communication, they could better coordinate and address the needs of children and families. Through coordination they were able to overcome many of the disadvantages of a compartmentalized service delivery system. Eventually, this growing group formed an organization, Connections, "to coordinate and enhance services for children, youth and families in Lincoln County," where North Platte is located.

Connections grew to 120 individual members and met quarterly as a whole group. In addition, its five teams—treatment, intervention, coordinating, prevention and education, and special projects—worked individually in their own areas. The prevention and education group worked on critical issues facing students and their families. They knew that there were many latchkey kids in empty homes after school until their parents returned from their workdays. They were aware that working parents had difficulty finding and paying for quality after-school care for their children. This group also knew that the high school was over 50 years old and inadequate. A bond issue for a new high school had been defeated twice in the 1990s. They wanted to find a way to meet more of students' needs within their limited budgets.

PLANNING THE FUTURE SEARCH CONFERENCE

Every year, Connections held a professionally facilitated strategic planning day at which they reviewed the past year and set their goals for the upcoming one. In 1997, Connections' coordinating team was looking for a process for its annual strategic planning session to stimulate new energy, bring in more community members and organizations, and meet the new

Nebraska funding guidelines that stressed coordination among agencies. Ken Seeley, executive director of The Colorado Foundation for Families and Children, was working with Connections to help them develop a local collaborative action plan to address the new state agencies' funding requirements. His thoughtful description of future search principles, its process, and his experiences in facilitating future searches in other educational settings convinced the team that future search was worth exploring.

The coordinating team became a steering group. After careful consideration, the steering group agreed that a future search would provide a solid foundation for their work. The steering group struggled to create a theme that would capture their dreams and desires for their community. They finally agreed that the theme of their future search would be "The Coming Together Conference: Action Planning for Assuring the Continued Quality of Life in Lincoln County." Maintaining and growing social capital was the underlying theme of the future search, although the term *social capital* was not widely used at the time.

This community had a long history with social capital. From its pioneer heritage when helping neighbors was a necessity of survival to the present day when neighbors still looked out for each other, a norm of social connections and interactions existed. People pitched in to help when needed, knowing that when they needed help, someone would provide it. As Putnam (2000) has found, "Social capital, social networks and the associated norms of reciprocity" (p. 21) are strong in Nebraska. "Statistically, the correlation between high social capital and positive child development (and therefore school success) is as close to perfect as social scientists ever find in data analysis of this sort. States such as . . . Nebraska . . . have healthy civic adults and healthy well-adjusted kids" (p. 297). Connections wanted to stimulate even more social capital on a large scale for the benefit of the entire community.

The future search conference would look at and plan for the future of the entire community, not only for the school system. It would look at how to enrich all aspects of the community: health and mental health, economic development, community pride, recreation, and transportation, as well as education. The steering group brainstormed all of the stakeholders who needed to be involved and clustered them into eight stakeholder groups: education, health, agriculture, business and industry, human services, community volunteers, criminal justice, and youth. Because all of

Lincoln County had to be represented, participants were of diverse age, gender, occupation, culture, economics, and interests. They included youth, seniors, movers and shakers, old-timers and newcomers, the faith community, and other citizens.

THE FUTURE SEARCH CONFERENCE

The future search conference was exciting and exhausting. Participants worked hard to listen to and learn from each other. Their time lines graphically illustrated the connectedness in the community. "The future search brought old-timers, newcomers, and everyone in between to a greater understanding of their community. With the time lines and the mind map, everyone in the room was on the same page," a participant said as she recalled the event five years later. The mind map of the present emphasized the current challenges of the many community needs that were not being addressed. The vivid future scenarios were fun and motivating. They left participants dissatisfied with their current reality.

At the conclusion of the future search conference, participants were excited. They realized that, together, they could accomplish the goals they had individually dreamed about. People discovered that others shared many of their ideas. The right people were in the room—a cross-section of citizens was dedicated to make positive changes. School Superintendent Dr. James Merritt and Mayor Jim Whitaker were both ready to tackle difficult issues. A willingness to implement new ideas and a commitment to change were palpable. Before people left, they volunteered to work on the following teams:

- Schools as centers.
- Youth and recreation.
- A treatment team to coordinate child abuse treatment and investigation teams.
- Integrated services to develop a mechanism for information gathering, and to coordinate, integrate, and expedite service delivery.
- An expanded tax base to bring in industry and commercial enterprises.
- Unified pride to engage the community and the Union Pacific Railroad, a major employer in the community.

- A coordinating team to locate funding, create an organization, and effectively manage Connections.

> This was the first meeting where lots of different community groups and people came together. It put people together in the same room, spinning dreams and celebrating history together.
>
> —future search participant

FUTURE SEARCH OUTCOMES

Volunteers and professionals are still working on these teams, although some team names and goals have changed. All teams have enjoyed considerable success. For example, the tax base has expanded considerably with the establishment of a Wal-Mart distribution center in town. During the future search conference, one of the early critics of the process was the director of economic development. By the last day he was won over, stating that he would build the economic development effort on the future search outcomes.

The Connections coordinating team's early effort was to apply for and receive a $100,000 grant from the Nebraska Foundation for Families and Children. They also changed their name to Community Connections. "After visualizing the future, we were no longer content with the present because we knew that the service could be better for kids and families," recalled the director of special education. "It was obvious that to create a better future we needed dedicated staff."

Community Connections hired a full-time executive director, Jayna Schaaf Swanson, to coordinate and support the work of the teams and to help find ways to turn their visions into reality. Today, Community Connections has three full-time members and one part-time staff member and 25 after-school staff members. This umbrella organization facilitates communication, cooperation, and coordination among more than 70 participating organizations and numerous at-large members. Community Connections, according to its brochure, is "dedicated to planning and implementing action that furthers the quality of life for children and families in Lincoln County." More than 260 Lincoln County residents volunteer their time and talents to accomplish team, committee, and program goals. Annually, approximately 615 families receive direct assistance and positive opportunities through Community Connections.

YOUTH

Youth played a very important role in the future search. This group of articulate and passionate young people made their voices heard in every future search activity. They let the adults know that their needs and goals were critical to the quality of life in the community and that they were an untapped resource. This group took on the task of publicizing activities for youth and working to provide more positive outlets for young people. Their contributions in the future search encouraged the superintendent to add one nonvoting youth to the school board.

EDUCATION

Dr. James Merritt, North Platte's new superintendent of schools, had only been in his position a few months before the Coming Together Conference. He was able to acquire an invaluable understanding of the history, challenges, opportunities, and people in his school district in the two-and-a-half days of the future search conference. He was also able to capture the enthusiasm of the future search to create a "schools-as-centers" program in his school system. This new school model would address the problems of fragmented child services while helping all children succeed in school. Schools would combine a range of educational, health, and social services to ensure that children would be ready and able—socially, physically, and emotionally—to learn. Welch (2001) describes the schools-as-centers model as "a proactive response to our new understanding about what all children need. We can no longer separate the child at school from the child after school and from the child at home. The well-being of the whole child is tied to the well-being of the whole community."

Dr. Merritt's vision, shared with many others at the future search conference, was to connect the community with the schools and to supplement traditional curriculum with new programs to enrich student experiences.

His hope was that this enrichment would not come solely from the school district budget.

The schools-as-centers program has grown to sponsor after-school programs at elementary schools, Asset programs (see description below), mentoring and tutoring at the middle schools, and tobacco prevention programs at the high school. "Schools as Centers came from a dream, from a skit at the future search. And now it's fabulous," exclaimed Lois Books, community activist and future search participant.

Schools as Centers

Schools as centers, or community schools, is a concept that is becoming widely accepted around the country. This notion of public school as something more than an academic institution has been advanced by many researchers, including Reginald Clark, Joy Dryfoos, Margot Welch (2000, pp. 14–17), and the late John Gardner. As stated in a position paper by the Public Education Network (2002), the key principles of schools as centers include the following:

- Public schools that offer access to a wide range of programs and supports are better able to fulfill their core academic mandate of student achievement. Faculty members can concentrate on teaching and learning when they have community partners to help children and their families overcome the many nonacademic barriers to learning.
- Public schools need to be part of communitywide coalitions that seek strong connections among community members, service and program providers, and community organizations to address academic and nonacademic barriers to student success. With public schools at the center of a coordinated effort to help children and youth become academically and socially successful, the fabric of community life is strengthened.
- A broad range of community stakeholders must be involved in assessing student and community needs and in determining how those needs should be addressed. The community has a rightful role in shaping schools as centers of community life; organizations and individuals— including nontraditional, often marginalized voices—must be engaged in communitywide strategic planning efforts to determine what pro-

grams and supports should be available at school, for whom, and how they should be delivered.

The North Platte program incorporates these principles and goals in its many programs and in its relationship with the community. The Community Connections board of directors and the board of education signed a memorandum of understanding to ensure that the program would run smoothly. It defines and clarifies roles and responsibilities of the involved agencies. Today, students' needs are met by school staff and supported by community volunteers, human service agency staff, and Community Connections staff. Many new programs and services are available at schools through the schools-as-centers programs:

K.I.D.S. (Kids Involved in Dynamic Stuff) Klub

This is an after-school program for elementary school children developed through the cooperative efforts of Community Connections and North Platte Public Schools, and initially funded by a grant from the Peter Kiewit Foundation. It provides a convenient and safe location for parents to leave their children, knowing they will be comfortable, well supervised, involved in fun activities, and expanding their learning beyond the classroom. The goal of the program is to establish an environment that creates a bridge between school and home. It offers experiences that not only enrich children but also reinforce basic skills. K.I.D.S. Klub provides a safe and relaxed environment for elementary school children before school and after school until 5:30 P.M. According to its administrator, Michael Davis, K.I.D.S. Klub has eliminated the latchkey problem that the Connections' prevention and education team had originally identified as a precipitating problem.

When President Bush announced the 21st Century Community Learning Center program under his No Child Left Behind Act, North Platte was in a position to receive monies. It already had all the necessary components—protocol, multiagency and community partnerships, and staff. Its K.I.D.S. Klub had a proven track record of meeting the goals of the president's new program. Community Connections used its successful grant-writing approach to obtain the 21st Century Community Learning Center $1.2 million grant to expand before-school, after-school, and summer-school programs. Buckland Consultants, a local firm, worked with Community Connections and 25 partner agencies to properly complete and submit the applications.

The Youth Asset Building Program

This program was introduced two years after the future search. The coordinating team brought representatives from the Search Institute to introduce its Forty Developmental Assets program to the community.

> The forty developmental assets are concrete, common sense, positive experiences and qualities essential to raising successful young people. These assets have the power during critical adolescent years to influence choices young people make and help them become caring, responsible adults. (Search Institute www.search-institute.org)

The Assets program, coordinated by Diann Weiss-Vargas, is now incorporated into the middle schools. Student asset teams at both middle schools promote the 40 developmental assets through school and community activities, which they initiate, organize, and supervise. These teams have sponsored family nights, talent shows, parties, and a booth at the Kids' Safety Saturday.

The Lincoln County Tobacco Coalition Program

This coalition protects and improves the health of the public by increasing community support and participation in local tobacco control in schools and the community. Funded by the Nebraska Health and Human Services System's Tobacco Free Nebraska and directed by Matthew Weiss, this program promotes clean indoor air policies as it partners with schools. It provides prevention instruction for middle school students and training for teachers while it works to increase compliance with state and local policies that prohibit tobacco sales to minors. For example, students helped with restaurant surveys to determine tobacco use policy. They honored smoke-free restaurants and encouraged others to improve their policies. They worked with asset team youth at a cleanup day called Tobacco Kick Butts. They provided civic and school presentations on tobacco prevention and even produced public service announcements aired on local radio and TV.

High Expectations Mentoring Program

Mentors spend at least four hours per month working with individual students in grades K–5 to provide them with experiences and opportunities not otherwise available. Youth and mentors also have the opportunity to spend time together at sponsored monthly group activities, such as game night, a magician presentation, and a visit to the North Platte Veterinary Clinic. In 2003, volunteer mentors contributed over 500 hours and worked with 25 youth and their families. Teachers report that these students have improved grades and attitudes. In a survey completed in July 2003, 100 percent of mentees reported an improved attitude toward school in general and better school attendance as a result of their relationship with their mentors.

The SWAT (Services With Activities for Teens) Team

This team evolved from the future search "youth and recreation" team. Youth in grades 6–12 initiate and implement fun, safe activities for themselves and their peers. Their efforts foster pride in their accomplishments while also producing a lot of fun. Their activities go beyond the typical movies and school activities. Last year over 400 people attended the SWAT-sponsored Battle of the Bands where four bands played original and popular music as they competed for cash prizes.

SWAT has formed a partnership with RSVP (Retired and Senior Volunteer Program) to provide community service activities. The two groups sponsored the "Fill the Ford" project to collect toiletries and hygiene items for those who could not afford them. A local Ford dealership loaned a Ford pickup truck, which was parked outside of Wal-Mart for shoppers to load with items not covered by food stamps. Together SWAT and RSVP members collected $800 worth of items.

The SWAT team is an example of how the younger generation is learning to build social capital. They are contributing their ideas and energy to the community while having fun. "I just want to be involved, to help people, to be looked at as a leader," said high school student Amy Neal, cochair of SWAT. "I like to have a lot of fun without getting into trouble."

Beyond Schools as Centers

The partnerships between the community and the schools have produced many benefits to the schools and community. The atmosphere in the community reflects its increased pride and ownership, with community members and organizations trusting school leadership and feeling pleased to be connected to the schools.

The future search was a catalyst for Dr. Merritt and others to access and extend social capital in the community. They wisely took advantage of heightened community interest to develop support to further meet educational needs. Examples of this are the bond issue, volunteers, and interagency support.

Bond Issue

Shortly before Dr. Merritt became superintendent, the voters had defeated three bond issues for construction of a new high school. Despite this record, Dr. Merritt decided to try again to enlist the support of the community to replace or remodel the 1930s-era high school. This time he would bring the community into the process from the very beginning.

Dr. Merritt asked a group of 60 people, including both supporters and opponents, to tell him what needed to be done about the high school. This group led an 18-month effort to determine the best solution. In a very open process, citizens had an opportunity to ask questions, give opinions, and learn about options. After working with other citizens and learning about finances, remodeling, repairing, mechanical components, and facility and construction issues, the original group of 60 developed a list of 22 criteria that needed to be met for them to approve any plan. Their architect provided them with cost estimates for each of nine proposals that met their given criteria. With 85 percent agreement, the group supported one plan for a new high school.

After the group agreed on the plan, they and others went to the community to ask for its approval. More than 1,000 people in a town of 24,000 were involved in this major effort. On April 4, 2000, the town voted. The $29 million bond issue passed with a 54 percent approval, carrying every precinct. After the bond issue had passed, town citizens publicly demonstrated their pride and support by purchasing 800 signature bricks for

$100 or $500. The passage of the bond issue signaled a positive change in the community to a "can-do" ethic. In August 2003 the town celebrated the dedication and opening of their new high school. It had been a long time coming; collective pride in this effort was very justified and visible.

Volunteers

School personnel know that they can call upon community volunteers to provide services to help students. They are using volunteers to combat tardiness and absenteeism problems at the middle schools. Although school staff were able to call students' homes when they were late for school, they often discovered that the parents were at work and the students had no way of getting to school. The school enlisted the help of parents who were willing, on very short notice, to pick up students and bring them to school. Once the students were in school, they were able to learn in the classroom and also discuss their tardiness problems with school staff.

Interagency Collaboration

The community has become a true partner with the schools. More agencies, departments, and organizations are now offering their unique contributions in the schools to students and staff. They supplement the curriculum with invaluable resources, information, and role models. Following is a partial list of the programs that community agencies and citizens provide in the schools:

- Probation and police officers work as adjuncts to the educational teams.
- Fire officials work in schools to educate students and teachers about prevention.
- Staff from human and health services provide educational programs to students.
- The Rape and Domestic Abuse Team provides anger management sessions, healthy relationship sessions, and dining manners instruction for students.
- Community Connections and North Platte Community College provides adult basic education for non-English-speaking parents and

English as a Second Language instruction for their children as a family in an evening after-school program.

- University of Nebraska extension educators provide units of instruction on better nutrition and healthy snacks. These educators teach Character Counts, a character-building program to elementary and middle school students and K.I.D.S. Klub. Through community donations the extension educators raised money to construct brick murals representing the six pillars of character on a wall of their new high school.

CHALLENGES

Although North Platte has enjoyed major successes, major challenges still remain. Community Connections is trying to find ways to address the continuing needs of students and families. Professionals and volunteers know that their work will never be over. Sustainability is a key focus. Local financial support must be established so that the program is not totally dependent on grants and awards. The program must leverage its dollars to get the most out of its monies. It must continue to build partnerships and find new community volunteers and resources.

The local school budget has been cut and state aid has been reduced while student and family needs are growing. Now more than ever, this community must work together to maintain its high quality of community and life.

REFLECTIONS ON THIS SUCCESS

Bringing everyone together, strong leadership, and the activation of social capital are three major factors that contributed to the success of this project. "In this small town, we have to support each others' projects, contribute and celebrate together. The future search helped us appreciate this," commented a future search participant. Community Connections has kept everyone together by nourishing the spirit of cooperation and understanding that emerged in the future search. It distributes a regular newsletter with notification of events and actively looks for public relations opportunities. Between 50 and 100 people attend the annual planning day to examine needs and develop solutions. They celebrate their accomplishments, review and renew old goals, and develop new ones.

Leadership in this community has come from many sources. Both the then-new mayor and superintendent utilized the vision, enthusiasm, and public participation from the future search to implement new initiatives. The superintendent set the tone for public involvement and community partnerships. His actions encouraged citizens to become leaders of various committees and projects. The funding and hiring of a dedicated executive director to lead Community Connections was critical in the system changes and in maintaining the momentum established in the future search.

Future search was both a tool and a catalyst for bringing the citizens of North Platte together to appreciate their social capital and to invest it wisely in improving the quality of life in their schools and community. By connecting to shared values and working together to implement specific projects, community members now know that they can make their community better for everyone. They have institutionalized the basics of social capital in their organizations and are educating their youth to build more social capital. These social investors continue their fine work and have a thriving community of which they are very proud.

CONCLUSION

North Platte has "developed innovative, bold and creative collaborations to address the needs of children and youth. . . . They support the high value of local collaborations between and among city governments, county governments, school systems and others in mobilizing neighborhoods and communities to provide services and foster environments supportive of children, youth and families," stated the National League of Cities upon selecting Community Connections as one of seven U.S. communities for its Award for Excellence in Community Collaboration for Children and Youth (*Nation's Cities Weekly*, 1999). The future search was a significant factor in helping the community earn this award. When it comes to social capital, North Platte is a very wealthy community.

7

Building Community Capacity to Support Quality Education

Nancy Aronson, Emily Axelrod, and Mary Ann Bobosky

INTRODUCTION

Imagine knowing that a tax increase is needed for your local school district and being faced with the following conditions:

- Close to 65 percent of the voters in the district do not have children in school.
- The community has been hard hit by the economic downturn, particularly in the once-thriving high-tech field.
- Approximately 75 percent of the school referendums in Illinois failed in 2002.
- In 1994 a similar referendum in your district was soundly defeated.

These were the exact conditions faced by the members of the referendum committee of Naperville Community School District 203 in March 2002. Yet in spite of this, they were able to mobilize 1,000 members of the community to get out the vote and pass the tax increase.

How did they achieve this remarkable feat? One of the major contributing factors was the relationships that were built among stakeholder groups when they were brought together at the future search conference of March 1998. As David Griffith, the Naperville unit education association president, remarked, "The future search started the ball rolling." At the conference, trust was built and the student voice was heard. These important seeds—the network of relationships, trust between the district and the community, and the focus on what was good for kids—were planted by 288 stakeholders at the future search conference and nourished by those participants and many others in subsequent years.

BACKGROUND

The Decision to Have a Future Search Conference

During the winter of 1997 when the idea for a community conversation about student learning in the twenty-first century first surfaced, District 203 had a good reputation. Test scores were high, partnerships with the community were formed, parents and other community members were involved in the schools, and a school improvement process existed in each of the 21 schools in the district. Given these circumstances, why have a future search conference? The idea was initiated and promoted by two school board members. Responsibility for establishing a vision for the school district rests with the board. They saw the future search as an opportunity to involve the community in the conversation about the vision. The board members involved Superintendent Donald E. Weber in sponsoring the effort. They tapped Mary Ann Bobosky, director of planning and community relations and coauthor of this chapter, as the person with responsibility for implementing this community conversation. The future search conference was chosen as the way to involve many voices in a short period of time and reach common ground on a vision.

The Planning Group

District leadership took care in identifying a planning group. The group of 20 included union leadership (professional and support staff), teachers, parents, building administrators, district office administration, school board members, students, community members, support staff, and senior citizens. This group had many important conversations and made decisions that shaped how the process would unfold. As this group talked about the purpose of the conference, it saw the effort as a way to further reduce the "us versus them" tension between the district and the community and between the administration and the teaching staff. It was also a way to engage community leaders more directly in the future of the school district. As Mary Ann Bobosky saw it, "The future search represented the next step of getting the parents and community together with us." The goals of the future search were to

- Develop a shared understanding of our current education system.
- Develop a common vision of the opportunity for learning in the future.
- Commit to community action necessary to move the education system into the twenty-first century.

The planning group made the decision to run four parallel conferences (four rooms) and engage close to 300 people. They used such a complex process because

- They wanted to engage all facets of the school/community in the dialogue.
- They wanted to bring as much of the community leadership to the table as possible.
- They realized that there were many agendas in the community, and that it would be important to hear people out and see where there was common ground.
- The larger number of participants would preclude any one individual or small group from dominating the outcomes.

They put a lot of careful thought and attention into the process, deciding who to invite and the variety of voices needed in each room and at each table. For example, an article in the daily community newspaper encouraged and invited citizens to participate. Jeri Stodola, a member of the planning group, was the wizard of tables. Her belief was that "we needed to have mixes that enabled people to do the jobs they were there to do."

A Key Ingredient for Success

During planning, the group realized that no predetermined outcome or hidden agenda existed. They questioned this often. The purpose of the conference—creating a vision for the twenty-first century—was clear. It was also understood that the future search would provide the structure that would take the school and community on a journey to identify common-ground directions for the future of District 203. But what the directions would be was not set prior to the conference. The planning group came to trust that the future search conference was not an exercise in bringing people to a conclusion that top leadership had already reached! This seemingly obvious and very important distinction would prove to be a crucial element in what happened during and after the conference.

OUTCOMES

The future search conference was held in April 1998. It yielded both concrete, tangible outcomes and what might be called intangible outcomes. Both impacted future actions taken by members of the school and the community. Distinctions are drawn below between these two types of outcomes for the purposes of discussion, with the full knowledge that they are intertwined.

Concrete, Tangible Outcomes

The future search conference yielded 11 common-ground themes. These themes formed the basis for the district beliefs, the district vision, and a modification of the district's mission:

- Meet the individual and unique learning needs of each student.
- Continue to include basic skills in the curriculum.
- Emphasize respect and responsibility.
- Integrate the real world into learning and expand the development of life skills in leadership, teamwork, communication, critical thinking, and problem solving in a student-centered curriculum.
- Support the teacher's expanding role as facilitator and coordinator.
- Use up-to-date technology as a tool for everyday learning.
- Employ flexibility in the use of educational resources, such as scheduling, curriculum, and personnel, and in the use of methods of instruction and assessment.

- Develop nontraditional and alternative assessments for systems and individuals.
- Create opportunities for increased communication, collaboration, and participation among all constituencies in the community.
- Foster a community of lifelong learners.
- Develop financial and community resources.

Based on the common-ground themes, a representative steering group highlighted four core beliefs that seemed to both underpin the common ground and reflect the dialogue that had occurred at the future search: excellence in education, dignity and uniqueness of each individual, responsible citizenship, and partnership with the community. They also crafted a vision statement: a passion for lifelong learning.

Partnership with the Community

As a result of this conference the district mission statement was amended to include the partnership with the community. Following is the mission statement:

> Our mission is to graduate students who think critically, solve problems, make decisions, and have the skills necessary for productive citizenship and lifelong learning by providing excellent, comprehensive programs and services *in partnership with the community.*

The last few additional words communicated an important intent on the part of the district. Many of the actions that followed in subsequent years were aligned with this intent.

Common-Ground Action Teams

At the conference, action teams were formed around the common themes to generate recommendations. These went to the planning group to assist with implementation. A number of the action teams became part of existing groups or developed into district committees. The beliefs, vision, and mission became foundational for other major initiatives and continuous improvement efforts. A sample of action team recommendations that were implemented included the following:

- A big effort was made by the Naperville Education Foundation to communicate with and solicit the alumni for their support. The short-term result was an updated alumni directory and contributions to the foundation. In 2003, the foundation received a $500,000 grant from an individual recognizing his parents' education in the 1930s in Naperville. The expanded Naperville Education Foundation grant program has provided support for teachers' innovative ideas.
- The district used all of the information that was gathered from research and member input, particularly about meeting the unique needs of students, to help develop three critical goals for the district: 1) Develop a shared understanding of the need for continuous improvement based on school district beliefs, vision, and mission; 2) design quality work for learners; and 3) develop leadership capacity. The district also used the data to assess the school district against 10 standards developed by the Center for Leadership in School Reform in Louisville, KY.
- The technology team recommended and developed a program to institute curriculum in the high school for students to give technology support. They also suggested compiling a guide for all facets of technology—a directory of programs, services, personnel, and opportunities for training. The directory would be shared with all personnel and students in the district, helping people use the available technology more wisely and more often.
- Increased connections in the community have led to business mentorships for teachers and have helped link teachers to the community and businesspeople with specialized knowledge and skills. There was particular emphasis on reaching out to more retirees and business-people and forming partnerships with civic groups such as Kiwanis, Lions Clubs, the League of Women Voters, H.U.R.R.A.H. (Happy Upbeat Recycled Retirees Actively Helping), and The American Association of University Women.
- Changes were proposed and instituted to increase flexibility in scheduling at the high schools.
- The junior high schools instituted a program to reduce bullying.
- Conversations in one action team led to a districtwide diversity plan.
- Freshman academies were established at the high school. These are school within a school structures for at-risk students.
- The district refined the math and literacy curricula.

Using the Beliefs, Mission, and Vision

The beliefs, mission, and vision were foundational for other initiatives, in particular, the Standard-Bearer Process. Briefly, the Standard-Bearer Process was an initiative developed by the Center for Leadership in School Reform (Center for Leadership and Reform, Louisville, KY, Dr. Phillip Schlechty, www.clsr.org). District 203 was selected as one of 14 pilot school districts across the United States. The purpose of Standard-Bearer is to use a system framework to assess the capacity of the district to support and sustain innovation and improve performance. District 203 was particularly interested in more completely meeting the educational needs of all students, particularly those in the two middle quartiles. Figure 7.1 illustrates the process.

During the future search, the community developed the information for the outer ring—their shared beliefs, vision, mission, and values. The information and outcomes became a frequent frame of reference for the work of the Standard-Bearer committees as the district worked on "Organizing for Results" and the schools worked on the "School Improvement Process" (SIP). Connecting the future search with the Standard-Bearer Process was important because future search participants could see that their results were being used. In addition, the intentional connection between the future search conference and the Standard-Bearer Process reduced the fragmented way that people frequently experience initiatives.

The beliefs, mission, and vision also formed the backdrop for the building-level school improvement process. Even five years after the future search conference all committees must align their work with the beliefs, mission, and vision.

Intangible Outcomes

The invisible threads of a compelling vision weave a tapestry that binds people together more powerfully than any strategic plan. And people, not the business plan alone, determine the outcome. Success depends on what an organization's people care about, what they do and how they work together. (Goleman et al., 2002, p. 209)

For the purpose of writing this chapter, the coauthors convened a reunion meeting for the original planning group in the spring of 2003, five

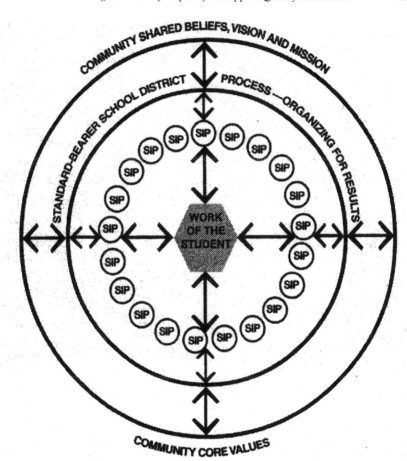

Figure 7.1. Standard-Bearer Process (Data from Naperville Community Unit School District document, 2003)

years after the future search conference. Ten members, representing all the stakeholders except the school board, engaged in a lively dialogue, sharing their perspectives on the impact of the future search conference. Although they contributed information about many of the tangible results that have already been outlined, most of their conversation was about the intangibles—those factors that contribute to the culture and fabric of their organization but are hard to quantify. It was from their stories that we really got a sense of how pivotal the future search had been and the wide-ranging nature of its impact.

The intangible outcomes included increased trust, empowerment and ownership of the outcomes by the school and community, a connected network of stakeholders, and increased leadership capacity in both the district and the community.

Intangible Outcome 1: Trust

A positive, constructive cycle of increasing trust began at the conference. Dennis Reina and Michelle Reina call this *transactional trust* (1999, p. 82). They define transactional trust as managing expectations, establishing clear boundaries, delegating appropriately, encouraging mutually serving intentions, keeping agreements, and being congruent in our behavior. We developed figure 7.2 to illustrate the cycle of behaviors that we observed after the future search. These behaviors were repeated over time as more efforts were initiated and the circle of involvement widened.

At the conference, stakeholders created links with other groups as they engaged in conversations and shared their perspectives. Dave Griffith, president of the Naperville Unit Education Association (National Education Association affiliate) commented, "The school district had a history of confrontation, us versus them. The future search allowed us to talk and realize we had more in common than we thought." This spirit of open information sharing was also carried throughout the Standard-Bearer Process.

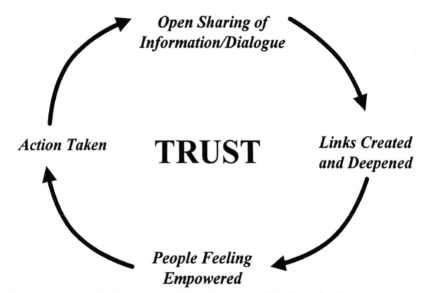

Figure 7.2.   Trust Cycle (Courtesy Nancy Aronson and Emily Axelrod)

This important districtwide effort involving hundreds and hundreds of stakeholders also reinforced the cycle because it was so inclusive.

One example of increasing trust was how the administration candidly shared its budget information during the referendum. Two financial experts from the business community joined the referendum committee to uncover money that they believed might really be available, but they were unable to find any excess money! They affirmed that the district had accurately portrayed the financial picture. As Ruth Cross, an elementary principal, pointed out, "This was important because the community then understood the tax increase was not a matter of poor money management."

The increased trust among the central office, the board of education, and the teachers was also confirmed as the district prepared for the 2002 referendum. To ensure that the financial projections were accurate and the proposed tax increase was credible, the union agreed to early negotiations. This flexibility enabled the district to project the actual teacher salaries, a large part of any school district's budget. The union's action was unprecedented in Naperville. The relationships that have formed and the trust that has been built have allowed the system to adapt.

Intangible Outcome 2: Ownership of the Outcomes and Empowerment

As the planning group talked about the impact of the future search, the word *empowerment* kept coming up to describe the shift in participation that had occurred, particularly on the part of the community. Empowerment has become a cliché in some circles in education, but in District 203 it has important meaning. In the past, committees could have a rubber-stamp feel. People were brought together to discuss and confirm what had already been decided. The community was asked to support a specific initiative or to fill a specific need, for example, to volunteer for an activity. This shifted dramatically. A sample of the comments from members of the planning group illustrates this point:

> Community participation moved from being involved as a volunteer, for example, to being empowered—on a committee meaningfully shaping what happens.
>
> —John Schmitt, Realtor and chair of the
> Naperville Area Chamber of Commerce

> During the future search process, what people said was valued. So
> people more readily signed up for committees.
>
> —Mary Ann Bobosky, director of planning and community relations

Members of the planning group talked of the defining moment in the future search. It was on the last morning of the conference. The large group, which included everyone from the four parallel conferences, had just confirmed the common ground. The facilitators were shifting the activity toward action planning. As the facilitators explained how this would be done, there were many questions, many more than usual. Something wasn't flowing right for participants! As the facilitators initiated the activity, resistance was palpable. It soon became clear that the approach to action planning was not what this community wanted.

After a little more discussion in the large group, the facilitators called a break, met with the planning group, and redesigned the activity. When the community heard the redesign, they reengaged with energy and focus. This was a defining moment in two major ways. First, participants realized that there were no preset outcomes and that they could truly influence what happened, which reinforced trust in the process and influenced subsequent participation on district committees. Mark Paztor, a junior high school principal, explained, "The future search was a shot in the arm for committee work. People knew that if they got involved in committees, they were really part of something—not just going through the motions." Second, it accelerated ownership of the outcomes. People had given input and seen it change the design of the conference. They owned the design. As one participant said, "We feel like we own what we created and it has shown up in the work we do in the district."

Intangible Outcome 3: A Connected Network of Stakeholders

The future search conference was a forum for community dialogue and decision making. It provided the opportunity for diverse stakeholders to understand their links more clearly and to deepen their connections. These connections positively impacted

- The ability of the community to come together, share ideas, and have its collective voice heard.

- The nature of the partnerships between the district and the community, including parents, senior citizens (retirees), and business partners.
- Collaboration and the tapping of stakeholder expertise for particular issues as they arose.

Opportunities were created for stakeholders to come together to share ideas and to celebrate success. Following the conference, action teams met for approximately six months. Three-quarters of the way through their work, a large group meeting was held to share their progress, get feedback, and then continue working with the knowledge of what others in the system were doing. Community breakfasts were held several times a year to share information and celebrate the contributions of individuals and various community and business groups.

The community also came together at critical times to exert influence and have their collective voice heard. In one example, the school board had taken action related to not renewing the superintendent's contract. The community felt that the circumstances surrounding the decision and the way it was being handled were not aligned with their values. Approximately 500 members of the community, including a broad spectrum of leadership, unified to influence the school board to change its decision. The board listened, and a majority of the members voted to reverse the decision.

Partnerships between the district and the community expanded, both qualitatively and quantitatively, following the future search. The term *expanded* is used because partnerships have always been important to District 203. Individual schools already had business partners and retirees had a group called H.U.R.R.A.H., which organized senior citizen volunteers across the district.

There are numerous examples of partnerships with the business community. These relationships are becoming increasingly more collaborative. The business partners are expanding the ways that they offer their expertise and resources to the educational process. For example:

- Members of an architectural firm worked with mathematics students. They offered everyday, practical applications for the concepts being taught. This firm also offered expertise for the school remodeling effort. They drew up blueprints for a whole new pattern of flooring and tile.

- A business specializing in solar panels not only helped by installing solar panels on the roof of the school but also trained four teachers in solar energy—concepts that enhanced the science curriculum.

Intangible Outcome 4: Leadership Capacity

The future search was a catalyst for leadership development in the district and with members of the community. It helped people see the big picture, fostered risk taking, and enabled personal connections to be made. This increased capacity amplified the ability of the organization to take action.

Tim Wierenga, a high school math teacher at the start of this effort, described his experience thus: "During the conference, I worked outside my box. I saw I could have a bigger influence. This stepped me into becoming the math department chair, a role I was unwilling to consider in the past." Tim transferred his learning from the future search to his leadership in the department. He took the lead in revamping curriculum planning in the district. Instead of fragmenting the planning by level, he brought the whole system, K–12, in the room together. He knew it was imperative for educators at the various levels to see the big picture and their interconnections as they developed the curriculum.

Pat Franzen, a teacher, provided this personal anecdote: "Coming out of the future search conference, I felt pride and trust. This encouraged me to take risks. When I heard about TIMSS (Third International Mathematics and Science Study), I went back to my colleagues and said, 'I think we can do something with this.'" Indeed they did. With the support of the superintendent, Dr. Donald E. Weber, all 1,300 eighth-grade students from District 203 participated in this international benchmarking examination. All other teams were from other countries. Naperville proudly placed first in science and sixth in math in this worldwide event!

Outcomes of the Conference Impact Leadership and Action

Mark Paztor said, "This had an impact. There was positive energy, a sense of trust, and an understanding of where the district was going that influenced action happening." The sense of direction also built a collective leadership capacity and confidence. Participants from the future search were spread out across the community and across working groups in the district. For example, many of the chairs of the Standard-Bearer committees had been participants at the future search.

Michael Fullan states, "Shared meaning and organization connectedness are the long term assets of high performing systems" (1999, p. 28). The tangible outcomes—the common ground—represented where this district and its community had shared meaning. The intangible outcomes exemplified this connectedness. Taken together they created a strong and flexible foundation. This foundation made many things possible—from some with smaller impact, such as a parent teaching an after-school course, to others with widespread systemic impact, such as the passing of a tax increase.

CONCLUSION

Future search was a significant tool for creating a strong foundation for the next level of growth and development for District 203. The planning group offers the following reflections and advice in hopes that they might be helpful to others as they embark on systemic change:

- Alignment between the school board and the superintendent is important. Have a governance structure in place that supports and has the capacity for this kind of work.
- Much was accomplished. The intangibles plus building critical mass were crucial. There were enough leaders in the district holding the focus, enough people feeling empowered, and enough meaningful links and connections created to take the work forward.
- The seed of a conversation started at a conference can take hold years later. The union president described the new teacher evaluation document. It reflects that the professional community is the entire school, not just one's classroom. There is an expectation that a teacher will contribute to his or her professional community. This expectation represents a fairly significant shift in participation. This conversation started the idea and the awareness was developed at the future search.
- Future search is not a cookbook approach to strategic planning. As Don Weber, the superintendent, noted, "The three-day future search

conference brought people together, gave us direction, but did not give us tactical information for a strategic plan. The model doesn't map out how to use the results. We had to figure most of that out ourselves."

- Clarify your purposes and desired outcomes.
- Include and listen to the student voice. Not only can students offer good ideas and provide an important reality check, adults may hear things from students that will stay with them for years to come.
- Trust that people can come together for this type of conversation.

Paradoxically, future search is a relatively simple process that can handle the complexity of these times. As two members of the planning group said, "This was a town meeting. The democratic process works. Never underestimate the power of a large group."

8

Supporting Health and Mental Health So Students Can Learn in San Gabriel, California

Jean Katz and Vera Jashni

INTRODUCTION

The story of the San Gabriel Family Resource Center is a story of collaboration—beyond the school district to city government, the community hospital, health and social agencies, and a historic church. This collaboration created a system that supports the general health and mental health needs of students and their families. This system continues to serve the students, school district, and community beyond its original intent.

WHY THE FUTURE SEARCH?

The San Gabriel Family Resource Center is the direct outcome of a future search in 1999 to change the way fundamental services are delivered to students and their families in the San Gabriel Unified School District (SGUSD) and the city of San Gabriel.

San Gabriel Unified School District leaders pursued a Healthy Start Grant from the State of California Department of Education to respond to research showing that sick, hungry, frightened, and emotionally troubled students cannot focus on learning. The leaders knew that providing for these fundamental needs was a prerequisite for meeting the district's mission: to serve students' academic learning needs and prepare them for the world of work and for citizenship in a democratic society. Leaders also knew that the changing community demographics were increasing the need for these fundamental services.

The ethnicity of the San Gabriel population has shifted dramatically over the last decade. Until 1990 it was a predominantly white and Hispanic community. Asians now represent the community's largest ethnic group. Even within large population groupings such as Asian, there are subpopulations of Chinese, Korean, Filipino, Japanese, and Vietnamese families. Among Latino residents, new immigrants from Mexico and Central America now outnumber the long-standing families of Mexican descent. More than one-third of students have a low rate of English language proficiency based on testing. Many families are entrenched in intergenerational poverty with a widening gap between the haves and have nots. More than 25.4 percent of the residents live at or below the federal poverty level. Many children of low-income families are sufficiently needy to qualify for Temporary Assistance to Needy Families (TANF) yet do not qualify because of their parents' marginal employment. At Gabrielino High School and Jefferson Middle School, for example, 20 percent of students received TANF in the 1998–1999 school year, while up to 60.7 percent qualified for the National Free Lunch Program. On the other hand, the north end of San Gabriel borders on San Marino, which is one of the wealthiest communities in the Los Angeles region.

San Gabriel, 15 miles east of downtown Los Angeles, is an ethnically and socioeconomically diverse community of more than 41,230 residents. At the time of the future search, the population was 35.1 percent Asian, 32.6 percent Latino, and 30.6 percent white. The San Gabriel Unified School District has 5,326 students enrolled in five elementary schools, a middle school, a high school, and an alternative community education center. Due, in part, to language and cultural barriers, there is limited parental involvement in schools. Adolescents face enormous stresses including drugs, gangs, and racial tensions. In 1999, there were 210 juvenile arrests and 238 reported cases of child abuse, a ratio of 16.4 per 1,000 children. During 1997, there were 70 births to women less than 20 years of age.

BEFORE THE FUTURE SEARCH:
THE BEGINNING OF COLLABORATION

The San Gabriel Healthy Start Collaborative (SGHSC) began in the spring of 1998 when a concerned group of school counselors, school nurses, and parents met to discuss ways in which they could bring additional services to youth in the district. They applied twice to the California State Department of Education to receive a Healthy Start Planning Grant. The grant was not funded because there were no existing collaborations for health and mental health services for students and families.

To begin creating this collaborative, in 1998 the district hired Antonia Clark, a school nurse, as a health services manager. From the beginning she had a vision of what the Healthy Start Collaborative might become. Her first outreach was to San Gabriel Valley Medical Center. Leaders of the district and the hospital agreed that they would provide space for meetings in both the district and the hospital to enhance conversation. They also agreed to provide additional services to each other. The Healthy Start Collaborative began as more agencies joined. Together, they identified common issues.

The collaborative put itself in a position to receive the grant. The core group realized that a broad cross-section from education, human services, parents, students, and community members was needed for their efforts to take hold. It hired Pam Solomon, a grant writer, as a consultant to identify other necessary agencies and partners and to develop the third grant application. It recruited new members. Two school board members were strong supporters for the project and assisted in forming the collaborations. By the end of the year, the group had recruited a total of 15 additional parents, teachers, and students. The expanded group forged links to local city agencies and community-based organizations in the interest of informing and coordinating available resources for students and their families.

The SGHSC members met monthly in the first year to learn about each other's organizations, gain trust, and discuss the community's common dreams, hopes, and visions for community children and families. The results of a community assessment conducted before the first grant application were used to delineate the goals. Every goal was driven by the desire to see students do well in school and to enhance learning support systems that would help them perform at a higher level. The goals that the collaborative selected after reviewing and prioritizing the community assessment are to improve the academic achievement of students through mentoring and tutoring, to provide low-cost and free medical and related health services, to improve the economic well-being of youth and families, and to ensure the health and functioning of pregnant and parenting teens.

While this collaboration was being formed, a group of executive leaders also began meeting to establish the San Gabriel Foundation to support the health, social, and educational needs of children and families in San Gabriel. Canon Denis O'Pray, pastor of the Church of Our Saviour, invited Superintendent of Schools Dr. Gary Goodson, Steve Fallows, CEO of San Gabriel Valley Medical Center, and San Gabriel City Manager Michael Paules to a series of dinner meetings to discuss creating a foundation. Canon O'Pray and his church have a long history of supporting the larger community in their nonsectarian agenda, contributing over $10 million over 20 years to service agencies in the San Gabriel Valley.

BEGINNING THE FUTURE SEARCH

In the autumn of 1998 Superintendent Dr. Gary Goodson invited Jean Katz, facilitator of districtwide strategic planning, to facilitate a planning process connected to a third Healthy Start planning grant proposal, and later, a Healthy Start operational grant proposal. Mrs. Katz proposed the future search model because it engages the largest number of collaborators to develop the framework for the plan. Together they agreed that the purpose of the conference would be to develop a vision for the Healthy Start Project, determine the areas of primary focus, begin action planning in those areas, and kick off a further community assessment process. The planning process began with collaborative members, Mrs. Katz, and cofacilitator Dr. Vera Jashni, former deputy superintendent of schools in Culver City, CA, and president of the board of Didi Hirsch Community Mental Health Center.

More than 70 stakeholders, representing a wide range of those interested in the physical and mental health and well-being of students, attended the future search conference in the social hall of the Church of Our Saviour in 1999. The eight stakeholder groups included students, parents, teachers, administrators, health care providers, counselors, mental health providers, and government services like police and parks and recreation.

THE FUTURE SEARCH CONFERENCE

The conference began with this quote from Margaret Mead, "Never doubt that a small group of thoughtful committed citizens can change the world. Indeed, it's the only thing that ever has." "Healthy Youth in Healthy Families" was the theme. The intensive work at the future search resulted in the following:

- Vision and mission statements were developed for a collaborative approach to help San Gabriel youth and their families. The vision was a "one-stop shop" coordinated center, meeting the health, mental health, and social needs of students and families, leading to greater academic achievement. The mission statement reads: "To promote the healthy development of youth and their families through community partnerships that support full academic, social, personal, and emotional growth."
- Broad goals were established and action planning began in the areas of academic achievement, health care, mental health, economic well-being, teen pregnancy prevention and services to pregnant teen mothers, after-school programs and safe neighborhoods, fund development and sustainability, and evaluation.
- A Healthy Start planning task force was established to gather demographic and resource information, ensuring extensive input from students and parents.
- Action teams were established to review current service delivery systems, identify untapped assets in specific areas of need, and recommend action plans for addressing priority issues. The action teams focused on teen pregnancy, health, mental health, after-school services, safe neighborhoods, and academic improvement.
- Participants committed to involve themselves on at least one action team and to recruit other parents, students, and community members.
- The vision was expanded for a new San Gabriel Community Foundation that would build an endowment to sustain programs and services for youth.

The future search conference was the first time that all the stakeholders had an opportunity to meet each other and learn of each other's needs and wishes.

AFTER THE FUTURE SEARCH: WIDENING THE CIRCLE AND RECEIVING THE GRANTS

Shortly after the future search, San Gabriel Unified School District began the application process for a Healthy Start planning grant of $50,000. It would focus on the needs and strengths of adolescents and explore the causes and consequences of barriers to students' access to needed services. Parents, teachers, and students of Jefferson Middle School, Gabrielino High School, and the community education center, together with community representatives and city staff, contributed hundreds of hours developing the Healthy Start planning grant proposal. It was awarded a few months later.

As soon as the collaborative received the planning grant, it began to develop the application for the implementation grant. The infectious enthusiasm generated at the future search conference carried over to the indepth community assessment process and other action team activities. Building on perceptions of needs and resources identified at the future search, the Healthy Start Planning Task Force worked with students, parents, and school personnel to develop needs assessment instruments and to interpret the results.

Collaborative members analyzed the results of written surveys and focus groups, dissected current information to identify needed improvements and strategies, and developed action plans to align program goals and integrate services from schools, the district, and community agencies. They were ready to implement programs to dislodge the interrelated obstacles to academic success: poverty, inadequate access to health care and other professional services, and language and cultural barriers.

Special efforts were made to ensure that the collaborative would be inclusive. School site and district office personnel (e.g., teachers, administrators, schools nurses, and teaching aides); ethnic and racial groups, including subpopulations (e.g., Vietnamese, Central American, and Mexican); religious organizations; human services agencies; social and civic clubs; as well as city, county, and state agency representatives were all included. Each member provided a critical link toward the shared goal of capitalizing on community strengths to achieve positive youth development. The SGHSC partners would be leaders, planners, designers, implementers, trainers, administrators, evaluators, and overseers of the initiative.

All of this outreach and data gathering paid off the following year in March 2000, when the district applied for and received a three-year Healthy Start operational grant of $400,000 for the Family Resource Center (FRC), and a second Healthy Start planning grant of $50,000 to study the needs of children and families attending the three qualifying elementary schools in the district.

STARTING THE HEALTHY START FAMILY RESOURCE CENTER

Launching the San Gabriel Family Resource Center would require a massive effort. The program would need a coordinator, staff, policies, procedures, systems, and a building. The new health services manager and family resource center coordinator began by meeting with the collaborative partners and their staffs to review the grant and identify areas for focus. The action teams for teen pregnancy, health, mental health, afterschool services, safe neighborhoods, and academic improvement were reconvened. The FRC coordinator met with each action team while participants facilitated their own meetings. This was her opportunity to learn what they were doing yet leave them with their own pride of leadership and initiative.

A marketing professional offered his services to help develop a brochure with a logo and graphics describing the services offered. It was distributed at schools, the district office, the collaborative meetings, the coordination council (a coalition of nonprofits and community agencies for the community at large), city government, and other nonprofits, as well as at health fairs.

By looking at other case management systems in the region, a case management system was developed for students and families in need of counseling and multiple services. A protocol was designed for referral of students and families. Referrals began to come from schools and collaborating agencies that would refer clients to the FRC and take referrals from them.

An executive committee was formed to make policy decisions for the FRC. It was made up of the superintendent, the health services manager, the FRC coordinator, representatives from the city of San Gabriel Parks and Recreation Department and from the San Gabriel Valley Medical Center, and a high school counselor.

The coordinator and the health services manager attended school meetings to inform teachers and aides about FRC services. They also informed the administrative council, the counselors at the high school and middle school, and the elementary schools of the FRC services.

MENTAL HEALTH AND SAFETY SERVICES

The FRC offers a variety of mental health and safety services. Soon after its opening, the FRC had more referrals than it could handle. When even the coordinator started seeing counseling clients, she realized that she needed more case managers. A school nurse was hired part-time as a case manager. Still the caseload grew too large. Many referrals were sent to and received from collaborating social agencies. An example of the two-way referrals is the Los Angeles Commission on Assaults Against Women (LACAAW). The FRC and LACAAW are offering a joint program of self-defense classes for 20 at-risk girls and their parents. This relationship came about when the LACAAW director reported that two or three clients who were referred to Healthy Start received counseling on intimate personal and family issues.

LACAAW offers date rape prevention classes at Gabrielino High School, the continuation high school, and Jefferson Middle School. The classes are offered in Spanish as well as English. LACAAW refers Asian-language clients for counseling and education to the Asian Pacific Family Center. LACAAW also offers mini-self-defense classes at Gabrielino High School in the physical education program. LACAAW is seeking funding to set up four-hour classes for women and will repeat them for youth. Weekly classes in Spanish are provided for parents of students. The classes include education regarding domestic violence and how it affects children.

Recently Pacific Clinics have become partners with the FRC. They offer four interns to do mental health counseling. The interns are working toward social work or psychology licenses and are building up supervised hours at the FRC.

The health services manager reported that a family with three generations who have been in gangs lives across the street from the FRC. One of the children, enrolled in a school in the district, was referred to the School Attendance Review Board (SARB) for 37 days' absence. With the resources of the FRC, the health services manager was able to get Medi-Cal (California's version of Medicaid) for all three children and help the family find better housing and emergency food.

HEALTH SERVICES

After forming the Health Action Team, the FRC applied for and received an L.A. Care Grant to develop a health clinic. Various community agencies and individuals provided further help. The clinic was opened in January 2002 with a celebration and press coverage. The clinic provides services for uninsured students. It gives general physical check-ups to uninsured students and parents, as well as immunizations and TB tests. It provides sports physicals for high school student athletes. Two mornings per week a physician from Yu Care Medical Group provides medical services to 30 people.

The health services manager learned about some student and family medical needs through her participation on the School Attendance Review Board. She was able to get immediate medical appointments and taxi vouchers or other transportation for their appointments. An immigrant mother who was referred from a rape prevention and treatment program was able to get health insurance and free dental work through contacts made by the FRC. After their basic health needs have been met, students are able to turn their attention to school learning.

FEEDING AND TUTORING

The program was greatly enhanced when the FRC hired Roy Rossell as a family advocate. His work demonstrates how much can be accomplished by a dedicated and focused individual who is not a certificated employee of the district. Mr. Rossell had been providing Parent Institute parenting classes for Spanish-speaking parents, and volunteered to tutor, counsel, and mentor some students. As a family advocate he noticed that many of the students' families in the community needed food. Mr. Rossell had been spending his own money to buy food for the families. The superintendent of schools advised him to enlist the aid of other agencies.

Several agencies contributed food that was old, in dented cans and boxes. Mr. Rossell was dissatisfied with the poor presentation. He located Dove Ministries International (DMI), a nonprofit agency that provided new food and gift items. DMI receives food and gifts from all over the United States and packages it to make a nice presentation. The superintendent wrote a letter of endorsement, promising that volunteers would be provided from the FRC in return for the food contributions. Mr. Rossell recruited many parents, who had received the food and gifts, to be volunteer packers at the warehouse. Even after developing this program, the growing need for food by parents and families far exceeded supplies. Now he picks up food from other organizations as well.

Students directly contribute to the FRC as well as benefiting from it. High school students were invited to the FRC as tutors. Some were drawn from the Interact Club, a high school club sponsored by Rotary International. One Vietnamese American boy from the club, a volunteer tutor, noted that student-tutoring services were delivered in an uncoordinated manner. He decided to organize the student tutors with schedules and firm time commitments. After getting the tutoring program established on a firm schedule, he made a report to the board of education. Members were amazed that such organization could come from student initiative and leadership.

Tutoring was named by almost everyone interviewed for this chapter as the strongest contributor to improved student academic performance. An example is Maria (not her real name), a 15-year-old girl who had a difficult relationship with her mother. She received counseling for several months at the FRC and also participated in the tutoring program. Her attitude and grades improved. She won an award at the high school for the best grade point average improvement. Maria is now involved in the volunteer service program at the center.

AFTER-SCHOOL PROGRAMS

After-school recreation and sports programs have a positive impact on the mental health and well-being of students. The Parks and Recreation Department was an early partner in the Healthy Start planning process. The relationship between the district and the Parks and Recreation Department goes back 45 to 50 years, but programming was enhanced and expanded after the future search and development of the FRC. The Parks and Recreation Department now provides after-school recreation and traditional after-school sports on school campuses in addition to city park facilities. The district provides the facilities; Parks and Recreation provides the programming. The working relationship between the school district and city government is unique in San Gabriel.

PREVENTION OF PREGNANCY, SERVICES TO PREGNANT TEENS AND TEEN MOTHERS

There has been a systemic expansion of services for pregnancy prevention and services to pregnant teens and teen mothers as the school district, the hospital, San Gabriel Mission, and a myriad of other agencies and community-based organizations all work together, with services intertwined.

Work has now begun to prevent teen pregnancies and to serve teen mothers and their babies through direct education, role models, creation of hope, and collaborations. The basic money for the pregnancy prevention and pregnancy care programs comes from the San Gabriel Valley Medical Center (SGVMC). Associated with Catholic Health Care West, the mission of SGVMC is to take care of the community, not only hospital patients. SGVMC also collaborates with a community service club, Soroptomist, and with the California Employment Department's Career Partners, in a mentoring and internship program for pregnant and at-risk teens.

Rebecca Bigler, RN, lactation consultant and teen liaison from the San Gabriel Valley Medical Center, provides much of the service to teens at risk of pregnancy, pregnant teens, and teen mothers. She supports, educates, and mentors pregnant and parenting teens to ensure a healthy outcome for mother and baby. Using the Teen Outreach Program Service

(TOPS), she meets in the high school and middle school to educate students about at-risk issues. In the summer, she offers a perinatal summer program for parenting teens. She offers guest speakers, healthy mother and baby programs, and plans for health care for teen mothers and babies. The program is free with funding supplied by SGVMC and Family Support Services of Los Angeles County.

Twenty-two former students in Ms. Bigler's programs have purchased their own homes while working and going to school following high school graduation. One is working for a CEO at Warner Bros. movie studios.

Ms. Bigler's attendance at Healthy Start Collaborative meetings has maintained the hospital's link with the school district, opening doors in both institutions to benefit students and their families. Education, role modeling, and the creation of hope occur wherever the services are delivered.

MORE GRANTS, MORE SERVICES

Pam Solomon, the grant writer, is the current acting FRC coordinator. In partnership with the staff of the FRC, she has continued to identify and apply for grants to enhance and expand the services of the center. In addition to the Healthy Start planning and operational grants, which paid for salaries for the coordinator, family advocate, and two clerks, Medi-Cal reimbursement has paid for the medical administration and case management and some other medical expenses. Some collaborating agencies fund programs and services that they offer at the center. A Healthy Families grant pays for staff to provide application assistance for families whose children may qualify for Healthy Families, Medi-Cal, or other low- or no-cost medical insurance. L.A. CARE helps support the health clinic. A Federal Substance Abuse and Mental Health Administration grant will soon provide elementary school counseling. A Federal 21st Century Grant for the Middle School provides after-school academic tutoring and enrichment. The Education Division of the Los Angeles County Performing Arts Center has provided performing arts programs in the schools. Performing arts have been shown in research to enhance the mental health and academic achievement of students. The Santa Anita

Family Services Collaborative received a grant to track teen pregnancy data for 51 agencies.

A relationship has been established with the California Community Foundation to continue to seek other private funding. The Educational Foundation of the Los Angeles County Office of Education has just agreed to provide 501(c)(3) status for the FRC, allowing the center to apply for certain grants that are only available to nonprofit organizations and not to public institutions like school districts. San Gabriel has an Education Foundation, which provides funding for certain needs not covered in the school district budget. The San Gabriel Women's Club raised $300,000, which they contributed to the San Gabriel Foundation to be distributed for scholarships for Gabrielino High School students.

After the future search, the San Gabriel Community Foundation was legally formed with a $25,000 contribution each from the city, the school district, the hospital, and the Church of Our Saviour. The California Community Foundation administers the foundation. The San Gabriel Foundation is building an endowment fund to support projects like the FRC. In spring 2003 they made their first $25,000 grant to the FRC. Since the Healthy Start operational grant expired in June 2003, Mrs. Solomon and the staff of the FRC continue an active search for grants and other resources to sustain the fine programs that are being implemented.

CURRENT SERVICES AND PARTNERS

As of October 2003, the San Gabriel Healthy Start Family Resource Center provides the following services: medical care, dental referrals, free immunization clinics, Healthy Families/Medi-Cal medical insurance assistance, English as a Second Language classes, legal assistance referrals, transportation assistance, mental health services and referrals, health education classes, parent education, after-school tutoring and mentoring, and emergency food services. Collaborative partners provide services for students and their families, either at the center, in the schools, or on referral to their own facilities. Partners include those in education, counseling, medical services, career education, recreation, law enforcement, parenting, and funding and grant writing.

ADVICE FROM A SCHOOL BOARD MEMBER

When interviewing key stakeholders for this chapter, we asked, "What else should we be asking so someone in your job across the country could read this chapter and start to replicate your accomplishment?" Cristina Alvarado, who was a board member before and after the future search but was out of town and off the board at the time of the conference, replied, "It is critical to have expertise to know how to navigate the system. It helped so much to hire a grant writer and a facilitator. We couldn't do it alone. It is like bringing in an architect and engineer to build a building. Just as it is important to emphasize the need for some *expert* help in preparing grants and developing a comprehensive and inclusive plan for moving forward, I believe it is equally important to lay out what to expect from the group process. In other words, a community that has not experienced collaboration will struggle with the group process a bit. It will most definitely experience *forming, storming, norming, performing.* People should not give up because of individual agendas or personality clashes. It is important that the future search process be followed *(trust the process)* and that the group allows itself growing pains."

REFLECTIONS ON SUCCESS

In her seminal work *Leadership and the New Science*, Margaret J. Wheatley described organizational reality: "There are no recipes or formulae, no checklists or advice that describe 'reality.' There is only what we create through our engagement with others and with events" (1992, p. 7). The engagement and sharing between San Gabriel community members and the San Gabriel Unified School District personnel were critical in developing new programs and resources to meet growing needs. Both were ready and willing to share needed information and resources to improve health and mental health services for students and families. The SGHS Collaborative has continued to meet monthly since 1998 to report and monitor progress and recommend new strategies and resources. It has become a key venue for community networking and for maintaining and sustaining the program through very difficult fiscal times in the state of California.

The San Gabriel Healthy Start Family Resource Center is now considered a model of coordinated and collaborative services in L.A. County. Each direct service and referral raises the possibility that involved students can now be academically successful. Factors contributing to success include leadership from multiple sources, vision, passion, persistence, existing relationships across the community, professional skills, input from all stakeholder groups, continuous outreach, enthusiasm, and humor.

9

Creating a Community for Healthy Learners in Minneapolis, Minnesota

Catherine M. Perme and Sara E. Stoltzfus Mullett

Every child is guaranteed access to a quality education. Healthy Learners Board has created greater equity and access for needy families around what should also be an entitlement and a right—quality health care.

—Carol Johnson, former superintendent of
Minneapolis Public Schools

BACKGROUND

This is the story of how the stirrings of a labor–management issue spawned a future search that resulted in a momentous school–community partnership that has improved the overall health of school children in Minneapolis Public Schools since 1998.

In the spring of 1995, the Health Services Department of Minneapolis Public Schools was on the verge of internal collapse. There were serious labor–management and communication problems that made service delivery difficult. At the same time, the department was under increasing pressure to respond to the rising health needs of 45,000 students in 88 schools.

It seemed that the world had changed significantly for the district in the preceding 10 years. By 1995, over 60 percent of its student population was in poverty. Twelve percent had chronic illnesses. Almost 500 children had significant health conditions that required frequent monitoring and adjustment of life support systems while in school. Licensed school nurses and paraprofessionals were faced with 4,000 visits per week for episodic care. Many children lacked health insurance and had no connection to primary health care. Children were coming to school unhealthy and not ready to learn, and the problem was getting worse.

Like many departments in the district, continuing budget cuts had plagued Health Related Services (HRS). The department had responded by cutting nursing hours and trying to stretch its services with the use of paraprofessionals. By 1995, only 25 members of its staff of 180 people were licensed school nurses; over two-thirds were part-time paraprofessionals, otherwise known as health assistants.

Major conflict occurred in 1994. The union representing the health assistants appealed for a review of their job classification. Union members felt that since they were doing the job of nurses, they should be paid more money. Disagreements emerged between nursing administration and the union about the actual depth and breadth of the paraprofessionals' responsibilities and authorities. The result of the job study conducted by the district's Human Resources Department provided little change to the job classification. Communication was strained, the health services administrator had quit, and larger issues remained. To resolve this crisis, a labor–management committee was formed to repair relationships and answer questions about how the department should be structured to deliver services more effectively.

ASSESSMENT

Catherine Perme, one of the coauthors of this chapter, was hired to conduct an assessment in the fall of 1995. The assessment included focus groups with school nurses, paraprofessionals, and administration, as well as direct observation of staff and committee meetings and a documentation review. The assessment found the following:

Work overload. It was obvious that people were dedicated to the health of children and doing the best they could. However, morale was low, safety appeared to be compromised, and the potential for disaster seemed high.

Role confusion. Focus groups and documentation indicated that confusion existed between the role of the school nurse and the paraprofessional. Nurses were delegating more and more procedures to paraprofessionals, who may or may not have been well trained or adequately supervised.

Serious liability exposure. According to guidelines published by the National Council of State Boards of Nursing (1990), essential principles of appropriate nursing delegation were that (a) quality nursing care could not be provided in isolation by unlicensed persons functioning independently of the nurse and (b) a limited (or costly) supply of licensed nurses could not be used as an excuse for inappropriate delegation. Focus group discussions and job study documentation indicated that both of these principles were being compromised, exposing the district to liability.

Lack of structure. A supporting structure was needed to assist people in working in a coordinated and cohesive manner. At all levels, people assigned all of their time to work tasks with no time for supervision, coordination, planning, or communication. Communication and decision-making tasks received short shrift. Management tasks were not clearly defined and received a low priority. Paraprofessionals reported to two different functions, creating confusion and inconsistency.

Lack of personal communication and connection. People at all levels talked about isolation, lack of support, and lack of communication. Weekly newsletters were well read and daily hotlines well used. However, communication at this point was not personal. People most often craved acknowledgment, connection, participation, and dialogue.

Unclear departmental role. The big issue that needed to be addressed was the role of Health Related Services in the schools and the changing larger community. The purpose of HRS needed to be clearly articulated and accepted by stakeholders in the school and community in order for expectations and staffing levels to be better matched.

INTERVENTION PLAN

A consulting team headed by Catherine Perme and supported by a multidisciplinary team of external consultants was created to assist the department through the end of the 1995 school year. The team was composed of specialists in conflict resolution, team development, public health, strategic planning, and project management. The approach focused initially on improving communication and teamwork within the current structure to reduce isolation and liability exposure. Some key elements of the plan follow:

Conflict management training for the labor–management committee. Because of communication breakdowns and hostility, it was important to start with resolving interpersonal conflicts on the labor–management committee and teaching members how to communicate with one another more effectively. We believed (and were proven correct) that improving the functioning of this group would have a ripple effect on the rest of the organization and smooth the way for further work.

Engaging all stakeholders to create a new vision and role for Health Related Services. HRS could not solve its problems alone. What was needed was the engagement of the community at large to help envision a new path. The consultant recommended a future search (Weisbord & Janoff, 1995) at the beginning of the restructuring process. A major medical foundation, the Allina Foundation, provided a grant of $20,000.

A cross-functional planning team for restructuring the department. A group of 20 to 25 people was charged with fleshing out the details of a new structural plan after a new vision was established at the future search conference. Members would be drawn from those who attended the future search, including representation from all unions and stakeholders.

PLANNING THE FUTURE SEARCH CONFERENCE

A design committee of 15 members was launched in December 1995 to design, plan, and conduct the future search conference in less than two months. Participants included many members of the initial labor–management committee, as well as stakeholders from the city, county, and health care communities. All members of the committee were highly aware that not only the future of the department was at stake, but also the health of schoolchildren. There was a sense of urgency to find a solution. The group decided to focus on the future of health care for school-age children and the roles of the school and community in helping to provide it.

As the design committee struggled with whom to invite, some increasingly difficult dynamics emerged. Committee members began to understand the depth of concern about potential outsourcing that was expressed by the paraprofessional union. There was a great deal of resistance to inviting any private sector health care providers to the future search, and deep-rooted skepticism about the motive of the foundation that provided funds for the event. After heated discussion, the future search principle of the whole system in the room won out, and these parties were invited, albeit with expressed mistrust from the union.

THE FUTURE SEARCH CONFERENCE BEGINS

The future search conference began on a bright, cold February morning. The 72 participants included representatives from HRS staff, unions, parents, health care providers, government agencies, school administrators, private foundations, and community activists.

The time lines of past events and the discussions surrounding them proved fruitful. The group relaxed a bit. Everyone was coming up to speed quickly on *why* the department was struggling to provide service. These activities generated a wide range of data for everyone to consider. The data showed how seemingly unrelated events had affected the current state of affairs, such as war on many continents (and the resulting boom in immigration to the city of Minneapolis), laws and court decisions (which decreed mainstreaming of students with special needs), and industry trends (such as managed care). The mind map (see the introduction for a general description) experience nearly brought people to the brink of despair as they considered an unchanging future. Clearly, a new model was needed, but the task seemed almost too daunting.

PROCESS BREAKTHROUGHS

The first major breakthrough occurred as a few staff and union members revealed their concerns about being blamed for the situation and potentially being outsourced. In response, other stakeholder groups helped staff and union members to understand that the future search was not about them but about the children—and that, as staff, they were counted on to be part of the solution. After this, the visioning session took off with a great deal of renewed energy and focus.

The second major breakthrough was a "nail-biter." The conference was closing at the end of day two after an energizing, vision-filled afternoon. Participants had dreamed big. Their visions commonly focused on a seamless flow of information, assistance, and services among schools, health care providers, and community resources. They came to a dead stop when one of the participants said, "Who will *do* all this?" There was a chorus of concern; over 80 percent of the people there had that same question. Clarification revealed that they did not believe that they had enough power to make their vision a reality, and suspected that the people who *did* were not in the room.

Our hearts were racing. Remembering the endless hours that the design team had spent on selecting invitees, it was hard to imagine that they had left many stones unturned. And 90 percent of those invited were participating at that moment. The facilitator asked the group to take a good look at each other, at the community that they represented, at themselves as individuals, and then asked them to name who else should have been in the room. After some discussion, the facilitator told the group that the future was up to them, that *they* were the people who could choose to make it happen. And if they loved that vision enough, by golly, come the next day and commit to *start doing something*.

That evening the design team was depressed. We wondered if anyone would come to the next—Saturday!—session. The facilitator questioned her own words, wondering if she had been too harsh, or if she perhaps had driven people away. To our great relief, nearly 75 percent of participants returned the final day.

What we realized was that the dependency and powerlessness that the group experienced was endemic to their culture; being direct and clear about boundaries and responsibilities helped to shift the group into a different place. In addition, the opportunity of having another night to sleep on things (inherent in a three-day design) was an important part of giving participants the time to make a commitment.

FUTURE SEARCH RESULTS

An enormous outpouring of community support resulted from the future search. The vision that was produced was very supportive of a continued health care presence in schools, albeit in a different form than the current one. The mood of the department shifted as people realized they were no longer alone in their efforts for children's health. Liz Zeno, a nurse manager within the department, said, "The most significant result of the future search and the ensuing partnership was the feeling of our staff that we no longer had to do everything on our own, and that we were connected to the community." The key themes that emerged as common ground were

- A common, clear mission dedicated to promoting the health of schoolchildren.
- A broad definition of health (focusing on the entire lifespan).
- Partnership between Minneapolis Public Schools and community health care organizations and providers.
- Consumer-friendly, seamless systems between schools and providers.
- Accountability and outcome measures for evaluating student health and its impact on student learning.
- A focus on prevention and early intervention.

Immediately after the future search conference, the Health Related Services Department spent three to four months redesigning itself to become more focused on preventive care, early intervention, and internal and external collaboration. It redesigned its mission and, using vision-based conference results, designed a new management and organizational structure. Then the department returned to its community partners with goals for review and support.

EARLY IMPLEMENTATION—FITS AND STARTS

At the opening of the following school year (1996–1997), an implementation council was formed to oversee and coordinate the change process. Half of the original planning council served on the implementation council, taking leadership positions in various work groups. Additional staff and community partners who could provide a fresh look and support for the implementation effort joined them.

The year was difficult. The scope of the effort made it difficult to find a starting point, and the group sometimes floundered. The union, still distrustful, continued to resist initiatives and plans. Despite this, the department continued to use the participative and whole system processes that it had learned and was able to accomplish the following in that school year:

- It focused its goals and strategies on improving the overall health of students and partnering with the community to provide direct care for individual students. This was done using a nationally recognized public health model cocreated by Joyce Essien, who worked on this effort. Joyce was a consultant from Emory University affiliated with the Centers for Disease Control (CDC) and a coauthor of the book *The Public Health Competency Handbook* (2002).
- It identified four key outcomes for itself and the community that would have the most impact on student attendance and achievement. A healthy learner 1) is in school and ready to learn; 2) has access to preventive health care; 3) understands and uses information to make health-promoting decisions; and 4) achieves full potential physically, socially, emotionally, and academically.
- It established a partnership with the City of Minneapolis Health Department to conduct a needs assessment of the kinds of data and systems required to make these outcomes possible. It learned through this effort that 1) there were no good baseline data from which to assess overall student health or progress against outcomes, and 2) there was virtually no technology employed to support this effort.
- The department restructured as follows: 1) It changed the lead management position from an administrator to a director and lengthened the work year from 10 to 12 months. Sara Mullett, one of this chapter's coauthors, competed for and won the position of director of health related services. Up to this point she had been the acting administrator and during that time had shepherded the department through the future search and the intervention. 2) It included a new, interdisciplinary management team to provide coordination, supervision, and support to the 150-plus staff in the department. 3) It redefined all job descriptions in light of the new direction. 4) It increased

efforts to build the competencies of staff at all levels of the organization.

Through the use of the whole system perspective that it had learned from future search, the department was able to build an internal structure that made it easier for the community to connect with the department (and vice versa) and to build relationships to support student health.

A first big test of this new direction occurred in May 1997 when the district, union, and city health department all underwent leadership changes. It is noteworthy that not only did the vision survive but also new leadership continued to support and broaden its implementation. For example:

- The new superintendent had had positive experiences with major health care organizations in her prior school district. She broadened the implementation to include executive and policy level involvement.
- The union representing the health assistants elected a new president, who brought a more moderate perspective to the union.
- Finally, the new health commissioner for the city of Minneapolis not only adopted the burgeoning partnership but became actively involved and directed his managers and staff to continue work with the school district in support of the vision.

THE RIPPLE EXPANDS

During the 1997–1998 school year, the implementation council realized that a successful partnership would need to generate the types of outcomes that would appeal to both the private sector (characterized as being action oriented with a focus on quick progress) and the public sector (characterized as process oriented with a focus on balancing the needs of multiple stakeholders). It defined the following design criteria for an effective partnership:

- A focus on initiatives that would bring everyone together and provide focused impact and success.
- Participation from a high-enough level in member organizations to influence resources and budgets.
- Goals that were win-win for schools and for the health care community.

INITIATIVES

All of the initiatives that were selected had a high degree of benefit both for the school system and the Minneapolis health care community. In keeping with future search principles, these initiatives were the common ground on which all partners could work for collective as well as personal benefit.

Connecting Students to Primary Care

The first initiative was to help students and their families get connected to primary care—an important piece of the overall vision and a key defined outcome for a healthy learner. A partnership with the Allina Foundation provided funds for multilingual teams to assist families new to the district to find appropriate health care providers and insurance. The Minneapolis Department of Health provided key leadership and support to help families overcome barriers to using health care systems due to language skills, literacy, homelessness, documentation, or other multiple stressors. A grant from the Children's Defense Fund through the Robert Wood Johnson Foundation has helped to sustain this initiative to this day.

Immunizations: "No Shots, No School"

A change in state law allowed the district greater flexibility to improve the current 67 percent immunization rate. The implementation council saw the change in law as an opportunity to leverage major change and used it as a catalyst to jump-start the school–community partnership. At that time, an inordinate amount of staff time was spent trying to track down immunizations in the first 45 days of each school year, the previous deadline. Despite this effort, usually a number of students were still excluded at the 45-day cut off because they did not have their immunizations current. This midterm exclusion was extremely disruptive to the students' learning.

The new goal was that 100 percent of the students in the Minneapolis School District would enter school in September (less than four months away) with their immunizations complete. The superintendent put out a call for action to the future search partners to assist with this effort. A planning group identified not only the focus but also the people who needed to be at the table to start work on this initiative, both at the executive and technical levels.

The magnitude of the partnership that emerged was unprecedented. An immunization task force emerged to spearhead the initiative. Work groups were identified and commissioned to tackle the four areas considered the biggest obstacles to success: access, communications, data, and assurance.

Access. The group worked closely with the health care community to develop the concept of "healthy learner clinics"—designated city clinics that provided immunizations before school started, *for no fee*. These clinics also provided walk-in services, translators, and assistance with transportation.

Communications. A "No Shots, No School" media campaign was launched citywide. A "Hot Shot Line" provided information about what immunizations an individual student still needed. A targeted mailing, in English and native languages, provided further information.

Up-to-date information. The group worked with the Hennepin County Health Department to connect school immunization data to the metrowide immunization registry.

Assurance. School principals were contacted to help them understand the reasons for the change in policy and how to implement at the school site.

Results

By the end of the first week of school, 98 percent of the student body had been immunized. Nonimmunized students were able to walk into a clinic on the first or second day of school and get immunized on the spot. First-week immunization rates have remained at 97 percent or above.

The Healthy Learners Board also emerged from this initiative. This school–community partnership has become the fundamental structure that sponsors, supports, and implements public health initiatives for the betterment of students in Minneapolis Public Schools.

Healthy Learners Asthma Initiative

Buoyed by their success with the immunization initiative, the Healthy Learners Board decided to tackle a more complex subject in the 1999–

2000 school year—dealing with chronic illnesses such as asthma, diabetes, and life-threatening allergies. It was estimated that one out of eight children in Minneapolis Public Schools—or more than 5,000 students—had some type of chronic illness, which was a significant factor in attendance and performance.

A three-year project was created to improve outcomes for students with chronic illnesses, with an initial focus on asthma. The project's goals were to increase attendance for students with asthma by 50 percent and reduce hospitalizations by 50 percent. Seed funding of $500,000 came from the Healthy Learners Board partners themselves. A large portion of this money was earmarked for evaluation of both process outcomes (system changes) and student outcomes. The board believed that if an effective model could be created for managing asthma, it could be used to manage other chronic conditions. Steps included hiring an evaluator, an overall project coordinator, and school resource nurses. To move the asthma initiative forward, the following structure was put in place:

- The Asthma Planning Group, consisting of representatives from the district, Children's Hospital, the Department of Health, a health plan, a health care provider, and the evaluator, was given responsibility for providing overall direction to the asthma initiative. Their work included ensuring congruency of effort and consistency of messages within and between work groups, as well as providing oversight as the evaluation took shape.
- Two work groups were formed in conjunction with community provider groups to address the clinical aspects of the initiative, one for clinical practice and operations and one for clinical program elements.
- Four work groups focused on activities within the schools, including the School Asthma Group, the School Policy and Practice Workgroup, the Education Workgroup, and the Environment Workgroup.

Results

Although the asthma initiative did not reach its lofty goals of reducing absences and hospitalizations by 50 percent, the initiative *did* have a major impact on student health and attendance. According to the final evaluation report, in a follow-up survey conducted in January 2002: "Data showed significant reductions in nighttime breathing problems and school days missed, and improvement in asthma control score. More students had written action plans from their doctor; and a small, but positive change was found in hospitalizations" (Splett & Associates, 2002, p. iv). In addition, 20 "great, unexpected outcomes" were identified, including the following:

- Health office staff, families, and providers were speaking a common language about asthma.
- Health office staff expressed pride and confidence in their knowledge and ability to care for children with asthma.
- Families were coming to clinics because of notes sent from school, such as an "Asthma Visit Notification" from a school nurse or health assistant.
- The manager of the asthma initiative, as well as the Healthy Learners Board, received the 2001 Shering/Key Asthma Leadership Award from the National Association of School Nurses.

A grant from the CDC awarded to the Lung Association of Minnesota and the Healthy Learners Board is now sustaining and further developing this initiative. In addition, the coordinator for this initiative is working with the State of Minnesota Department of Health to incorporate key components of the asthma initiative into a statewide school asthma program, also funded by the CDC.

New Initiatives in Progress

The Healthy Learners Board identified two initiatives to begin developing in 2003 for implementation in the 2003–2004 school year: vision and hearing screenings and mental health.

INFRASTRUCTURE

The all-volunteer Healthy Learners Board and Partnership has become the basic infrastructure to sustain the vision, focus, and energy of community efforts. Ongoing membership is by organization, not by individual participation. Figure 9.1 is an overview of the Healthy Learners Board and Partnership structure.

The board is composed of 28 high-level decision makers from organizations representing schools, providers, public health, elected officials, and the community. It is responsible for developing overall strategy; selecting, implementing, and evaluating initiatives; forming public and private policy positions; and raising funds and committing resources. The board meets four times per year and has four work groups: fund-raising, planning, policy, and administration.

Healthy Learners Strategies Management

The strategies management group includes staff from the Healthy Learners Board Administration Team as well as chairs and coordinators of ongoing and new initiatives. This group's job is to develop and recommend implementation strategies for various initiatives and to ensure coordination of activities. The group meets monthly to solve problems, ensure management of processes, and coordinate internal and external communications for the general community and throughout the partnership.

Initiative Task Forces

Each new initiative has a planning team and various task forces and staff as needed for implementation. Membership on these teams is not restricted to partners—any person or organization that is interested, willing, and able to contribute to its implementation is welcomed. Once an initiative becomes operational, the goal is to obtain sustainable resources to integrate it into the existing systems. At that point, Healthy Learners Board involvement is reduced or eliminated.

What Makes This Work So Well?

It is noteworthy that the Healthy Learners Board is completely voluntary and started with no resources other than what the partners were willing to provide. One answer to its five-year viability lies in the vision that was created at the future search conference. A recent review of board members showed that over half the organizations that participated in the original future search

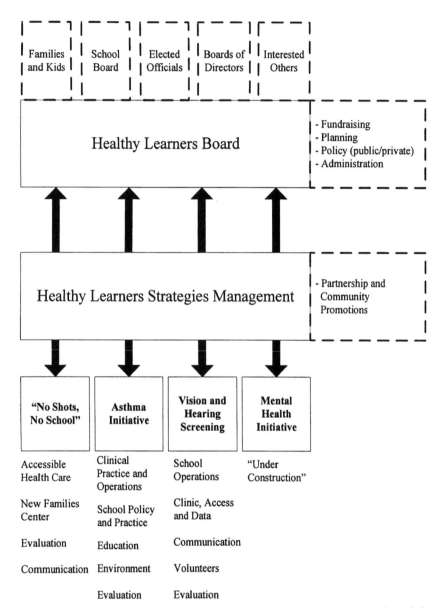

Figure 9.1. Overview of the Healthy Learner Partnership Structure (Adapted by Catherine Perme from Healthy Learners Board brochure)

are still represented on the Healthy Learners Board. Another answer lies in the guiding principles of the partnership:

Focus on the future. The Healthy Learners Board keeps itself firmly focused on its vision of optimal health and academic success for children in Minneapolis, seeking creative ways to engage the community and change the larger system.

Whole system participation. On the Healthy Learners Board, there is representation from every stakeholder group. Critical to this is the involvement of high-profile health leaders who are in a position to influence changes in their own organizations or the overall system.

Picking the right business opportunity. The Healthy Learners Board has carefully selected initiatives that were timely, doable, win-win, and able to generate enthusiasm.

Common ground rather than conflict management. The partner organizations and the people who represent them are encouraged to bring their diverse views to the table. In addition, the focus on achieving practical, win-win outcomes changes the nature of the initiatives from a tendency toward blaming and competition to one based on learning and collaboration.

Self-management. The management and implementation level of the Healthy Learners Board is fluid. Partners have complete control over when, what, and how many resources they provide and how they organize internally to support initiatives. Within the partnership, shared leadership is the norm as well as a structural component.

Another answer to why this has worked so well over time is that the Healthy Learners Board has created an organizational model that propagates and focuses energy in a way that is important for long-term sustainability. This is based on research in the field of human system dynamics, which identified the basic building blocks of self-organization known as the CDE model. This model was developed by Dr. Glenda Eoyang in her research on sustainable communities as described in her dissertation (Eoyang, 2002), and in *Facilitating Organizational Change: Lessons from Complexity Science* (Olson & Eoyang, 2001).

- The Healthy Learners Board and Partnership created a clear "container" to bound and focus its work with a clearly defined common vision; guiding ideas and operating principles; and clearly defined roles and responsibilities at various levels of operation.

- The board invites and promotes diversity in its broadest sense, encouraging a wide variety of partners and stakeholders to join and share differing views.
- The board created mechanisms for exchange with feedback loops within its structure, the evaluation of outcomes, data gathering with focus groups, and partnership and community promotions.

LESSONS LEARNED

The Future Search Process Works

Even with future search primary facilitators who lacked background in health care and had limited experience with future search, the process worked very well; sticking to the basic principles of the process yielded results.

Whole System Representation Is Crucial

What provoked the future search and the entire intervention (and no doubt the outsourcing fears of union members) was a question posed by the superintendent, who in response to the labor–management problems asked, "What is the role of health care in schools, anyway? Is there a different way to do this?"

Had the design team not engaged private sector health care providers in the initial future search because of its anxiety about outsourcing, the results would have been completely different today. It has been the partnership of *three* sectors (education, public health, and private sector health care) and parents that has truly changed school health care systems in Minneapolis for the betterment of kids.

Time Spent with the Union Is Time Well Spent

Listening to union members, understanding their perspectives and concerns, and engaging them as active participants in building the future (versus treating them as an afterthought or a contract negotiation) was another key to successful transformation.

Building a new level of trust took a long time. The future search was just the first step. It was important to continually inform all staff about what was happening and why, as quickly and objectively as possible, keeping facts out in front, and being honest with everyone. When union members themselves saw the larger picture and the need to get the community involved, tensions were reduced. When they were affirmed for their role in caring for schoolchildren and saw a place for themselves in the future, they began to tenuously trust the process.

First Things First

In retrospect, the district might have seemed slow moving in building a partnership with the community. It was more than two years after the future search that the first major public initiative was launched and the Healthy Learners Board and Partnership was created. However, without the work that Health Related Services did to restructure itself and build its own internal capacity, it is doubtful that it could have successfully participated in as broad a partnership. That partners assisted them with funding and resources to do this work and waited for them to complete it was also a result of the future search.

Valuing Differences and Finding Common Ground among Vested Interests

Acknowledging and valuing the different sectors' perspectives, processes, and problems as equally important was (and continues to be) both the frustration and the blessing of the Healthy Learners Board. It is hard work to listen deeply, suspend judgment, and find common ground. It is harder work to value those differences and use them effectively over time. The Healthy Learners Board has spent a great deal of time listening to one another and thinking strategically about their differences, because this is such an important building block in sustaining a long-term relationship.

Closing system gaps has been achieved by linking the various stakeholders' interests together in ways that had never before been considered, and by selecting initiatives that had solid benefits for all. For instance, asthma costs in urgent care, emergency departments, and hospitalization were escalating, and insurance providers wanted to see how to lessen these costs. Partnering with Minneapolis Public Schools, the county, and other public health agencies was one avenue to control costs as well as improve outcomes for kids.

Focus on Outcomes, Not Structure

Had the Healthy Learners Board spent time structuring itself first (i.e., charter, membership, governance structure, etc.), we doubt it would have been as effective as it is now. The partnership structure has emerged over time as a way to coordinate resources, funds, and system changes as they relate to new initiatives. The initiatives came first; and the structure was created later to help partners dynamically adjust to new needs and initiatives.

Leadership at All Levels and in All Forms

There was (and is) so much work to do that creating a structure in which only a limited number of people played leadership roles would have slowed productivity and the implementation of initiatives. People at all organizational levels are able to take leadership roles within task forces and work groups, without regard to their status in their partner organizations. At the same time, there is no substitute for sustained and passionate leadership at some level to keep things moving. The director of Health Related Services has played the role of chief strategist and community builder. The sponsorship and participation of the superintendent as cochair of the Healthy Learners Board has demonstrated the school system's commitment to partnership and change.

Evaluation-Based Outcomes

Since they were walking a new path, the partnership needed a feedback mechanism to assess their progress and to help focus their energy and resources. As a result, measurable initiatives have become the norm rather than the exception. Again, in its own words, the Healthy Learners Board (brochure, 2002) describes its process:

> A collective, sweeping vision which cannot be tied to reality remains a dream without action. Healthy Learners Board did not need to know all the

answers in the beginning, but its members were willing to explore and discover. Healthy Learners Board learned through trial and error and evaluation that one must travel unruffled and optimistically down an unmarked road. And if, at some point, the wrong path is chosen, turn around, reinnovate and set out again.

In these initiatives, clear, measurable outcomes directed the specific steps required for positive results. . . . Measurable successes have taught Healthy Learners Board to begin with minimal health care interventions and move to a more complex overall response to the health needs of children (p. 13).

Appropriate Use of Resources

Another critical success factor for this partnership has been the willingness to purchase expertise and technical support when it was needed. The partnership was able to move much faster and experience success earlier with the help of targeted expertise in the areas of health care strategy, research and evaluation, and organization development than if it had tried to struggle through these issues with limited knowledge and background.

Change Does Not Always Mean Cutting Services

There is a tendency for school districts to cut auxiliary services (such as transportation, food services, health care, etc.) when faced with budget crunches in order to protect the academic core. Problems occur when cuts are made without thinking about potential repercussions, which might include liability issues that may be far more costly in the long run.

What we have learned is that there is another way: being fundamentally clear about the role of an auxiliary service and finding partnerships to leverage the internal resources. What has been the most surprising and affirming is the level of partnership at which community members are willing to engage, finding common ground within vested interests.

CONCLUSION

There is no doubt that the future search employed in this intervention was critical to the impressive outcomes in student health. This event helped all stakeholders see the big picture, embrace the complexity of the situation very quickly, and build a solid foundation for future work. The partnerships and the community support generated by the future search formed the cornerstone of today's efforts. The strong success of each initiative demonstrates the power of future search for system change.

It is equally true that this transformation would have failed without the benefit of committed leadership from all sectors to prepare the way and support the implementation. The lure of large group events is that they *can* be truly transformational. Yet participants must be willing to be transformed and be willing to work hard to make the transformation a reality. The leadership, commitment, and passion for children's health were the true leverage points in this intervention process. We just helped those levers reach as far as they could.

Part 4

INCLUDING STUDENT VOICES

One of the fundamental principles of a future search is to "get the whole system in the room." We do this by working with a planning team that ideally represents the whole system. Interestingly, the group that typically eludes the planning team is the one that is most affected by the work of school districts—children and youth. Some people feel that young people under the age of 16 cannot handle a future search and that it would not be responsible to demand this of them. They worry that the children would not be comfortable speaking up in such a setting. Invariably the youth participants become the "truth tellers" and the ones who raise the really important issues, or ask very provocative, simple questions that enable the whole conference to move to a deeper level.

If youth are important stakeholders in the outcome, they need to be involved in the planning team, as they are mindful of youth needs. Getting youth participants to attend the conference often presents some additional challenges to the conference planning team. Arranging transportation and securing parental permission and support is vital. The planning team must enlist a diversity of youth: the young people who look "good" to adults, the young people who are respected by their peers, and the young people who are outsiders and not being well served. The three chapters in this section illustrate the influence children and youth were able to have.

In Santa Monica, CA (chapter 10), student voices were heard, student leadership was acknowledged, and the issue of equity and equality for *all* students shifted in a positive direction. A key focus of this district's new strategic plan is to close the achievement gap that is documented in achievement scores and distrust—the gap that appears between rich and poor, between whites and Hispanics, blacks, and other people of color living in Santa Monica.

At the Novato School District Future Search Conference in California (chapter 11), there had been no students on the planning committee. The student participants had not been informed about the structure or principles of the process and fought it because they had no confidence that their voices would be heard. At the most critical part of the conference, the students threatened to walk out! Other voices resonated and were sympathetic to student concerns. How this was handled as well as how this school district successfully used future search to respond to charges of racism are described in this chapter.

In Montreal, QC (chapter 12), the story about students is not found so much in what happened during the conference but rather in what happened afterward. One of the six action groups from this future search formed a central student committee, ensuring that students are full educational partners in this district. These central student committees—still a rarity in the education world although most individual schools have student committees—are gaining in popularity as students are speaking up and having a greater influence on their education. This chapter also includes discussions on leadership, broad commitment to follow-up, and meaningful coincidence.

10

Finding the Rainbow in a Coat of Many Colors: A Districtwide Strategic Planning Process

Shelley Sweet and Jean Katz

INTRODUCTION

In the midst of California's budget crisis, it is remarkable how much progress occurred during the first year of implementation of the Santa Monica–Malibu Unified School District (SMMUSD) Strategic Plan. Since the strategic plan was adopted in June 2002, there have been continual cutbacks as over 80 percent of educational funding comes from the state. The community anticipated the initial cutback and worked diligently to promote a parcel tax on local real estate to supplement the state's dwindling resources. Unfortunately, the November 2002 vote failed to meet the 66 percent approval needed to pass. Yet committed administrators, teachers, parents, and students in the SMMUSD created real changes in equity and equality, instructional strategies, curriculum, and early childhood education despite severe financial restraints.

The future search conference in SMMUSD was a pivotal point in a larger strategic planning process. The future search and the strategic planning process heralded a new way of working in the district. During this yearlong process the system began to change in planned and unplanned ways. The issue of equity and equality for all students shifted in a positive direction. School–community relationships developed and became more inclusive. Student voices were heard and student leadership was acknowledged. This chapter describes the journey toward those changes, the results that occurred in implementation, and what was learned in the process.

Santa Monica–Malibu Unified School District, one of 82 school districts in Los Angeles County, has a total enrollment of 12,499 students in 11 elementary schools, two middle schools, two high schools, and a continuation high school. In addition there is a child development program with state preschools, Head Start, and an adult education program. The district stretches along the Pacific Coast from Malibu, a predominantly upper-class and upper-middle-class population area, to the south end where some families are living on welfare. The ethnic diversity mirrors southern California, including African Americans, Latinos, Asians, Anglos, and students of Middle Eastern background.

GETTING STARTED, JUNE 2001

The superintendent was in the middle of his first 100 days, meeting hundreds of people, when he first met Shelley Sweet, coauthor of this chapter. Mr. Deasy was clear about the overriding purpose of the district's challenge and his work—to improve student achievement. In his first year he wanted to build his leadership team, model educational practices in the classroom, and build a community-driven strategic plan. He and the board of education contracted with Shelley to develop a detailed strategic plan with four to six initiatives that would be adopted in June 2002. Based on the purposes and desired outcomes, Shelley outlined a five-stage process (illustrated in figure 10.1) and a planning calendar (see table 10.1).

PLAN THE PROCESS

The first step was to form a design team whose primary responsibility was to oversee all the phases of the strategic planning process. The district recruited the design team through an open public process using local newspapers and e-mail. Right from the start the school board wanted to be in-

Figure 10.1.   Five-Step Planning Process (Courtesy Shelley Sweet)

clusive and encouraged all citizens to apply for this team. A subcommittee of the board interviewed the only 12 people who applied and accepted them all. The design team members would help plan the process, lead it, and get the right people to attend key events and conferences.

The design team first met in September 2001. The 12 members represented several stakeholder groups, including parents, community members, a principal, a teacher, a student, district administration, the superintendent, and a board of education member. The team did not reflect the full diversity of the community. Shelley introduced them to the five-stage plan and to some of the guiding principles and guideposts for the planning process:

- The five-stage plan would involve many different stakeholders, with new people introduced at each stage to expand the circle of involvement.

Table 10.1.   Planning Calendar (Courtesy Shelley Sweet and Jean Katz)

Planning Stage	Participants	Expected Time Frame
Plan the process	Design team (The superintendent and board of education member were members of this team.)	Sept. 2001 to June 2002
Assess the current situation	Members of the community and design team members	Oct. to Nov. 2001
Prepare for and conduct the future search conference	Members of the community and design team members	Dec. 2001 to Feb. 2002
Strategic work groups develop specific action plans for each initiative	Members of the community, community cochairs, and design team members; culminating in a summit meeting to share the results with the community at large	March to May 2002
Adopt and celebrate (prepare for and present to the board of education and celebrate adoption)	Design team members	June 2002

- The assessment phase was designed as a series of interviews with the community to determine the district's strengths, cherished values, and successful programs.
- A large three-day conference was planned for February 2002. It would include 140 people, with participants from all community stakeholder groups mirroring the district. It would be conducted as two concurrent conferences of 70 people each. In that conference the participants would create the four to six common goals and form action teams to begin working on the details of those goals.
- The design team would reflect on what had been learned at each stage and use that information to plan the next stage.

Now with a full understanding of future search principles, the design team recognized that it needed to expand its membership to be more representative. The team grew to 18 people and had much more diversity by the second meeting.

ASSESS THE CURRENT SITUATION

Stage two, assessing the current situation, used Appreciative Inquiry (Cooperrider & Whitney, 1999) interviews to discover themes about participant successes for building the future. More than 100 people were involved. The session was enthusiastic and spirited. Trust was built through paired interviews followed by small-group summaries of themes. Translators were available for multiple language interpretation. Because of the conclusions drawn by the participants at that meeting, the design team conducted more interviews. Their outreach throughout the community resulted in the desired broad stakeholder involvement.

The assessment process concluded with the design team reading and summarizing all interviews. Community members were again invited to participate. The team organized the themes in a short document, using these five categories: 1) optimize the learning experience for all; 2) maintain and enhance specific programs; 3) manage and allocate resources equitably; 4) ensure administrative and management accountability; and 5) foster communication, outreach, and empowerment. The two examples in table 10.2 provide a partial representation of findings for each category. Additionally, the themes of achievement for all students and the difficulty of getting diverse representation of stakeholder groups came out of the assessment as major concerns.

THE FUTURE SEARCH CONFERENCE

The design team formulated the conference topic based on learnings from the assessment phase. It titled the conference "Designing the Class of the Future: Excellence in Learning and Equality of Opportunity." In planning for the future search conference, the team faced many obstacles, including the lack of funding, the difficulty of finding and paying conference managers and support people who mirrored the district's demographics, and the legal requirement to open the conference to the public.

The design team customized the standard future search process to respond to the unique concerns and conditions of the SMMUSD. Knowing that board of education members and elected officials wanted to attend but could not stay the entire time, the design team devised a workable compromise: they placed a visitors' table near the door in each conference area. A member of the conference staff greeted and oriented visitors, gave them materials, explained the conference guidelines, and sat with them. Each day these board members, the mayor, and the visiting public could speak to the conference for a limited number of minutes.

After looking deeply at the past and the present and envisioning their desired future, stakeholders affirmed their desired outcome: a classroom of the future that would create excellence in learning and equality of opportunity for all. The six goals, or initiatives, that had emerged during the conference included abundant resources; standards-based curriculum; differentiated instruction; schools as community centers; optimal class size; and universal access to quality early childhood education, family support programs, and after-school care.

During the dialogue, students and some parents raised their voices to include one important area they felt had been left out: equity and equality of education. The district now had seven common goals because of student and parent leadership and candor.

Table 10.2. Examples of Findings for Five Categories of Themes (Courtesy Shelley Sweet and Jean Katz)

Category	What Works Well	Areas for Improvement
Optimize the learning experience for all	Personal connections between teachers and learners are crucial and meaningful to the learning process.	There should be uniform standards and curricula across classrooms, grades, and schools.
Maintain and enhance specific programs	Art, music, and sports programs are an essential way the district provides "best experiences" that support inclusion and diversity naturally by helping students and parents value each others' strengths.	More proactive programs are needed for different learners/special education/gifted/English language learners.
Manage and allocate resources equitably	There is significant parent involvement, which provides access to varied enrichment for students.	There must be adequate and equitable resources (materials and equipment) across all sites to support the educational process.
Ensure administrative and management accountability	There is much optimism about the credibility and leadership of the new superintendent.	The physical and emotional safety of students within schools (e.g., sexual harassment, bullying, dress code enforcement, substance abuse) is paramount.
Foster communication, outreach, and empowerment	There are many opportunities to volunteer, leading to parents who are involved and feel supported and empowered.	Help must be provided to underserved, underperforming, and disenfranchised communities so they can better understand how the system, schools, paths to honors, and other classes and services work, as well as the roles they can play to be effective.

STRATEGIC WORK GROUPS

After the future search conference, seven strategic work groups convened regularly for more than two months to develop strategic action plans (outcomes, measures, strategies, tactics, accountability, budget, and quick wins) for each of the initiatives. The groups, along with additional community members, projected three years into the future.

One committee chair said, "The work group was where 'the rubber met the road,' and we created real plans to define each initiative. We were stretched by working in a three month time frame, but it was important not to let this drag on."

The strategic work groups presented their formal progress report on the initiative action plans to the general community in May 2002. Later that day the strategic work group members presented the results of their work to community members at the Santa Monica Arts Fair. This formal presentation and informal discussion gave the community an opportunity to hear about the specifics of each initiative, ask questions, and give input.

Next, the strategic work group chairs integrated the seven areas into one overall district plan. Their prepared materials showed how the strategic plan would work with current district programs. Since the 2002–2003 school year budget had already been approved, there would be no monies for initiatives that year. The strategic work group and the design team hoped that more money could be raised in years two and three.

The design team then reviewed the strategic plan, the seven initiative outcomes, the detailed plans, budget considerations, and a time line with the board of education. The team also recommended the formation of an implementation and accountability team to ensure implementation of the plan. After this review, the board of education adopted the strategic plan in June 2002.

IMPLEMENTATION OF THE SEVEN INITIATIVES: SEPTEMBER 2002 TO SEPTEMBER 2003

Implementation of initiatives began that fall. Community members, strategic work group chairs, and district staff led the effort. The programs and results listed below took place in the first year of implementation.

Initiative 1: Abundant Resources

The district's and community's attention to funding resources expanded as a direct result of the abundant resources initiative. The chair of this initiative and key committee members built community teams to address funding issues and specifically campaign for a parcel tax. In May 2003 the Abundant Resources Committee chairperson reported, "We went out to get more funding using a $300 parcel tax on the ballot in November 2002. The tax needed a 66 percent vote to pass; we got 61.18 percent. Not quite enough. Some say we asked for too much money. We are trying again, with a $225 parcel tax on the June 2003 ballot." The second funding measure passed in June.

Initiative 2: Standards-Based Curriculum

The standards-based curriculum initiative brought its focus to the schools in many ways. It analyzed English and language arts and mathematics because this was the year to adopt textbooks in these content areas. It adopted the Houghton Mifflin Language Arts series for grades K–5. It distributed the English and language arts and mathematics standards to all district teachers in all grades. Now most schools have posted the standards. The district now offers professional development on standards-based curriculum to principals, district office leadership, assistant principals, and teacher representatives. Additionally, new leadership coaches provide instruction in leadership training in intensive workshops to teachers.

Initiative 3: Differentiated Instruction

The differentiated instruction initiative, closely linked with the standards-based curriculum initiative, was partially funded by grants brought to the district by the superintendent. This initiative has a strong parent-leader who continues to convene her team and keep the initiative moving forward. The district provided training sessions on differentiated instruction for elementary teachers in the fall of 2002. Teachers started changing instructional strategies in the classroom within a few weeks after the training. Training for secondary teachers occurred in the winter and spring. During the second semester, teachers who did not receive that training were able to observe the trained teachers' use of differentiated instruction. A program has also been implemented at all the district elementary schools for literacy coaches to help teachers instruct reading more effectively. The director of data and assessment developed measurement protocols to gather information about levels of teacher implementation of differentiated instructional strategies.

Initiative 4: Schools as Community Centers

The coordinator of school and community partnerships is working with the schools on the community center initiative because these two efforts are so closely connected. This committee conducted a survey to understand existing resources and unmet needs at the sites. Relationships with existing community partners have been maintained and new ones have been developed, including the Promise Substance Abuse Treatment Program, which donated $12,800 to maintain intervention programs at the major high school after funding was cut. When a former agency partner indicated that it would no longer be able to provide counseling services at one of the schools, another agency was approached and agreed to fill the gap—at no cost to the district.

One aspect of this team's plan was to identify space to accommodate additional community resources at schools. When it seemed unlikely that space would be allocated in the tight economic environment, the committee developed creative, no-cost solutions to provide space, resources, and services to students and parents. For example, the district worked with the Boys and Girls Club to establish a facility at a middle school and at Malibu High School.

Initiative 5: Optimal Class Size

To create optimal class size, the district has limited out-of-district permit attendance and has updated an analysis to determine availability of space at each school.

Initiative 6: Universal Access to Quality Early Childhood Education, Family Support Programs, and After-School Care

This initiative has the longest name and the largest group of people actively involved. It has successfully merged with the district's Early Childhood Advisory Committee. It also benefits from the expertise and support of the Child Care Task Force, with which it overlaps in both membership and intent.

The district's child development services office is doing most of the actual work for this initiative. As planned, they have completed assessment tools for evaluating each child's readiness for kindergarten and await funding for implementation. The district currently provides full-day preschool for children from low-income families and is in the planning process to expand preschool to additional families. Professional development for early childhood teachers is ongoing.

Initiative 7: Equity and Equality of Education: Closing the Achievement Gap

The equity and equality of education initiative most explicitly challenges the district to finally close the achievement gap between the higher performance of Anglo and Asian students and the lower performance of African American and Latino students. This initiative stimulated the following activities to close this gap:

- The AVID program, available to all middle school students and parents, helps them learn skills for study and research. It is hoped that this program will enable greater numbers of underrepresented students to be successful in institutions of higher learning.
- The redesign of the major high school: A redesign committee for the major high school explored a range of structural and programmatic changes to turn the large, comprehensive Santa Monica High School into smaller schools-within-a-school. This change, implemented in the fall of 2003, focused on providing a more personalized education for students, with priority given to 9th and 10th graders at the high school level. Although the conference did not directly cause the high school redesign, it empowered an active student voice to propose the need for the redesign in the community. The future search process engaged all stakeholders in setting this as a district priority.
- Curriculum standards are being applied throughout the district at all grade levels. Expectations are high for all students at all sites, not just at some sites for some students.

- Honors and advanced placement classes at the high school are increasingly more inclusive of minority students.
- Child Development Services is working with the sites to provide families with information about kindergarten readiness prior to kindergarten enrollment.
- Parent education relating to college requirements.
- The new mathematics requirement—that all students take algebra by the eighth grade and that all students have four years of math in high school—raises the bar.
- The Student and Family Support Services Office focuses on achievement issues for individual schools and publishes data across the schools on the web.
- Four-year colleges: The high schools are encouraging students of color to apply to four-year colleges, whereas before the schools encouraged many of these students to apply to local two-year colleges.
- Performance targets have been established for every disaggregated group.

INCLUSION, RACE, EQUITY, SOCIAL CLASS, AND STUDENT ACHIEVEMENT

Two themes—diverse stakeholder inclusion through engagement and equity and equality for all students—intertwined to strengthen the strategic planning process and produce results in the first year of implementation.

In retrospect, these themes emerged early from Superintendent Deasy's focus, the board of education's visible public application process for the design team, and the inclusive collaborative processes built into each of the five phases of the strategic planning process. Mr. Deasy spoke of his values and the strategic plan publicly, "The plan's primary function is to improve student achievement. It's about instruction, it will always be about instruction, and nothing but the best quality customized instruction!"

The need for inclusion surfaced at the first design team meeting when Brent Kastenbaum, the high school student on the design team, spoke up for more diversity. He took a leadership role in suggesting additional people and enlisting them for the team. Right away an important student voice was heard; all the adults listened, as they did from then on. Later, Kastenbaum said that this moment on the design team was a critical point in the process: "This team was not going to be like every other team, and they were not going to sweep issues under the table."

The next call for inclusion came out of the current assessment process at Lincoln Middle School. The design team had worked very hard to make this first public assessment event a successful meeting. But when participants looked around the room and at the wall-sized stakeholder map, they realized that the participants that day were mostly educated women with family incomes above $100,000. In order to reach other stakeholders, the design team took the paired interview process on the road—to Malibu, to the Boys and Girls Club in Santa Monica, to business groups, to the district's website, and to meetings in many school locations. The circle of involvement expanded as more and more community members learned about and participated in the planning process.

Because of the assessment process, the design team knew it would take a big effort to get the right mix of people at the three-day future search conference. They selected and recruited key persons for each stakeholder group. They monitored acceptances as they came in, noting where they needed additional stakeholders and where there were too many. Then they personally invited others to fill the gaps.

The inclusiveness of the conference initiated a new way of being with each other. It showed that all the different groups could come together and find common goals. Later, one design team member said, "The conference was the best thing. It brought a mix of folks together in one room, each with their own input, to hash things out and find common ground."

With the whole community mirrored in the conference rooms, participants began talking about the unmentionables of race, equity, social class, and student achievement. In fact equity and equality became the issue that drew the most attention. When concerned African American and Hispanic students and their parents formulated the equity and equality goal, everyone experienced a new level of candor. When the students stood up and took leadership roles, they galvanized the whole conference. Not only were they instrumental in ensuring that equality and equity became a goal, but most of these students and their parents helped draft the initiative's initial plans that led to actual programmatic, organizational, and community changes.

The results of the equity and equality issues and principles pervaded the community and district in even more ways. Soon after the conference on April 30, 2003, a student-driven Achievement Gap Conference really emphasized the disparity in student achievement. Students had done their homework and brought the numbers to show how minority students were not achieving as successfully as whites. For example, only 10 percent of minority graduates were going to four-year colleges, whereas 80 percent of white graduates attended four-year colleges. One student leader said, "Students and adults stood up and took responsibility for their own education. And the faculty backed them. We knew that things were going to change."

Social justice has also been a major effort of the Equity and Equality Committee. Two students, both now attending different colleges, have reached back to the district to establish a scholarship for two high school students who have actively created opportunities for social access, equity, and excellence relating to social justice. One of those students served on the design team, and both attended the future search conference.

Mothers for Justice was formed and now serves as an advocate for students. At first the mothers were concerned about discipline. Now they are focused on closing the achievement gap. Many of the mothers attended the future search conference.

There was a controversy on the Race and Discipline Task Force regarding the actions of police on school campuses. Police expected to be in charge at schools. Now there is an ongoing series of community meetings, coordinated by neighborhood members including Mothers for Justice, to continue to address problems among the neighborhood, schools, and the police. The group wants to be an ongoing committee to refine and adjust policies and procedures as issues arise.

The concepts of equity and equality are now infused throughout the entire district. People refer to these principles in all areas of the district as they plan and work on the issues addressed in the other initiatives. The district values the voices of the diverse stakeholder base, recognizing the importance of the majority opinion while protecting the minority viewpoint. Teams evaluate themselves to see if they represent the range of diversity in the community. They recognize when voices are missing and team members personally solicit input from these voices in the community.

THE FINAL ANALYSIS

The district coalesced around the seven initiatives with a unified approach and a roadmap for implementation. The strategic plan is a tangible, public document that the board of education continues to use to set priorities and make decisions. Groups, such as the district advisory committees, are integrating their needs into the appropriate areas. As the superintendent said, "We have created a common language and common set of expectations about student achievement." There are some areas that might have worked better. For instance:

- The Implementation and Accountability Team, recommended and approved by the board of education with the strategic plan, was never convened. The superintendent put one staff person in charge of implementation. She attended most of the initiative meetings and wrote a report to the board outlining implementation activities to date. However, she was not able to convene a group that would have overseen the implementation of the action plans and their integration into existing programs.
- Many teachers and students have not felt involved in the implementation of the strategic plan. They were not invited to determine ways to implement the plan at their sites and own the process of implementation.
- Some communication did not clearly link school initiatives and learning models to the strategic plan. For example, at the districtwide orientation in August 2002, the superintendent reviewed his principles of learning. Everybody received a copy of his presentation that tied the principles to district programs and services. However, principals and teachers felt that the strategic plan was not explicitly linked to the principles of learning. Professional development has been tied to the principles of learning but not explicitly to the strategic plan.
- Several recommendations of the Achievement Gap Conference have not been implemented because of budget cuts. The staff position to develop and implement policies and actions that would reduce the achievement gap and help students and families of color could not be funded. Funding cuts also precluded the ability to offer special college counseling for students of color.

On the other hand, the strategic plan has been the guiding framework for the board of education and the superintendent. The board has taken action on all initiatives except reduced class size. One board member said,

> The fact that the plan exists has been a calming factor in our fiscal crisis. There is a fiscal crisis in all of education. Now the district has structure for the future. We can concentrate on fiscal issues. We have a focus, not chaos.

The superintendent emphasized:

> We have built an accurate picture of the school district with the community. We have a quantifiable set of targets for the district, which get done and get measured. The plan helped to anchor us through all this budget stuff. Collaborative ways of working are more frequently the norm. Special issues are now more unified. There is less conversation by group and more by community. Now, instead of talking in individual groups, people know where to talk across groups, and do so.

Students were seen and respected as visible leaders on the design team, at the future search conference, and in the strategic work groups. Their voices were essential. Students from ages 8 to 18 stood up, gave their perspective, and commanded attention. They reminded all participants of the purpose of the work and the needs of their group.

Significant community involvement expanded the leadership pool available to the district. Fresh participants are now actively engaged with the district, with students, and across community organizations. Design team members have been elected to the board of education. Other community members are active on district committees or at specific schools. Involvement and inclusion deepened the level of engagement for most. As new participants brought multiple perspectives to the district's policy discussions, the ongoing conversation became more comprehensive. In June 2003 the superintendent said,

> Although no test score changes have been recorded yet, the process, especially the future search conference, legitimized the students' voices in ways we were not mindful of before, especially at the high school. The phrase, *plan to end achievement gap,* is reverberating in the community. Just making the unmentionables public was key.

Three months later, in September 2003, the district announced that test scores had shown dramatic gains. Overall English scores rose by 20 percent, African American students' English scores rose by 40 percent, and Latinos' scores rose by 50 percent. The superintendent was ecstatic. Mr. Deasy attributed the increase in scores to a combination of factors: 1) the great redesign work at the Santa Monica High School, 2) that teachers are more comfortable in their abilities, and 3) the community ownership of the vision of high achievement for all. He felt that the strategic plan was significant to the rise in scores, along with the work at the central office level. In addition, the board of education is focused and committed to the strategic plan.

Confronting Racism in the
Novato Unified School District

Kenoli Oleari

Whatever you can do or dream you can, begin it. Boldness has genius, power and magic in it.

—Goethe

PROLOGUE

It was a big deal. A predominantly black visiting high school basketball team believed they had heard the cheering section of the largely white home team shout out an offensively racist chant. In a less publicized incident, a largely white swim team wore sombreros to a swim meet with a predominantly Latino swim team. A community chorus arose charging "Racism!" There were accusations, denials, and demands that the district respond immediately.

Community members came down on both "sides" of the issue. Was this rampant racism, a misunderstanding, or innocent high school pranks? The media jumped into the fray, camping out round the clock, trying to capture the next incident for the evening news. Coverage went national. Other "racist" incidents were reported. For the district, this was a huge problem with legal ramifications.

FUTURE SEARCH

Jan Derby was an assistant superintendent of schools in Novato, California. Jan was dedicated to her students and committed to building a learning environment that met the needs of the Novato Unified School District. She was an effective leader willing to take initiative to realize a vision.

Annan Patterson was a guidance counselor in the Novato Unified School District. During the several years she had worked in the district, she had sought ways to support the students she counseled, both in her formal capacity and as a community volunteer. Jan and Annan had been involved for several years in a program to bring awareness of diversity issues to the schools in the district.

The incident at the basketball game had thrust these two leaders, along with other committed members of the community, into a vortex of public meetings, press conferences, appearances before the school board, and long extra hours of work. Fortunately Jan, Annan, and others working with them were up to the task. They began to focus their efforts on building something positive out of the experience.

Five months had passed since the first "racial" incident. The school board had directed the district Diversity Advisory Committee to propose a plan of action. This plan was to carry the district into a new era of racial awareness and respect. In her district capacity, Jan became the point person. As a key member of the Diversity Steering Committee, Annan was involved in finding a way to successfully bring the various voices to the table to accomplish this task. A date for a retreat was set and a planning team was chosen.

A member of the planning team had heard of future search through a friend who had once trained in the method and thought that it might give them what they needed. A little research told them it was worth exploring. Would it be possible to use future search to accomplish what they needed? There were only a few weeks until the retreat.

THE WAY IT STARTED

I was getting ready to leave on a trip I'd been looking forward to—traveling to Alaska via the Inside Passage—when I received the phone call. There had been some kind of racial incident at a local high school and some people in the district office wanted to hold a future search. A colleague and member of our local West Coast Future Search Network was calling to request my participation. The sponsor was the Novato Unified School District, located in a community near the high school from which I had graduated. I was sure we must have played a Novato school in some sporting event. The retreat was to occur within a few weeks and everybody was already invited. My gut reaction was, "This is all wrong." I was fairly new to future search and my training had told me that this was not enough time to properly plan a future search. In addition, how would we get the "right" stakeholders in the room if everyone had already been invited?

After a few phone calls and a meeting with the district staff, it was clear that they were going to do a future search with or without us. We scheduled a meeting and began to talk details. I was to partner with Shelley Sweet (see previous chapter), a whiz at dealing with details. This let me focus on the larger dynamics, my favorite piece of the puzzle. In addition, Helen Spector and Don Benson, also Future Search Network members, were to assist.

Shelley and I talked about the short time frame. We wondered if it was our responsibility as consultants to tell the client that this was not enough time to prepare for a future search. In the end, it was clear that this was a determined group. They were committed to work miracles. We decided to go ahead. I postponed my Alaska trip, we told the client we would work with them, and we scheduled our first planning team meeting. Was I making the classic novice mistake, letting myself get carried away by the enthusiasm of the group? I couldn't spend much time wondering; we were off and running.

BACKGROUND

We were filled in on some of the events that had brought us to Novato. The story began on February 13, 1998, at a basketball game hosted by Novato School District's San Marin High School against Tamalpais (Tam) High's predominantly black basketball team visiting from another district. The largely white San Marin cheering section had arrived wearing face paint and feathers, along with various other props, including, apparently, an "Afro" wig. The dress was intended to be reminiscent of San Francisco's 1960s, an era remembered by many of these youths' parents. During the warm-up, black players on the Tam team thought they heard the section hollering "N——, n——, n——." The team reacted and began to approach the Novato cheering section; their coach pulled them back and called a huddle. The San Marin principal was contacted, and he directed his administrators to cool down the cheering section.

Tam High was a mix of students. Some of the students came from Marin City, a largely black section of wealthy Marin County that had grown up from abandoned temporary housing left over from a World War II ship-building industry. Others were from Mill Valley, a particularly wealthy section of Marin County, largely white. On the other hand, Novato had roots as a predominantly white ranching community; only 1.9 percent of its population was black. It had experienced the arrival, over the last several decades, of families spreading out from San Francisco and other urban centers in the region. It had attracted a population of families of San Francisco police officers, as Novato fell just within the geographical boundaries within which members of that department were required to live. It had also attracted a number of families of guards from nearby San Quentin prison, a major California "correctional" facility.

By and large, Marin County regarded itself as a progressive or liberal community, with an identity as a "new age" spiritual center and a strong voice for the environment and other progressive causes. There were some in the county who had no reservations about disavowing Novato, and especially San Marin High School, as racially intolerant. Novato kids had been seen wearing confederate flags. Such things fed a perception of intolerance. Some said, "San Marin has done it again."

There was a clash of voices: black Tam students with the sensitivity of a black minority; "liberal" greater Marin voices; a more reactive voice from within the Novato community, some claiming the students "certainly wouldn't have done any such thing." Some people blamed the community reaction on "liberal" newcomers. Some thought it wasn't such a big deal, even if it had happened; others were shocked that it even might have taken place and would have no part in tolerating it if it had. The wagons had circled.

Later, San Marin staff and students in the cheering section would publicly recall that they had heard no such thing as "N——!" being shouted. Students had chanted, "Yanger, Yanger, Yanger" in support of a San Marin team member named "Yang." Others thought they had heard chants of "Chigger, chigger, chigger."

CNN did a piece; someone found a confederate flag in the 1997 San Marin yearbook. Headlines appeared in local papers proclaiming, "Racist hate does not exist at San Marin," "Cheers may have been misheard by Tam students," and "School officials at odds over alleged racial incident." San Marin received complaints from parents across the district. Charges and denials flew.

By February 24, Tam High had filed a formal complaint with the local high school athletic league. The complaint asserted that team members had seen a swastika in a bathroom on the day of the game and that students had confronted a coach in a threatening interaction in the parking lot. It described a generally hostile environment toward visiting players at San Marin High School. Other complaints were filed. San Marin was sanctioned by the league and put on a probationary status that prevented it from hosting home games.

Ultimately, an investigation by the Novato School District and Novato police determined from videotapes and interviews that at least one person in the cheering section had called out "N——." On October 9, several months after the future search, a student was cited for making the slur and charged with disturbing the peace. The Novato police chief announced that the student had admitted the action and said the investigation was continuing. The Novato School Board chairperson concurred, affirming that the slur and related incidents had actually occurred. There was never a formal determination that others had been involved in using the epithet. Much of the community came to accept that "it" had happened.

PLANNING THE FUTURE SEARCH

At our first planning meeting, we spent some time clarifying what the group wanted to achieve and going over future search principles. Because of the time frame, it looked like we were only going to have a few planning meetings before the conference.

We asked the group if there were any other people we needed to bring into the planning process. Youth was the first group identified as missing. The team decided it was probably too late to involve them but they would try. In the end, youth were not included on the planning team but were invited to attend the conference.

There was another critical stakeholder missing. The "liberal" planning team believed certain elements of the community held racist feelings and were in denial about the issue. The team realized this group needed to be involved but were not clear about how to bring them in. The team spent significant time talking about this. In addition, it turned out that this group tended to work at regular jobs that made it difficult to attend weekday meetings; the conference had been planned for three weekdays. The team identified a few people they felt could speak for this community perspective and who they thought might be available and want to participate.

The final issue was race; the planning team was all white. The team decided that it was too late to do anything about this in the time available. It also believed that the existing team could be sensitive to the issue of the participation of people of color. There were a number of people of color already committed to coming to the conference.

With a sense that the makeup of the planning team was the best we were going to get under the circumstances, we moved on to task. The group was clear that they wanted the task to focus on the kind of community they wanted to build, as opposed to taking on racism directly, a stance coherent with future search principles. In future search, we take on "process" issues like racism by assembling mixed groups of stakeholders in which people of different races and backgrounds work on issues that are important to all of them. If they had said they wanted to do a conference on racism, we would have counseled them to seek a larger common framework. In this case, we were already on the same track.

The group arrived at the task: "Creating and Sustaining a Just and Respectful Learning Environment in Novato Unified School District." With the task clarified, the group set out to make a list of participants. The situation we were dealing with presented a difficult issue regarding the selection of participants: People had already been invited to attend the retreat. In future search, it is important to select a group of "stakeholders" that effectively represents the range of voices needed to address the chosen task. How were we going to get the range of stakeholders we needed? As it turned out, I had worked in other contexts where the planning team felt they needed to include anyone who wanted to attend the conference. The way we had managed those events was to put out an invitation to the community involved, inviting anyone to sign up by a certain date. At this point, we closed off applications. We then looked at the list we had and invited the missing stakeholders. We adapted this model to work here. We could work with the invitees we had and expand the list to meet the stakeholder criteria. The group started making charts listing the existing conference attendees and matching them to the stakeholder categories they had identified. It then added names to this chart as necessary to get the desired stakeholder mix.

Another issue was the short turnaround for invitations and confirmations. The group did its best here as well. It attempted to reach people by mail with follow-up phone calls. Nevertheless, a handful of participants walked in the door on the day of the conference with no idea what a future search was or that they were going to be part of one.

A QUICK REFLECTION ON THE
MIRACLE OF SELF-CORRECTION

In spite of the challenges presented by the short time frame available for planning, we had decided to go ahead with the process and hope for the best. Our faith was confirmed through several incidents. As described below, the participants themselves acted to modify the conference task, adding a perspective that had been missing in the planning. In addition, pushback during the conference guided us as facilitators to make design choices on the fly. We did this by listening to the group and seeking a balance between the flow of the process and the direction the group seemed to want to go.

Much of the future search design reflects what people do naturally when they get together. Participants seem to know how to "do" future search and naturally adapt the process to work for them. While the process seems quite structured to many, it is always surprising to see how facile it is in responding to the discoveries of participants.

THE CONFERENCE

The day came for the future search conference, and people arrived. Many were confused by the setup in the meeting room. "What was this?" one wondered. "I've never been to a retreat that looked like this." The conference started and we described the agenda, ground rules, and principles. A number of participants took issue with the way the task was worded. The planning team had underestimated how physically threatened many felt by the racial incidents in the community. There was a short discussion; we discovered that adding the word "safe" would satisfy this concern. The task became: "Creating and Sustaining a Safe, Just, and Respectful Learning Environment in Novato Unified School District."

Next, participants were told that we would not be trying to solve conflicts but rather searching for common ground. Skeptical voices were raised, insisting that there were conflicts that had to be solved before anything could be done. Local activists were worried that common ground looked too much like compromise and felt uneasy. Students weren't sure that this wasn't just another adult way to steal their voices by controlling what they could or couldn't talk about.

An African American man was concerned that once again this would be a process that would avoid the important issues. He wanted to get down to it and look racism in the face. We took some more time to explain the concept of "common ground," the process of committing to discovering what we shared in common instead of focusing on solving our problems. The issue was discussed, and as people began to understand, they agreed to proceed; some still had reservations.

THE CONFERENCE CONTINUES

The rest of the first day proceeded well. People were involved and there were good group conversations. There were periodic rumblings that we were doing too much planning. Some in the group wanted to get down to action. On the second day, the mind map helped the group build a picture of the current issues. As the day proceeded, the group found the prouds and sorries particularly compelling. As usual, the future scenarios were entertaining and moving. One group wrote a beautiful poem that was a highlight of the activity. It was during the reality dialogue on the third day that resistance mounted.

TALKING-STICK CIRCLE

The students had met during a break and were threatening to walk out of the retreat. Jan Derby met with the students and reported back to the group. The students wanted a bigger voice or they were going to leave. This meeting was just more of the same and they felt they were not being heard. Other voices resonated or were sympathetic to student concerns. The tension rose. As facilitators, we stopped the process and suggested a talking-stick circle. In a talking-stick circle an object is passed clockwise around the circle of participants and each person gets a chance to speak. Only the person who holds the stick can speak and there is no cross talk allowed. The group agreed. The students agreed to join us. We made a big circle including everyone in the room. As the talking-stick was passed hand-to-hand, the tension about not being heard was released, and a consensus developed that the group wanted to move from planning into action. Propitiously, it was the time in the conference schedule to do just that. The energy in the room had shifted significantly. The students were again involved. We moved into action planning.

ACTION PLANNING

The reality dialogue had resulted in four themes: resources, safety, collaboration, and positive human relations. They had been derived from the following larger set of common-ground statements:

- Address those not taking responsibility, blaming others, and modeling racism.
- Address the political agenda designed to promote intolerance.
- Address the absence of parental supervision or parents and families.
- Access information from youth who are more aware and accepting of differences.
- Develop a willingness to acknowledge and talk about unspeakable things.

- Avoid violence as a solution.
- Review the use of language that adds to prejudice.
- Address the world as becoming a global village.
- Accept that personal safety concerns cause acting out of fear.
- Acknowledge that there is poor communication about race relations.
- Address the fact that there is polarization, rather than jumping into a discussion of morals and ethics.

The students caucused to decide how they wanted to participate in the action planning. There was some talk of working separately in a student contingent. They finally decided to spread out in action teams to make sure their voices got heard across the board.

A VARIATION ON A TRADITIONAL THEME

Rather than asking people to self-select into action teams, we decided to divide the group by common-ground themes for action planning. We wanted to avoid any tendency in this group to break out into action teams according to traditional affiliations. We also wanted to make sure people had a chance to work in associations they might not normally choose. In these groups, participants identified subthemes and implementation ideas. In some cases this took the form of projects, in some procedures, and in others recommendations to the district. We then had participants self-select into these groups to flesh out each action idea. The result was a range of ideas for projects. Some of the most resistant voices became excited about working with new partners.

As will be described below, these groups became "action committees" that would lead the district in its response to the events that had precipitated this retreat. By the afternoon, the room was full of enthusiasm.

FOLLOW-UP AND IMPLEMENTATION

One of the reasons this district was able to make effective use of the work it accomplished during the future search was its willingness to make an institutional commitment. During the remainder of 1998 and the first nine months of 1999, the Diversity Advisory Committee worked to forge the outcome of the future search into a plan that could guide the district. As a result of the new understandings gained from the future search, the committee expanded to include students and other missing stakeholders. They called their plan the Equity Action Plan. The group obtained feedback from the larger school community and integrated it into the plan. The stakeholder model and the concepts of inclusion and collaboration guided the feedback process.

Central to this effort was a set of implementation goals. The team established committees based on the common-ground themes. It utilized the action team members from the conference as the core members. Implementation matrices were created based on the common-ground themes from the future search and projects identified at the conference. Explicit goals and time frames were set according to the following categories: who, when, funding source, cost, completion date, student outcomes, and evaluation. To make sure there was long-term commitment to the goals of the program, the committee fashioned them into policy statements and recommended that the school board adopt them by formal action.

THE EQUITY ACTION PLAN ADOPTED

On September 21, 1999, the school board formally adopted the Equity Action Plan and established changes in district policy designed to ensure its implementation. In addition to the implementation matrices, the document included the prouds and sorries and the common-ground themes from the future search. Also included were the history of the district's work on diversity, the guiding philosophy, next steps, a budget proposal, and documentation of all of the board-level policy changes that had been put into place to implement the plan.

The Diversity Advisory Committee was responsible for overseeing the distribution and the implementation of the Equity Action Plan. To date, many of the goals and projects have been implemented. The plan continues to guide the district in its work on diversity.

LEARNINGS

Equity as a Key Concept

Annan Patterson remembers the following:

> There were many ripples from the future search. At first I wondered why we were calling the Equity Action Plan "equity" when it is about acceptance and respect. Now I see it is about equity not only between individuals but also between schools, richer and poorer neighborhoods, and who gets what level of staffing, materials and resources. Through these efforts we have become a cohesive whole, responsible to each other and no longer living by the credo, "I've got mine, now go away."

Centralization and Standardization

Up until the incident, the district functioned on a site-based orientation. Principals had a lot of power; the schools functioned as separate units. There was a feeling toward the district exemplified in expressions like "You can't touch us" and "That stupid district office." Now there is acceptance of more centralized coordination.

This incident rattled the institution to its bones; the school board brought in a new superintendent who shook things up, making personnel changes, establishing districtwide accountability, and developing districtwide cohesion. The Equity Action Plan was able to guide this change in direction with regard to diversity issues. The first African American was brought onto the school board. Annan reflected that through the process people realized that every kid in the district has to get the same message about respect and safety and learn the same things about the value of diversity, acceptance of difference, and mutual respect. People came to understand that it was not up to their neighborhood or principal to declare whether these things are respected; it was a matter of committing to values that support the greater good of the community as a whole.

Reflections on the Process

> The future search process was wonderful. It was all that I thought it would be. It was different. There were some big bumps. It was ardu-

ous emotionally. In the end, short and long run, what we got out of it took us so much further down the road. It gave us a sense of optimism and empowerment.

—Annan Patterson, Novato Unified School District psychologist

We are now looking at some new projects and are using the principles we learned in future search as a model. It works. In this case, the principle is, "what can we do to agree to disagree without attacking each other?" We are working on gay issues in the community. We've been able to meet across gender, religion and social and economic factors.

—Jan Derby, assistant superintendent of schools

OUTCOMES

In a recent interview, the following outcomes stood out for Jan Derby:

- The Equity Action Plan is still the reference point for our work on racism and other diversity issues. We refer to it constantly.
- Having the buy-in of all stakeholders established a long-term foundation that has not crumbled, but rather remained solid.
- Future search provided an action plan that we are still implementing. We are reviewing this right now with our Diversity Advisory Committee. We have made concrete changes from the board level down in how we operate based on these principles.
- Youth are now on the Diversity Advisory Committee.
- The Diversity Advisory Committee feels so empowered through the work it has done that it no longer feels shaken when it is publicly challenged.

Jan Derby reaffirmed: "I would highly recommend this to other school districts. It can give you a living action plan to help you resolve your issues, no matter what they are."

Jan left in the summer of 1999. The Diversity Advisory Board carried on the writing of the equity action plan using the future search data. It is still being referenced and implemented as of this writing. Jan has returned to her position and continues to commit her attention to diversity issues.

FEEDBACK FROM PARTICIPANTS

As a rule, future search does not request feedback from participants. We want participants to focus on what they did to reach success; not what future search did for them.

Having said this, the planning team took the initiative, for its own reasons, to ask for feedback at the end of the conference. Here is a summary of the responses:

Q: What did you appreciate?
A: Participants appreciated hearing from people with lots of different perspectives; looking at the past and present and dreaming about the future; being connected to the student action, the response to it, and the experience of the talking-stick circle.
Q. What would you have changed?
A. A handful of respondents felt the district staff was overrepresented and had too much control of the process. Several referred specifically to the lack of students involved in planning. Several comments noted other important people who were missing. There were a number of responses wanting more time for action planning. There were a number of comments about the retreat being too long, not having enough time to speak, and including too many participants.
Q. What are the recommendations for future "diversity work" in NUSD?
A. Primarily, the recommendations focused on inclusion: getting more people and voices involved. Additionally, there were a number of comments related to listening skills, quality of sharing, personal growth, and heart- and feelings-based projects.

POSTSCRIPT: GAY BASHING

Many of us who work with future search are idealists and would like to think that the method can work miracles. We are often disappointed when we learn that it has not solved a client's crisis in one fell swoop. During the fall immediately following the future search a Novato youth came out as gay. He was physically assaulted and injured. Some people came out in support of the youth; others attacked him. Some believed the young man injured himself to attract attention. Some again saw it as a canary in a coal mine. Even if he did it, what was he trying to say? Again there was national press. A school board member called it an urban legend. The issue was never resolved. Once again it caused turmoil for the district, San Marin High School, and the individuals involved. Other gay incidents occurred the following year.

Because of the work supported by the future search, the community and the Diversity Advisory Committee responded with a deepened sense of confidence. Students took the initiative to bolster gay/straight groups that had already been started in the schools and to expand this program. The district continued to implement the Equity Action Plan with confidence that it had broad support as an effective response to these and other acts of intolerance since the fall of 1998.

A FINAL LESSON

The response of the school community to the continued challenges in Novato is hugely hopeful and offers a lesson we probably all need to learn as individuals and communities. Life will always confront us with challenges; success is not avoiding those challenges, but rather building the capacity to meet them in a way that makes us and those we are involved with more whole. In the end, perhaps, this is the real hope. And it is fundamental to the system level impact of future search. If we can add to the robustness of our systems, there is great hope: *A robust system has less need to manifest itself in dysfunctional behavior.*

While it is ridiculous to imagine that the work we do in Novato or elsewhere would rid the region of intolerant attitudes, we know from experience that it can build a foundation and capacity for response that can truly transform a community. This story confirms this experience.

Success and System Readiness: Lester B. Pearson School Board and Its Commitment to Educational Excellence, Montreal, Quebec, Canada

Pat Deans, Kim Martens, and Ray Gordezky

What's been interesting about future search is that many initiatives like it have gone by the way but this one has not. People still see the power of sitting down together in the same room. It's a way that we can start working towards our vision and moving together; yet we are also able to continue to follow our own interests.

—Pat Deans, director of community services

INTRODUCTION

In 18 months, starting with a three-day future search conference in March 2002, the Lester B. Pearson School Board (LBPSB) was able to form a central students' committee, develop and launch an interactive community database, implement a "Peaceful Schools" program, pilot a work study mentorship program, collaboratively develop a board strategic plan, and draft the board's mission statement based upon the LBPSB vision and future search outcomes.

Not all future searches create such visible outcomes. Not all future searches create such visible outcomes. From this case, readers will learn how, in a short time, to create, encourage, and ensure constructive change.

THE CONTEXT

Quebec is one of 10 provinces (and 3 territories) in Canada. French is the first language for more than 80 percent of Quebecers. In schools, French is the teaching language except for certain pupils eligible for instruction in English. Quebec amended its Education Act in 1997 to eliminate denominational (religious) school boards, replacing its 156 denominational boards with 60 French- and 9 English-language boards. On the Island of Montreal, reform caused significant changes in student and staff populations. New linguistic school boards often were created from several denominational boards, each with separate policies on integration, French immersion, transportation, and so on. Many schools now operate under new, unfamiliar structures.

THE SCHOOL DISTRICT AND ITS FUTURE SEARCH

One of these newly created boards, the Lester B. Pearson School Board (LBPSB), serves over 30,000 students (primary, secondary, adult, and vocational) in 60 schools and centers. In its first few years, LBPSB consolidated six school boards, closing or amalgamating schools, selling buildings, and transferring educators and students. There was no time for long-term planning, and the board faced significant challenges in integrating diverse corporate cultures.

In December 2001, four years after its founding, LBPSB adopted a resolution to create "a long-term student-centred plan focusing on providing students with the skills needed to be successful in a changing world." As a catalyst to help bring the plan to fruition, the board's council of commissioners chose future search to create and implement a plan focused on "A Commitment to Educational Excellence."

The future search involved 65 diverse stakeholders from within the board and its partners from social services, business firms, and community groups. Participants envisioned changes 12 years into the future, from the time students enter kindergarten through their graduating high school. The board also held a follow-up conference two and a half months later in May 2002.

THE SYSTEM ONE AND A HALF YEARS LATER

I am thrilled that we [students] have become a full educational partner
and that the school board has been so supportive.

—A grade 11 student at Pierrefonds Comprehensive High School
and future search student stakeholder representative

Seven action groups were formed during the future search. Six continued
meeting regularly afterward, focusing on such key areas as fund-raising,
community links, flexibility in high schools, school safety, a central students' committee, and work study. These six groups shared a common philosophy: "Creating the best for our future best."

Here is a synopsis of board initiatives up to November 2003, indicating
the diversity of community involvement, the depth of creativity, and the
comprehensive nature of the action plans.

Community Links

A major consequence of future search came about in the fall of 2002.
LBPSB joined with three government agencies to create an interactive community database enabling teachers to tap community resources to help them
present exciting reality-based lessons and projects. Within six months, 86
companies had committed time and expertise to the 2,000 teachers and students, including guided tours, job shadowing, student interviews, guest
speakers for classrooms, teacher training, workshops, contest and exhibition
judges, equipment loans and donations, and participation in a career day.

Safety in Schools

The board has committed $100,000 toward this group's proposed antibul-
lying "Peaceful Schools" program. Training began in 11 schools and centers at the end of March 2003.

Work Study

This action group worked hard to establish a mentoring program for students aged 16 to 18 in the alternative programs that consist of a combina-

tion of academic and tech-vocational courses. Each week students spend three days on academic courses and two days on trades. LBPSB employees mentor students one-on-one in trades areas. In the last two years, mentoring programs have expanded significantly in all employee areas with much positive feedback from students and employees.

Fund-Raising

This action group joined with the Pearson Educational Foundation—a body that establishes partnerships with parents and business communities—to raise funds for school-based initiatives and to help individual students.

Central Students' Committee

> Central student committees—still a rarity in the education world although most individual schools have student committees—are gaining in popularity as students are pushing to have more say in their education.
>
> —Karen Siedman, reporter for the *Montreal Gazette*,
> media stakeholder at the future search

In an unprecedented step, this action team created a central students' committee (CSC) that was granted official status by the LBPSB Council of Commissioners. The CSC then received funding to promote student issues and governance. Being an official consultative body entailed tremendous responsibility. The group's members provide input to the board on policies being developed. In addition, the CSC developed its own logo and motto and went to work on a variety of important projects in the 2002–2003 school years to create flexible timetabling for the high school, to establish a link to the LBPSB website, to develop a constitution and code of conduct, and to organize a leadership conference.

The student group also met with Assistant Deputy Minister Mr. Noel Burke to discuss the students' vision for the future direction of education. They presented several ideas, including 1) involving students in determining what they learn and how they learn it (e.g., more course options, flexible timetables, etc.) and 2) providing more hands-on opportunities outside the classroom, (e.g., community work-study opportunities for course credit). These ideas met with strong support from other students and from the Ministère de l'Éducation du Québec (MEQ).

Flexibility in High Schools

This task force considered many innovative approaches to increase flexibility, including 1) four-day schooling with day five devoted to extracurricular tutoring, co-op, stages, sports, etc.; 2) year-round schooling; 3) a later morning start; and 4) additional options where students would develop their talents: leadership, sports skills, etc.

All high schools were included in the planning stage vis-à-vis flexibility. Bimonthly high school sector meetings including all high school administrators are presently discussing these issues. The action group addressed topics directly related to the Quebec education plan and curriculum reform, a key ingredient in the district's strategic plan, school success plans, and each school's educational project.

LEADERSHIP

> Leadership is about creating, day to day, a domain in which we and those around us continually deepen our understanding of reality and are able to participate in shaping the future. This, then, is the deeper territory of leadership—collectively "listening" to what is wanting to emerge in the world, and then having the courage to do what is required. (Jaworski, 1996, p. 182)

People within LBPSB have told us repeatedly that they recognize and value the diverse leadership within the various stakeholder groups—from students and community partners to teachers and staff, management, and school commissioners. There is also a shared respect for the leadership of Director General Leo La France. It is this leadership that is helping to sustain the change. "Leo is like the CEO of our board," Marcus Tabachnick, school board commissioner, explains, "Don't be fooled by his laid-back demeanour, he's tough. But he's patient with special people skills. He's a terrific leader." Peter Senge (1990) explains that:

> . . . leaders may start by pursuing their own vision, but as they learn to listen carefully to others' visions they begin to see that their own personal vi-

sion is part of something larger. This does not diminish any leader's sense of responsibility—if anything it deepens it. (p. 352)

Leo has been described as a person who consults, collaborates, and encourages people to bring issues to the table. Many mentioned his open-door policy and the way he welcomes everyone into his office. It is no surprise that despite his initial skepticism he came to use future search as a key milestone in strategic planning.

> What impacted me the most at the future search conference and the May reunion was the range of diverse stakeholders working together and sharing. There was a sense of trust. Initially I was concerned that the future search planning was evolving too slowly. I did not know where it was going until the first day of the conference. The two-and-a-half days with 65 people in the room were a very emotional time for me. I was overcome that people could share things so openly with each other. All stakeholders were feeling a trust in the process and each other. That also meant something of a risk. If you want to know what people think, you have to be prepared to hear whatever they say.

—Leo La France, LBPSB director general

Peter Koestenbaum (2000), a philosopher and business consultant, speaks of leadership as having four facets: vision, reality, service (ethics), and courage. We are struck by how these facets reflect underlying future search principles (see the introduction). Using principle-based structures and techniques, Leo La France was able to enhance his existing leadership skills by mobilizing a systemwide vision (focus on the future), creating a shared reality (common-ground dialogue), catalyzing mutual service (engaging whole persons, body and mind together) and supporting the courage to act among participants (self-management and personal and public responsibility).

BROAD COMMITMENT TO FOLLOW-UP

One striking aspect of future searches worldwide is the degree to which they engender sustained commitment to action. This widely documented phenomenon seems counterintuitive. How could LBPSB generate so much ongoing activity from a two-and-a-half-day future search conference?

One explanation we found useful is physicist David Bohm's description of the emergence of collective intelligence. Bohm suggests that "we're all connected through and operate within living fields of thought and perception" (in Jaworski, 1996, p. 109). He describes how changes evolve:

> At present, people create barriers between each other by their fragmentary thought. . . . Each one operates separately. When these barriers have dissolved, then there arises one mind, where . . . each person also retains his or her own individual awareness. That one mind will still exist when they separate, and when they come together, it will be as if they hadn't separated. . . . It's actually a single intelligence that works with people who are moving in relationship with one another. (Jaworski, 1996, p. 100)

How is this state nurtured so that people continue to meet following a future search? In some cases people continue to meet on their own regardless of support systems. Other initiatives need support. Inevitably some action teams fall by the wayside with or without coordinating structures. One thing we have noticed is that systems displaying the most visible changes tend to integrate both future search outcomes and principles into their day-to-day work. They tend to use simple structures and procedures for continued communication, networking, and shared learning. These include websites, newsletters, e-mail listservs, and periodic review meetings. Lester B. Pearson, in 2003, was using all of these methods to help people remain involved and effective.

Communication, Networking, and Shared Learning

In addition to structures and procedures, another effective follow-up factor is that of "community coordinator." Wenger, McDermott, and Snyder (2002) describe the role as follows:

> Good community coordinators are knowledgeable and passionate about the community's topic. They are well respected by their peers as practitioners, but they are generally not leading experts in their field. Since a coordinator's primary role is to link people, not give answers, being a leading expert can be a handicap. Good coordinators also need good interpersonal skills [and] must have the strategic and political savvy to create a bridge between the community and the formal organization. (pp. 81–82)

In this regard, LBPSB was fortunate to acquire the services of Pat Deans, director of community services. Though not able to attend the future search, she took on as part of her portfolio the follow-up work, buttressed by her background in education and organizational development and her personal people-centered philosophy.

> I am very interested in the linking of future search with other board initiatives. The alignment of who we are with where we want to go is critical. I feel people are important and do everything I can to bring people together. Everyone is a catalyst at one time or another. We need to recognize each other's talents and nurture leadership skills and opportunities. As people become involved and committed, we grow as an organization.
>
> —Pat Deans, director of community services

Integration into the System

The most obvious work required to implement a future search portfolio is supporting the many action groups. LBPSB has institutionalized this support through regular action group meetings at the school board, and by collecting and sharing action group reports. They also have been convening meetings of action group chairs two to three times per year and preparing biyearly reports for the council of commissioners.

Even this straightforward approach to integrating future search outcomes into the system is not without its challenges. In the 18 months following the future search, some action groups were working on their own, unconnected to the board's strategic direction. "We needed to make sure that everything discussed in action groups had a link and was aligned with board direction," the action group chairs replied when asked how things could be more streamlined.

The Board Mission Statement

LBPSB is also including the future search outcomes in its regular work. In January 2003, for example, less than one year after the conference, the management team met for two days to develop the board's mission statement and begin a strategic plan. Each future search action group's mission statement and the board's current vision statement were used as the basis for a new **LBPSB** mission statement. The following draft document was distributed to stakeholders for input and approved by the council of commissioners in late spring:

> The Lester B. Pearson School Board works with the community to provide a healthy, safe, respectful and inclusive learning environment in which there is the flexibility for all students to reach their full potential.
>
> The Lester B. Pearson School Board prepares individuals to assume their roles as responsible, competent and successful citizens who are capable of working cooperatively within an ever-changing society.
>
> The Lester B. Pearson School Board measures its actions and decisions against the core values stated in the Lester B. Pearson Vision Statement.

Developing the Strategic Plan

To cite another example, LBPSB by law has to implement a strategic plan. To begin this process, the timetable and basic concepts (based on Ministry of Education guidelines) were presented and discussed with all stakeholder groups during the winter of 2003. In March, the board again used future search principles to gather representative stakeholders and convene focus groups. These groups provided input concerning the board's openness to the community, the support offered to schools and centers, and satisfaction with services offered. The next stage included a meeting with representatives from each stakeholder group to analyze the priorities, based on data from many sources, including the future search initiatives already in place. In April an administration group/council of commissioners workshop was formed to review analysis results, set strategic directions, and draft objectives, strategies, and indicators. The management committee, which included all school and center administrators and managers, reviewed the draft before approval by the council of commissioners in May. By the fall of 2003 all stakeholder groups were commenting on the plan.

Boardwide Professional Development

Earlier, we quoted Leo La France on how future search has changed his practice. He mentioned as an example a boardwide professional development activity for all LBPSB employees held at the Palais des Congrès in downtown Montreal. The council of commissioners had modified the school calendar to include this day. All schools, adult and vocational education centers, services, and offices were closed on February 18, 2003. For the first time, all board employees shared a common professional development activity, bringing the whole system into the room to generate a sense of connection and a further shift toward a shared sense of *we*.

After staff breakfasts at each facility, buses took employees to the Palais. Each staff wore its school colors, carried banners, and sang songs. They re-created the days when riding the school bus was a daily experience. At the event, the electricity in the room was contagious. People sensed that something important was happening. Prior to the event, some had complained about the extravagant use of time and money. Now, people cheered, waved their banners, and hugged colleagues they had not seen for a long time. Pictures of LBPSB teachers and students of all ages flashed on the three big screens, along with the statement *We are the Board.* Leo La France's speech was inspiring. The motivational speakers (one in each of Canada's official languages) delivered messages that could be applied to teaching, working, and life. The bus rides back to the schools were filled with laughter, singing, and clapping. It was an organizational milestone which, we predict, will be recalled many times in the coming years as the moment when people recognized together the reality of the slogan: "*We* are the board."

PREPARING THE GROUND FOR MEANINGFUL COINCIDENCE

When we began working with this school board we were struck by the energy and commitment displayed by everyone we met. There was no doubt that all had a sense of pride in the parts they played in district education. What they missed was a shared purpose and trust among stakeholder groups.

With future search came a growing trust. In Canada, amalgamations and structural changes have put a strain on many boards and, in particular, the relationship between board management and teachers. This is not happening at LBPSB. The partnership and respect between these two stakeholder groups was evident in our conversations with system stakeholders. For the

Flexibility in High Schools Action Group to be still operational after 18 months is also a testimony to this partnership and to creating the best environment for kids. The changes being contemplated in this group could have significant impact on when and how teachers teach and would likely require adjustments to collective agreements. In other school districts even an exploration in this area would not be possible given the strained relationships.

The shared school district pride and persona was impossible to miss when we spoke with stakeholders 18 months after the conference. When we have returned to visit other systems where we have run a future search, we have found that when we ask members of one action group if they are aware of what is happening in other groups, they are not. But in this district people not only referred to the work that they were doing but were also aware of the work of others and spoke about it with a sense of pride and ownership. The magnitude and speed of this shift strikes us as among the most remarkable that we have seen.

Pearson's remarkable success stimulated us to look more deeply for contributing factors—structures, processes, leadership, and people—that might explain how the board achieved so much in such a short time. We made several surprising discoveries.

For example, where other organizations have been stymied by the appointment of a new executive leader during a future search process, LBPSB was able to take advantage of this change. Often a change in leadership means considerable anxiety. In this case we found an intriguing explanation for the explosion of creative energy in a new area of science pioneered by physicists to explain the nature of "self-organizing systems." That work, often referred to as chaos theory and emergence, offers useful insights into what we've seen happen at LBPSB.

Steven Johnson (2001) uses understandings from complexity and chaos theory to explain constructive alternatives to top-down change. He illustrates how individuals and groups connecting in new ways may create something wholly new. In this school district several things happened during the future search planning that contributed to the emergence of a new spirit in the district.

Choosing Future Search

The board invited the director general of the Ottawa–Carleton School Board (see chapter 4) to give a supper talk at a planning retreat in June

2001. His story of how a future search helped to catalyze the merger of two large school boards, including community partners in the process, stimulated the LBPSB director general to learn more about future search. By the time we were invited to discuss how we might help the board's plans, the three school commissioners and four school board managers had pretty well sold themselves on the process. The success of the Ottawa–Carleton future search, the timing of the Ottawa director general's dinner talk, and the ensuing strategic planning discussions all coalesced to point toward future search as the board's obvious next step.

Choosing the New Director General

At the same time, the board recognized that school district mergers inevitably lead to strained relationships. Many people at first feel displaced, even excluded. The new board leaders believed in the centrality of an organizational vision, values, and beliefs early in the merger process. They also realized that forcing a new initiative when people remained committed to their previous organizations could inhibit the development of a shared vision. People needed to be involved in creating the new system right up front. The leaders decided not to wait for system stabilization before going ahead with a future search.

During the planning, however, the director general (DG), Catherine Prokosh, who was the leading proponent of the future search, needed to absent herself for a few months. An assistant DG, Leo La France, took on the task of leading the project in her absence. During the first meeting, Leo admitted that he had doubts about the initiative and said he'd keep an open mind about what would come, and he did. Shortly after, the director general resigned. Leo was appointed interim director general, with full responsibility for leading the future search planning. He proved to be a skillful leader, negotiating to include important stakeholders and encouraging diverse perspectives within the planning team. How fortuitous, then, that only a few weeks before the future search conference, Leo La France, who brought with him strong people-centered values, became the new director general. Had a person been appointed who was not involved in the planning process, the entire experience might have been jeopardized. As Kurt Lewin explained over 60 years ago, people are much more likely to support plans they have had a hand in making than those turned over to them by others (in Weisbord & Janoff, 1995, p. 89).

In this case the district's organizational values and those of the director general were well aligned. After four years of putting new systems into place, the board's next priority was increasing collaboration among its many members. We saw Leo's timely emergence as the new board leader as wonderfully synchronistic. Leo's appointment felt like a small miracle to us. He valued the process of dialogue leading to shared vision. He modeled the principles of self-management and finding common ground in the way he included his colleagues in key decisions. He believed in the power of "we." He was ready to learn from the future search outcomes. Had an outsider been named at this juncture we doubt whether the future search could have accomplished so much. Joseph Jaworski (1996) has a description for this:

> We've all had those perfect moments, when things come together in an al-most unbelievable way, when events that could never be predicted, let alone controlled, remarkably seem to guide us along our path. The closest I have come to finding a word for what happens in these moments is *synchronic-ity.* (p. ix)

Choosing Members for the Planning Committee

The third critical event occurred during our initial meeting with LBPSB staff. We began by brainstorming a stakeholder list of those folks who affect and are affected by the system. We wanted, in the same room, people with authority, resources, expertise, information, and need. We narrowed this list down to those essential groups and individuals who had the greatest influence on the system. One key stakeholder group was the teachers' union, with whom the board was then in contract negotiations. This meant that union members could assume no extra duties such as future search planning.

Yet going ahead without union assistance would violate the whole system principle upon which future search is based. Union representatives were presented with the future search principles and the timing dilemma. They decided to put the issue to a vote of their constituents. The decision was that two union representatives would participate in the future search initiative despite a negotiating policy to the contrary. We do not know what sparked union representatives to present this opportunity to their constituents. We do know that the future search planning would have been significantly compromised without their participation. Many other stakeholders joined with equal enthusiasm.

Ann Svendsen and Myriam Laberge (2003), in their paper on stakeholder networks that foster learning and innovation, describe

> . . . a point where things have the power to bind . . . the point at which the parties involved can do things together that each party values, and recognize they could not achieve alone. . . . Such points of intersect provide the glue that binds the effort, and keeps it together (p. 11).

Such a point of intersection is precisely what future search makes possible. Indeed, future search's key principles embody this understanding. The first one, "getting the whole system in the room," recognizes that the right people have to be together for the task at hand. The second, "exploring the whole before fixing any part," acknowledges every person's contribution to a full understanding of the shared task. The third, "seeking common ground rather than reworking old problems and conflicts," leads to the discovery of creative intersections. Because consultants cannot do this for people, the fourth principle, "self-responsibility for action," becomes crucial. What consultants do provide are novel structures and unprecedented opportunities for people to do things they could not do before.

When we get a cross-section of system stakeholders into dialogue, change happens in the first planning meeting, often months or years before the two-and-a-half-day future search conference. Possibilities emerge that people never imagined. The system starts to shift as the planning team seeks to apply future search principles. The challenge for us is continuing to practice what we preach, holding the line on getting the whole system, investing time for sustained action, and people accepting responsibility for their task and action commitments.

> I am still inspired to do what we planned for our future . . . heck, I am planning on going in the front line, I think I might want to become a teacher, and I will teach the class of how our School Board used to be, and how it got this way! I've always kind of wanted to be a teacher, and if I do, I can really see if what we all worked on together is coming

through or not, and hopefully I will be a good example to those who want to learn. There's hope for the future yet, here I come!

—Student representative on the
planning committee for the future search

From complexity and chaos theory we also have become cognizant of how future search evokes a key phenomenon of effective systems called "strange attractors." These are turning points that arise in a system when many apparently unrelated factors within an organization and its environment become visible; they materialize when what is already present takes on shape and substance, flourish at times of adaptive challenge, and foster breakthroughs and outcomes that are unforeseen and unimaginable (Pascale, Millemann & Gioja, 2000, p. 75). Many future search techniques—time lines, mind maps, future scenarios—repeatedly evoke strange attractors.

> Future search is a people project. It encourages participants to come to their own conclusions as to new directions.
>
> —Marcus Tabachnick, board chairman

LEARNINGS AND REFLECTIONS

We have shown how committed leaders can use future search to enable transformation within an educational system. We need to point out that those who do so pay attention to the whole process—beginning with the planning all the way through to supporting follow-up. They do not view the conference or its attractive techniques as a quick-fix pill. Rather, they understand the ongoing requirement for energy and attention to sustain the work toward a shared vision. Future search is a great way to launch the boat. Follow-up processes and structures are required to sustain the voyage.

Nonetheless, we continue to be awed by the way synchronicity and fate played out so positively within this system. This is not to underplay the challenges that the system has faced but rather to acknowledge that the time for visible systemic transformation just seemed right. We cannot predict this alignment when we begin a future search. We do know, however, that a symbiotic relationship exists between future search and leadership.

Leaders will always play a key role in the success of a future search. In this case Leo La France fulfilled the requirement by fully supporting emerging changes and the structures needed to sustain them at the systems level, beyond that of individuals and groups. We know too that future search enables members of any system to emerge as leaders, often people that neither we nor they would have predicted had the interest or capacity until they found themselves acting in new ways.

This then is the challenge for those who would make the abstract notions of complexity and chaos theory practical in school systems. We believe that future search enables emergence, strange attractors, points of intersect, and synchronicity. We have learned from our review of events at the Lester B. Pearson School Board that these, under the right conditions, can enable educational transformations of the most constructive, long-lasting, and productive kind.

Part 5

<hr>

BEYOND THE DISTRICT

The four chapters in this section address issues related to school districts even though the events they describe are not districtwide future searches. The themes, processes, leadership issues, and follow-up efforts described in these chapters can be transferred to local school systems. The problem of financial constrains is another reason we have included these examples. For some, the leap to leading a future search seems too great a risk. The 12 previous chapters may have helped allay some of those fears. If you are still not convinced, then begin your future search journey by reading about opportunities to be a stakeholder in a future search. In all four of the examples in this section, the school district was a key stakeholder.

The impact of the future search in North Montgomery County Technical Career Center in Pennsylvania (chapter 13) transformed a failing, near-closing technical school into a model in technical career education. In this unique school fed by five different districts, partnerships with community employers, businesses, parents, and students have created innovative programs. Readers will learn how teachers have become leaders in taking initiative to improve education.

In Columbus, OH (chapter 14), very young children and their parents have benefited from the results of future searches and their follow-ups over a 10-year period. To increase services to this very important age group, nonprofit and governmental service providers have formed partnerships to be able to "blend funds" while still meeting funders' regulations. As the connection between early childhood education and student achievement is gaining more attention, communities can look to this chapter to learn about creative ways to leverage scarce resources as well as to imagine how a state-initiated future search could catalyze change at the school district level.

Chapter 15, set in the University of Southern California's Rossier School of Education, describes how a future search and subsequent activities led to a more coherent, less fragmented organization, which then produced measurable results, including balancing the budget, meeting enrollment targets, and increasing the student applicant pool. This chapter shows how the school created a structure to integrate and implement the outputs from its future search conference.

Chapter 16 tells the story of the Kansas State Department of Education's future search. It produced six strategic directions that now serve as a frame of reference for decision making and communication. Greater collaboration and partnerships with local school districts have been established. The future search principle of bringing the whole system into the planning process has been incorporated into how the department now operates. The state, along with the cooperation of local districts, has established a centralized data system that streamlines processes and provides more useful information. This chapter also describes the leadership dilemma of convening and attending a three-day future search in a time of budget shortfalls. "How can we afford to do this at a time like this?" "How can we afford *not* to do this at a time like this?" This chapter will be of interest to every school district that interfaces with a state department of education.

13

North Montgomery County Technical Career Center: Opening Up a System and Having Regional Impact

Nancy Aronson, Beverly Arsht, and Michael Erwin

INTRODUCTION

This is a story about changing attitudes and breaking stereotypes. It is a story about how vocational education evolved and became well respected in Northern Montgomery County in suburban Philadelphia. As you read this story you will see that although it focuses on one unique school fed by five different districts, this single school shares many issues with school districts. Both are concerned with mobilizing action in service to the student experience. Some of the themes that were of particular importance in this situation were the negative regional perceptions of the school, the need for higher expectations of students, the relevance of increased parent involvement, the formation of alliances with the community, and the development of teacher leadership. Using a future search conference to engage diverse stakeholders to reflect on the past, analyze the present, and shape the future directions of this technical career center directly mirrors how a school district would work toward making its aspirations for the future a reality.

In the spring of 1992, the North Montgomery County Area Vocational and Technical School was in trouble. The five home school districts, which sent students to the school and underwrote it financially, wanted to close the school. Although the school managed to survive, the staff had hard feelings. They had little hope for the future. When Dr. Mike Erwin became the director in January 1993, he knew the school had to change significantly or it might close. Although he believed that most of the staff were talented, the school had a serious image problem—inside its walls, outside in the community, and with the local school districts. This school embodied the county's negative perception of vocational-technical education.

An Image Problem

If an organization could be said to have low self-esteem, this one had it. The recent history of trying to close the school had left the teachers feeling chastised. They knew that other educators held them in low regard. In addition, some of the traditional negative stereotypes that are associated with vocational-technical education existed about this school, including the following:

- The school was a dumping ground for problem students or low achievers.
- Vocational education was for nonacademic students.
- Some parents who attended the vocational-technical school in the 1970s remember it having a drug culture—a stigma that still existed almost 30 years later.
- Industry viewed the school as out of touch with local labor needs.

Small Steps Make a Big Difference

From 1993 to 1995 the new leadership took steps to get the school moving in a positive direction. Steady progress was made. Most of the staff were open and willing to do things differently. They, too, realized that the school's future was not secure. As a significant part of this change, the director persuaded three to four key individuals to leave. The past actions and educational practices of these few had fueled, or at least typified, negative stereotypes about the faculty. The leader demonstrated his courage, decisiveness, and commitment to the school in dealing with the few key subordinates whose sustained poor performance was harming the school (Charan & Colvin, 1999). This step was needed for the future vitality and well-being of the school.

Soon thereafter, youth apprenticeship programs were started. Students began receiving relevant on-the-job experiences to augment their in-class learning. These programs were well received. Positive energy was beginning to build. The school was starting to evolve into a more contemporary technical career center. To reflect this development, the name was changed to North Montgomery County Technical Career Center (NMTCC or the Career Center). These early steps set the stage for strategic planning by signaling that business would not be continuing as usual.

STRATEGIC PLANNING: CHOOSING A FUTURE SEARCH

In early 1996 the state mandated NMTCC to complete a strategic planning process. The director saw this state requirement as an opportunity to listen to multiple stakeholder perspectives. The timing was right for a planning experience that would be pivotal in the life of the school. Indeed, because changes had started to occur in small, significant ways, there was enough hope, enough spark, to catch people's attention. The stakeholders who had wanted to close the school had needed to see some positive movement in order to commit their time and energy to creating the school's future. Much was at stake. A future search was chosen as the primary tool for strategic planning because its basic principles modeled opening up the system. All voices would be in the room and part of the planning.

THE PROCESS IS AS VALUABLE AS THE CONCRETE OUTCOMES

The Planning

The planning for the conference was crucial. It signaled NMTCC's desire for collaboration and openness. The steering committee, representing a mix of the school's stakeholders, spent time figuring out whom to bring to the future search. It invited participants representing nine stakeholder groups: students, parents, business and industry (current and potential partners), postsecondary schools, NMTCC staff, sending school staff, administration (including the NMTCC's board), community resources, and the community at large. NMTCC was fortunate to be able to include a partner from a technical school in Germany, a country that is a world leader in apprentice programs.

Steering committee members took great care in deciding which individuals to include. They ultimately selected a mix that represented the past, present, and future of vocational education in the county. For example, they invited some new staff members who seemed to have leadership potential in the hope that they would take future leadership roles in the school and in the community. Committee members took two other important steps related to participation. They made personal contacts to encourage attendance at the future search and insisted that invitees attend all three days. The activities and decisions of the steering committee sent a strong signal to the network of stakeholders about the importance of this conference.

The steering committee developed a theme and articulated purposes for the future search. The theme was "Innovative Approaches to Unlocking the Future." The purposes included

- Setting the directions for the future of NMTCC, as part of the strategic planning process.
- Acquiring and sharing information through the interaction of representatives of nine stakeholder groups.
- Expanding and strengthening relationships among NMTCC, its sending schools, local businesses, and community members.

OUTCOMES OF THE CONFERENCE:
GOALS FOR TECHNICAL CAREER EDUCATION

The goals identified at the future search conference were a central component of the strategic plan that had to be submitted to the Pennsylvania Department of Education. Dr. Don Burkins, a colleague of the consultants who was familiar with future search and the state requirements, worked with the assistant director of NMTCC, Dr. James Kraft, to compile a strategic plan that met the mandated requirements while supporting the actual organic, unfolding progress of this organization. NMTCC effectively managed the often-competing interests of organization relevance and state or federal government compliance. The goals that were developed are listed below:

- Career education: ongoing career education from kindergarten through adulthood.
- Curriculum: high standards for the changing needs of students and employers.
- Facility: maximizing all available resources to meet clients' needs.
- Global interconnections: cultural, technological, and business exchanges.
- Individual educational needs: meet individual needs utilizing all learning options.
- Partnerships: strengthen partnerships to enhance the training needed for all students.
- Technology: develop ongoing processes to anticipate change while staying current.

Ad Hoc Teams Replace Standing Committees

Action teams formed around these seven goals. Members of the teams met to develop their thinking and construct plans for implementation. The steering committee adopted the operating philosophy that teams and action plans would be based strictly on identified need, that they would be focused, short term, and have a definite end point. As priorities and issues arose in a goal area, ad hoc teams with appropriate stakeholders were formed, the priority was addressed, and the team disbanded when the work was completed. Using this process, NMTCC discovered how to keep alive the vitality between planning and results. This approach to teams and goals became part of the culture. As the director described, "It was not planning for planning's sake." Over time, it became expected that staff would be active on these ad hoc groups. Continuous improvement and widespread staff involvement became the norm for how business was done in this organization.

The Impact of Getting the Stakeholders in the Room

Opening up the system and getting the stakeholders together to have conversations about the future of vocational education had a major impact on the system. It influenced the actions of individuals and groups, created a climate of possibility for the future, and led to many concrete programs. It led to shifts in perceptions about what was possible for technical career education in the region.

Visibility in the Community

In addition to the visibility of the school at the future search, the director was able to network and make connections to open doors for future opportunities. For example, the head of the Rotary Club recruited him to speak to many groups in the community about what was happening with technical education in the county and at NMTCC in particular.

What Ifs Become Reality

During the discussions at the conference, people from business and industry offered new possibilities—what ifs—for ways of making things happen for students. "What if we came to the school site and partnered with faculty to do training?" "What if we brought students to the work site to take advantage of state-of-the-art equipment that would be too costly for the school to own?"

Hearing these conversations energized the faculty. The what ifs offered exciting possibilities for the future as they communicated an interest in the school on the part of the business community. As one participant described the conference, "The energy was magic. Many of these *what ifs* became reality."

The Image Begins to Change

The future search was an opportunity for outside stakeholders, including industry, to discover more about the school. People became more familiar with the programs. Outside stakeholders met and interacted with the staff and the students. Students were actively engaged, forthright, and constructive. Students' consistent demonstration of these positive skills helped shift some of the stereotypes and negative assumptions some people had about the school.

A Major Message from Parents

One major, influential message coming out of the conference was from parents. They wanted their children to have the choice to pursue a technical path or an academic path after high school. This dual importance of the technical skills and the academics was part of subsequent conversations for years to come. A signature of this school today is the integration of these paths. For example:

- The school evolved from a traditional vo-tech school to a technical career center.
- Two biotechnology students were accepted to Penn State on full scholarships. One of these students received a $100,000 ROTC scholarship from the Marine Corps.
- PSSA (Pennsylvania's statewide, standardized tests) scores increased as a result of teaching students in a contextual manner. Specifically, the average scores for youth apprenticeship students went up 200 points on these PSSA tests. These scores improved in part because academics and technical skills became intertwined. Math and reading skills began to be taught within the context of students' technical training where there was a high degree of interest and motivation to find solutions and think critically.
- A teacher from heating, ventilation, and air conditioning (HVAC), a skilled technician, returned for certification in math, science, and English. He now teaches academics using the contextual approach mentioned above.
- Technical students started taking more challenging and rigorous academic course work. For example, previously machine shop students were not required to take specific, higher academic courses and would take general math. Following the future search, students and parents received, for the first time, a pathway outlining the academic courses the student must take to prepare for a successful career. Students who wanted to be machinists began taking geometry, trigonometry, and calculus.

In addition to the parent perspective, the business and industry voices in the room were also important to the future of the school. As we will discuss in the next section, partnerships were launched and deepened. These partnerships created richer opportunities for student learning and positively impacted the perception of vocational education in the region.

THE IMPACT OF THE PARTNERSHIPS

Given the role of NMTCC as the bellwether for vocational education, strong partnerships with other stakeholder groups were critical if the school was to thrive and grow. Fortunately, the seeds of collaborative relationships that were sown and nurtured at the future search led to many positive changes:

- As teachers made contact with vendors at the future search, they exchanged ideas and began to think in new and different ways. Some ideas took hold. Following the conference, teachers took the lead in acquiring state-of-the-art equipment from different businesses. For example, a major automotive equipment manufacturer consigned $150,000 worth of its products to the school's automotive technology lab for student use. This was a win-win arrangement for the manufacturer and the school. Students had the opportunity to be trained on the same state-of-the-art equipment found in modern automotive dealership service departments. The manufacturer was able to bring potential buyers to the school where they could see the equipment being used.
- Opportunities for student work-based learning experiences were expanded beyond the local neighborhoods. Apprentices began working for service and manufacturing firms across the entire Delaware Valley region.
- New programming was created. One example was the Biotechnology Pathway. In partnership with major pharmaceutical firms, a biotechnology lab was established in the school to serve both high school students and adults.
- The school became more relevant. The knowledge and skills that students learned and experienced at NMTCC became directly connected to the workplace. As a result of the future search, the

school's occupational advisory committee was revitalized. The committee recruited additional members from business and industry to help guide decisions related to curriculum, facilities, and equipment.

- Postsecondary linkages created paths for students. The school formalized over 40 articulation agreements with colleges across the state. This means that secondary and postsecondary schools sign articulation agreements which give advanced credit for coursework taken in high school to students who elect to continue their studies at the postsecondary level. This eliminates redundant coursework and enables students to take more advanced or elective courses in college. For example, engineering technology students can receive up to 15 college credits for fundamental technology classes they took in high school when they matriculate into a community college technology program that has an articulation agreement with the students' school. When students take the Cisco Networking program at the technical school they can become industry certified or have the networking coursework waived at the college level where articulation agreements exist.

- Industry partnerships resulted in numerous unique opportunities for students. As a result of the partnership with the automotive service equipment manufacturer, various trade groups began to hold workshops at NMTCC during the school day. On one occasion, area service managers for Porsche held a workshop dealing with the newly introduced Boxster. Five service managers each drove a Boxster to the meeting. When students entered the lab, they noticed the Boxsters lined up across the lab. Imagine their interest! One of the service managers made a presentation to the students about the mechanics of the car. Students were totally engaged with the presentation and had the opportunity to learn about state-of-the-art technology from an industry expert. Without the partnership, the chances of NMTCC students experiencing this type of lesson would have been small.

- Improved relationships with feeder schools positively impacted enrollment. Enrollment went from 420 in 1992–1993 to 1,300 in 2002–2003. Today, there is a waiting list!

ADDITIONAL BY-PRODUCTS OF THE FUTURE SEARCH

In addition to the successes already mentioned, the future search was pivotal in other ways. It shifted perceptions, encouraged leadership, and modeled new ways of thinking about change and convening task meetings that are now part of how NMTCC does business.

Full Plates

The activities of the future search helped teachers shift their view about current initiatives and new activities. Prior to the conference, teachers talked about having too many things on their plates. Seeing the big picture, experiencing the larger context, and hearing from other stakeholders altered their perceptions. Although the number of items on their plates was not reduced, teachers were better able to make connections and understand how various parts fit together. Metaphorically, they were able to look at the landscape from an airplane at 10,000 feet instead of seeing only individual trees as they walked through the forest. This created a palpable emotional shift in how staff felt about their work and how much energy they had to make new things happen.

Distributed Leadership

This organization had a good deal of talent, but like most systems, much of it had not been fully utilized. Michael Fullan (2001) talks about the importance of teacher leadership and the vast, mostly untapped resource it represents. The future search served as a catalyst to release the energy and talent of the faculty as well as other stakeholders. Because of this conference, many individuals and groups started to take initiative, inspire others, and make improvements in order to expand and enrich the possibilities for students.

Teacher Leadership

Teachers who participated in the future search became teacher leaders in the school. This by-product of the conference resulted in significant advances in the services the school offers. Teachers taking the lead to further develop their programs became widespread. For example:

- In the years following the future search, the teachers in the power and transportation cluster worked together to get all of their programs nationally certified through the Automotive Service Excellence (ASE) Program. The automotive technology programs also obtained the necessary support from local employers to qualify their programs and students for the Automotive Youth Educational System (AYES). These certifications were the direct result of the five teachers in the cluster. To obtain the certifications, the staff created partnerships with local automotive dealerships and repair shops. Their efforts resulted in significant equipment donations and excellent job placement opportunities for students and graduates. The approach taken by the power and transportation cluster became a model in the state for what was possible.
- The school nurse, who participated in the future search, ultimately obtained a teaching certificate and created a hospital-based program for high-achieving seniors who were interested in entering the health care field. Through her efforts, health care professionals in a hospital mentored students in the program. The students experienced and learned about specific careers in the health field. All of the students enrolled in the program entered the health field and approximately a quarter of them entered medical degree programs.
- The graphic arts teacher, who participated in the future search, voluntarily got involved with a Macintosh Computer user group in the community to become more skilled with Mac computers. He also decided to obtain national skill certification through the Printing Institute of America.
- NMTCC staff also demonstrated shared leadership in obtaining International Standards Operation (ISO) certification, a well-known and well-respected status in the national and international business community recognizing companies achieving stringent global quality standards.

These are just a few examples of how the staff stretched their programs after the future search. The efforts they displayed went well beyond the everyday, routine responsibilities of teaching. They invested significant amounts of time and energy, much at their own expense. Their efforts resulted in major enrollment growth and recognition. They were part of building a school that was vibrant and effective. In the years following the future search, the staff earned incentive grants from the Pennsylvania Department of Education for improving student academic performance, high placement rates, and high attendance rates.

Advocates

Others also stepped up on behalf of the school and technical education. For example, a former executive in a Fortune 500 company became president of the parent/teacher organization. He used his position as a vehicle for speaking about the school and technical education in the county. He participated in a teacher in-service day that was coordinated by the five principals from the feeder high schools. His belief in and passion for technical education helped build the credibility of the program for both the traditional technical student and a new population of college-bound students interested in merging technical skills with their academics. This type of advocacy contributed to changing the perceptions of vocational programming and had more students considering courses of study that required postsecondary education. For example, the Allied Health Program started attracting students who were interested in pursuing careers in the medical field and the health sciences. Cisco Networking attracted students interested in computer science or computer information systems. Engineering and biotechnology programs at the Career Center became fields of interest for many college-bound students.

Incorporating Future Search Principles

Many of the principles of future search have been incorporated into NMTCC. Stakeholder involvement continues to be important to the organization. Who needs to be at the table is a common question that gets asked. Large group meetings with multiple stakeholders have been used to chart paths forward.

- A biotechnology summit was held in November 1997 to explore the feasibility of creating a biotechnology career path for students. This summit proceeded against formidable odds. As the planning for this idea was launched, an important stakeholder from a pharmaceutical company claimed that having a program of this type at a technical career center was impossible. The leadership and the consultants believed that the resistance existed because this was an entirely new way of thinking; biotechnology education at the high school level was novel. They believed that the shortage of labor in the field warranted this type of program. As the conversation unfolded, participants more deeply understood the opportunity that was presenting itself and began to envision what could happen at the school. This was the beginning of the biotechnology pathway that starts at the secondary level and proceeds through either a two-year or a four-year postsecondary degree program. Today, this career path has been so successful that it is a model for biotechnical initiatives throughout the state.

- A public review meeting was held 24 months after the future search. Participants were invited back for this meeting to share successes and challenges and to chart progress across groups. New ideas and possibilities were also solicited.

Faculty and staff were very involved in both the future search and the following strategic planning process. Today, they continue to have a strong voice in shaping the decisions at the school level. In 2002, another future search was held to chart the course for the next phase of development for technical career education for the school and for the region. This second future search explored issues of growth and ways to further expand opportunities for students. What a dramatic change from the possibility of closing which preceded the first future search!

LEADERSHIP REFLECTIONS

As we were preparing this chapter, we asked the director what he had learned from his experience as the leader of this process. Two things in particular stood out to him. One was that opening the system to include stakeholder voices is a powerful communication—literally and symbolically. "By involving members of the community in shaping the directions,

NMTCC instilled a sense of shared ownership for the school's success." The second insight was that collaboration is critical. According to the director:

> If you don't hear candidly from your stakeholders, you are working in a vacuum. Working in a vacuum leads to failure. It is critical to open the system up and create opportunities for dialogue across groups. Using this approach, you will get valuable feedback on current offerings. You will hear constructive, creative ideas for improvement. Involve staff in these conversations. They will gain a greater understanding and appreciation of community needs along with the role of the organization in meeting them. This information enables staff to take active leadership roles in moving the organization forward.

CLOSING THOUGHTS

The perception of vocational education in this region continues to shift in positive ways. Enrollment at NMTCC is up, and a technical career/academic path is becoming a more viable choice for more students. This school also offers important clues to what helps more students be more successful, more of the time. Imagine the possibilities for young people if stereotypes continue to be broken and attitudes continue to change about technical career education.

14

Community Collaboration: A 10-Year Journey for Young Children

Chris Kloth and Rebecca Love

Ancient wisdom suggests that "it takes a village to raise a child." When community leaders and citizens in Columbus, OH, embraced this ancient wisdom they realized that allowing children to grow into adaptive, life-long learners required cultivating adaptive systems. Our story will explore how, over a period of 10 years, they moved from theory to action.

INTRODUCTION

Upon learning that the editors were preparing a book on enlisting the whole system for positive change across school districts we were both excited and resistant. We were excited because it is clear to us how our work in Ohio's child-care and early education "system" (CC/EE) has affected the extent to which many children in Columbus, especially those faced with the challenges of poverty and disabilities, enter the public education system ready to learn. We were also excited because the public education systems on the state and local level, especially the Columbus Public Schools (CPS), have been partners in our work.

The resistance was rooted in our own experiences, and those reported by colleagues, suggesting that economic and political pressure, as well as the bureaucratic and other regulatory requirements, faced by CC/EE systems and school districts throughout the United States continue to make it difficult for system leaders to work together, despite the fact that the two systems are significantly interdependent, sharing families and children and often experiencing repercussions from the environment in a similar way.

In the change process described in this chapter the stakeholders from the education system were part of the work throughout the process. The shift that took place in the first of three future searches involving our children is one that is similar in future searches that have been run for school districts. This chapter offers an example of how future search was used to transform and sustain whole-system change over a 12-year period (1991–2003) and how it continues to do so to this day; it is an example that could be reproduced not only in a school district but also at the state or provincial level.

Our story began in 1991 with the first of three future search conferences. The scope of the first conference was the state of Ohio. The change process continued with another future search focusing on communitywide change in a large urban area. The third focused on strategic planning for a nonprofit agency involved in the first two conferences. At this writing, in 2003, the change process is continuing with concrete results that were unanticipated by the first event, but which clearly embody the vision and values embedded in each of the three future search conferences.

APPROACH

Whenever we talk with people who have been involved in, or directly affected by, this work they start with a story . . . usually about the circumstances that drew them into the work, or about the day they had their epiphany related to the work. This chapter is presented in a narrative storyline.

1991: CITIZENS INFLUENCE STATE
PRIORITIES—LAYING THE FOUNDATION

In 1991 Ohio's child-care and early education system (CC/EE), especially its Head Start programs, had received national recognition from organizations like the federal Administration for Children, Youth and Families (ACYF), the Children's Defense Fund, and the National Association for Young Children. Data provided by the ACYF indicated that, among 56 entities receiving federal Head Start (HS) dollars, Ohio was fourth in total enrollment and seventh in federal funding. Further, among the 12 states that added state dollars to the federal dollars, Ohio ranked first in both HS funding and the number of children served. At the state and local levels Ohio HS programs had received special grants to fund a variety of pilot projects, including the U.S. Department of Health and Human Services grant for this project.

However, CC/EE professionals (focused on children from birth to kindergarten) and families who were consumers of their services were not satisfied. They knew that large numbers of children and families still did not have access to services and that low-income households were especially hard hit by the shortage. They also knew that, except for the most basic health and safety requirements, there were few clear, consistent, systemwide guidelines to assure that adequately trained people were providing developmentally appropriate care and activities to foster the emotional, physical, and intellectual growth of young children.

Further aggravating the situation was the perception that, while Ohio was a leader in funding HS, the overall allocation of dollars allocated for EE/CC at both the federal and state levels was paltry compared to other state budget priorities. For example, public funders, most private purchasers of services (families), and the few family-friendly employers that have helped provide care have established reimbursement levels so low that wages for CC/EE workers typically have been barely above poverty level. Attracting and retaining qualified staff in such an environment was difficult.

A vicious cycle was created in which the cost paid for services became the basis for establishing the perceived value of the services. Driven by a scarcity-based view of the world, providers competed fiercely for very meager resources. As long as providers believed that dollars available for CC/EE could not or would not increase they continued to offer services at an artificially low rate.

In this context, Ohio's governor leveraged his relationship with the Reagan administration to access federal resources to create his Family and

Children First (FCF) Initiative. In his State of the State message on March 5, 1991, Governor George Voinovich said:

> Our aim is . . . to make an unprecedented commitment to one priority that I believe ranks above all others—the health and education of our children. The only way to do it is to pick one generation of children—draw a line in the sand—and say to all: "This is where it stops. Today is where it stops."

The First Future Search

During the summer of 1991 Chris Kloth attended Marvin Weisbord and Sandra Janoff's first effort to teach others how to manage a future search. Upon returning from the training Kloth reviewed a document that indicated the governor's office had contracted to begin the Children and Family First Initiative in 1992 with a strategic plan. The description of the planning process reflected a traditional top-down, expert-driven approach.

Kloth contacted Chris Stoneburner, the director of the governor's Head Start–State of Ohio Collaboration Project. He suggested to Stone-burner that they use a future search to create a set of parameters to inform the planning process and increase the possibility of gaining broad-based stakeholder support. Stoneburner consulted with the Ohio Head Start Association (OHSA) and arranged for a presentation on future search to a group of OHSA leaders and state officials. Based upon the congruence between future search and the commitment to build a collaborative strategy, the OHSA and the governor decided to cosponsor an event December 10–12, 1991. Thus began a journey that continues to this day.

Planning for the Conference

In this case external system pressures left only eight weeks to plan and conduct this future search, not much time to ensure the desired inclusion. It was also not much time for a group of state officials to rethink their original plan and incorporate this new process, especially if it was going to include people whom some might consider problematic or attached to a specific agenda. While collaboration and inclusion seemed like valuable concepts on an intellectual level, few expected to have to make these terms actionable quite so soon.

A previously planned event created an opening for conducting a planning session that included the key decision makers in state government, HS program executives, teachers from urban and rural areas around the state, local educators, and nonprofit agencies involved in serving young children. As this planning group considered who should be invited it became clear that there were strong feelings among different groups about who should and who should not be included in public policy conversations of the type that would occur at the future search. In particular, there was considerable friction generated when the planners considered two groups: HS mothers and CC/EE advocates who had been vocal opponents of the governor during his recent election campaign.

There was an intense dialogue among the planners about who was qualified to participate, who would understand the process, and who could be trusted. This conversation was a critical test of the potential viability of the future search process for this event. Fortunately, Stoneburner and the OHSA director, Barbara Haxton, were committed to the process and to inclusion. In the end, the planners agreed to include HS mothers and some of the governor's political opponents.

Key Events and Outputs of the Conference

The powerful impact of the decision to include these groups, and the wisdom of inclusion as a minimum critical specification for any future search, was most obvious in a dramatic moment during the future search when stakeholder groups were reporting their prouds and sorries. The table of top-level state government officials had just finished reporting on the challenges they had faced and the lessons they had learned from past mistakes, as well as the considerable pride they felt about the positive national attention given to Ohio for its CC/EE system, especially related to HS. During the brief pause after they finished one HS mother said, "That's all really good, but it's still scary as hell raising a kid out there." The brief pause turned into an extended, electric moment of silence.

There was a palpable shift in the room. The moment of silence was followed by a conversation in which people stopped talking from their official roles and began talking from their perspectives as parents, grandparents, aunts, uncles, and friends of young children. It became crystal clear that this entire group had found the common ground they needed for their work. Children were no longer simply a unit of measure or unit of service; the group began talking about *our children* and about their hopes and fears for *our children.*

In the end the participants produced a document called *A Shared Vision of Collaborative Service Delivery.* The document included 17 core values that all participants agreed the governor's plan should include if he wanted their active support of the plan. Taken together they described a system that demonstrates that children are truly valued by being inclusive, holistic, collaborative, and accountable in delivering a comprehensive range of high-quality services. The document also included 24 minimum critical specifications that every person in the room agreed ought to be re-flected in the strategic plan when it was completed. These specifications stressed the provision of the best combination of available services, a meaningful partnership with the family, accessibility to services, and re-duction of duplication of services and processes. Moreover, all partici-pants said that if these criteria were met they would actively support the governor's plan, despite any past opposition.

After the Conference

The report was delivered to the governor by a group of participants se-lected during the future search, including an HS mother. The governor passed it to the strategic planning team. The governor also met with this same group of future search participants when the strategic plan was com-pleted. The plan reflected their input and continues to influence state policy.

Modeling partnership at the state level, the new Republican governor carried over an interdisciplinary family cabinet from the previous Demo-cratic administration and made the FCF Initiative one of its responsibili-ties. The family cabinet continues to function. In addition, the state plan resulted in legislation that created an FCF Council in each Ohio county. Each county council is made up of families, public officials, and CC/EE professionals. They ensure that the core values and minimum critical specifications continue to guide local policy and adapt the state plan to lo-cal conditions.

The governor who initiated the first future search has been replaced, but the legacy of the event is embedded in policies and practices that continue to affect Ohio's CC/EE system. Few workers are aware that this first future search conference even occurred. None of the parents who are present today were part of the future search. But many can and do articulate in their own ways the core values and attributes from that first event through their words and actions.

1993: IMPROVING THE QUALITY OF CC/EE IN CENTRAL OHIO

While there was a good deal of excitement generated by the plan, there were many who wondered what would be done to make the plan real and whether the reality would measure up to the lofty aspirations of the plan.

Once the results of the first event became apparent, one of the participants decided the time was right to take the work further, to make it real on a regional level. As the executive director of Action For Children (AFC) in Columbus, the 15th largest U.S. city and Ohio's state capital, Diane Bennett wanted to build common ground and energy for action on CC/EE issues throughout the entire Central Ohio region. Leveraging the energy generated when the state-level plan was published, she convened a diverse stakeholder group to engage in a dialogue focused on its potential benefits to Central Ohio children and families. The group became known as the Franklin County Childcare and Early Education Council.

The Second Future Search

In November 1993 AFC sponsored a future search focused on building common ground for improving the quality of CC/EE in Central Ohio. The result was the identification of four key areas of concern: access, quality, affordability, and public awareness. These became the focus and criteria for the work that followed.

The participants in the second future search committed to create a comprehensive community plan to focus and guide their work in the future. The council created task groups for the four areas of concern and charged them with creating a vision, core values, goals, and strategies for each area. Consistent with the parameters that guided the governor's plan, collaboration emerged as both a core value and core strategy.

In the summer of 1994 The Child Care Action Plan for Franklin County was released at a large, widely covered outdoor event at the Ohio statehouse.

It outlined specific strategies and steps for making the ideals of the state plan operational on the local level. Community leaders delivered speeches while hundreds of children from child-care centers throughout the community participated by creating jigsaw-style "Pieces of the Plan." "I'm a Piece of the Plan" buttons were created and distributed to match the puzzle pieces. People in child care and early education still refer to being "part of the plan."

1994: CREATING ACTION FOR CHILDREN'S STRATEGIC PLAN

The Third Future Search

Meanwhile, with an eye on increasing "public awareness" as an outcome related to both internal and external publics, AFC's board decided to leverage the agency's high visibility and credibility among many CC/EE professionals, families, and employers to ensure that a broader, ongoing dialogue would occur throughout the community. In 1994 they began their regular three-year strategic planning cycle. Having been through the previous future search events, and being a collaborator at heart, Diane Bennett recommended that AFC use a future search to drive the planning process. They included members of the council, local and state officials, nonprofit and for-profit providers, home-based providers, the public school system, members of the business community, and other stakeholders in shaping the AFC strategic plan.

One result was that the board committed considerable agency resources to incorporating the system vision, values, goals, and strategies into all the agency's public information and education efforts. In effect, they took a leadership role in shaping messages to the larger community about the county plan. AFC also committed agency resources to support its expanding role as a neutral convener of dialogues about ongoing and emerging CC/EE issues and the plan. They hosted meetings of the council, maintained its minutes and, when needed, arranged for external facilitation. They also created safe space in which specific conflicts, such as the differential impact of policies on stakeholders, could be resolved.

In an effort to model the values of community collaboration and partnership, AFC also took the counterintuitive approach of highlighting the work of other individuals and groups, making its own role less prominent.

If AFC helped facilitate conflict resolution in a particular situation it made sure the parties in conflict were given public credit for their effort, rather than publicizing the agency's role as convener. With considerable difficulty and tenacity, AFC invested time and energy in developing its own accountability measures so the board could see the impact AFC was having on the larger system and see how helping others look good and get credit was essential to achieving the mission and vision.

One very significant aspect of AFC's role as convener and communicator was its clear commitment to both pushing the system to change and allowing it to progress at a pace it could sustain. For example, as CC/EE providers continued to make services available to children and families, they worked hard to identify, endorse, and implement shared quality standards that would "raise the bar" for the entire system. Some providers, including most of the HS-approved centers, already met or exceeded the new standards. Others were able and willing to begin to incorporate the standards into their programs. However, others found that the investment required to implement the new standards would increase their costs and undermine their commitment to increasing access, especially for those most in need. Where progress was being made and gaining momentum, AFC simply made sure people kept meeting, working, and making progress. And in areas where progress was slower or more difficult they tried to facilitate experimentation.

1995: IMPLEMENTING "BLENDED FUNDING" AND COLLABORATION

One concept from the county plan, referred to as "blended funding," raised issues related to trust, power, and control and seemed to undermine each design that had been piloted. Agency executives and boards resisted sharing internal financial management strategies and, especially, their actual budgets until the design was complete and approved by all.

Some organizations tried working with others in a variety of new ways. Others insisted that working together was nothing new and that they had been collaborating for many years. Closer examination revealed that the quality of working together among different partners varied dramatically. For example, one set of collaborators made sure that the buses from each agency did not all arrive in a neighborhood at the same time, while another found ways to send one bus to pick up all the children in a particular neighborhood. People began to express a loss of hope that they would ever find the perfect model they could all support to operationalize "blended funding."

Finally, AFC and the Franklin County Department Job and Family Services (JFS), the biggest funder of subsidized care, changed the frame. In the new frame the focus shifted from "getting it right" to allowing multiple experiments and learning from mistakes. John Haan, then director of JFS, announced that the agency would consider funding any collaborative project that conformed to the council's vision and values and would demonstrate alternative ways of sharing funding. He agreed to allow AFC to evaluate proposals on behalf of JFS and council members.

Keeping in mind that these nonprofits were working from the mental model of scarcity mentioned earlier, risk taking related to funding in general and sharing funds in particular was rare. However, one group of partners did submit a proposal to JFS. It involved the YWCA, one of the HS organizations, a small Lutheran Church, and T.E.A.C.H., a grassroots neighborhood organization formed to help residents take control of a housing complex that had come to be known as "Uzi Alley" for the violence, drug dealing, and other crime in the area. Each had worked with at least one of the new partners in another setting and believed that the experience would allow them to stretch.

The project got off to a quick start. A high degree of commitment to the collaborative nature of the project, especially by the YWCA and HS, allowed each partner to share resources to remodel a facility that needed a lot of work before it could be approved to open and operate. Unfortunately, they spent so much time getting the facility open in time to enroll children at the beginning of the school year that they had done very little in the way of role clarification and relationship building. The YWCA and HS had participated in all three future search events and, as a result, had developed considerable commitment to and experience with collaboration. The other two organizations had not. Eventually the project folded.

With strong support from her agency's administration, Rebecca Love, director of early childhood for the Franklin County Board of Mental Retardation and Developmental Disabilities, had begun working with HS in 1985 to ensure that very young children with special needs were served with nonhandicapped peers of the same age. By 1991, when the first event occurred, she and her staff had achieved a high degree of personal and professional credibility in the community as advocates and service providers for the children and families they serve. In addition, they were seen as good partners when working with others.

The vision and values that emerged from all three conferences resonated deeply with Love, her administration, and her staff. The events opened up vistas of possibility that allowed her to expand her own view of interdependence to include the larger system. It also provided her with access to a broader set of relationships as she worked with others.

While she understood the potential benefits of the emerging shifts in the CC/EE system for all children, Love was deeply committed to finding ways to leverage the resources of the larger system for her constituents. Collaboration was particularly important to her. She believed that an environment that included children of typical and nontypical ability, and of many cultural and economic backgrounds, could benefit all children.

The Ohio Department of Mental Retardation and Developmental Disabilities (MR/DD) solicited proposals to expand existing early childhood centers. The County Board of MR/DD bid for, and in 1995 received, a $1.5 million matching grant from the state. With the combined state and county leadership and resources as a base, Love immediately invited a broad base of local CC/EE professionals to create a truly inclusive and collaborative child-care and family center.

Adding to successful partnerships established with several EE/CC programs throughout the county, Love designed two parallel strategies. MR/DD and one of the HS agencies agreed to collaborate in operating the Early Childhood Learning Community (ECLC) at Marburn. It served typical and nontypical children in the same classrooms. ECLC/Marburn became a lab for learning what would be required for human systems to work together seamlessly, which they defined as operating in such a way that children and families experienced the staff, programming, and services as if they were all provided by a single agency while allowing each agency to maintain its organizational integrity.

In 1997 plans began for building a new facility that would be able to collaboratively serve 700 children and their families. The Reggio Emilia Model (New, 1990; Edwards, Gandini & Forman, 1993) was selected to frame their future operation. This model has community as its central metaphor. It recognizes that spirit, form, and function must all be linked from the earliest phases of design. The building, the program, and the relationships are conceived as an integrated whole.

Love and several other partners, including Jean Gordon, the project's lead architect for locally based Moody/Nolan, traveled to the town in Northern Italy that inspired the Reggio Emilia Model. The level of leadership support that had already developed among the partner agencies was evident in the fact that so many of the partners were able to participate in the trip, especially given the environment of scarcity at this time. As a result of the trip people felt validated and excited about their plan. They could see how the core values that emerged from the first two future search events could be realized in a single facility. Even the architect realized that he could (and did) create a space that would support the spirit and aspirations of the partners. Partners' commitment to a new way of doing business grew as they implemented the pilot at ECLC/Marburn and planned the new building.

Consistent with the commitment to authentic participation and implicit in the principles and practice of future search, a group was formed to shape and guide the implementation of the new center. It became known as the Family Partnership. It contributed to the selection of the operating model, the design of the building, and the governance model for the facility. By involving the partners in her vision so early in the process Love had made clear that she was serious about collaborating on a deeper level than they had ever experienced before.

2000–2002: THE BREAKTHROUGH—ELEMENTS OF SUCCESS

In January 2000 the Family Partnership knew that their work was about to become more difficult. From their experience at ECLC/Marburn they knew that when the building opened in September 2001, the human systems would have to be in place to create a caring learning community that would have the capacity to grow into their highest values and vision for children, families, professionals, and the community. They faced decisions about shared staffing, shared funding, shared space, and other contractual arrangements that would begin to affect each agency's bottom line.

The Breakthrough

When the JFS-funded pilot project closed, Kloth conducted a process evaluation and debriefing of the experience. Referring back to coordination, cooperation, and collaboration in the governor's original document, it became clear that these terms are often used interchangeably. It was found that there had been an inconsistent interpretation of what these words meant to each partner. The opportunities and traps inherent in each approach in this and other situations frequently undermine efforts to work together. The evaluation and debriefing findings were consistent with the experiences of Kloth and his colleagues in many community and organization settings. These experiences articulated an emerging typology for distinguishing among distinct ways of working together (Kloth, 2000). In particular, this typology demonstrates that as individuals, organizations, and systems begin to work together more closely they begin to face the benefits and threats of boundary permeability (see figure 14.1).

For many of the partners this continuum of ways to work together proved to be enlightening and empowering on several levels. First, there

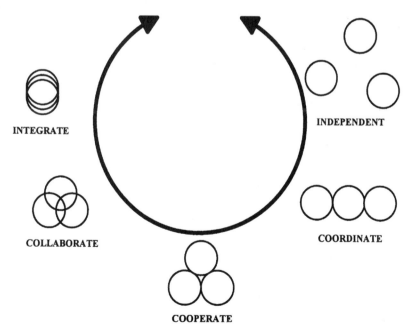

Figure 14.1. Emerging Typology of Working Together (Courtesy Chris Kloth)

was considerable outside pressure to "collaborate." They had all committed long ago to working together in a variety of ways and settings. Most had tried to do so. However, they had more stories of frustration than success. Closer examination of the frustrations revealed that partners often began working together, using the term *collaboration*, only to discover that one intended to coordinate and the other intended to integrate.

Another feature of this typology was reported to be quite valuable because it was seen as rooted in the culture of the EE/CC professionals. Referring to the concept of legitimate interdependence, none of these is considered inherently better than another. Rather, depending on the situation, each of these types may be applicable in the same relationship.

Elements of Success

The Family Partnership also reviewed learning from pilot projects over the previous years. This learning included six key elements of working together that had emerged from the evaluations and reflections on those pilots (Kloth, 2000): 1) shared goals, 2) a shared view of legitimate interdependence, 3) shared power, 4) shared control, 5) shared accountability, and 6) mutual respect and trust (see figure 14.2). These elements have continued to frame their work.

While these terms were familiar to the partners from many years of workshops and articles, they reported that this framing helped them understand past frustrations and successes. It allowed them to create a more explicit agenda for building partnership. Three particular elements were consistently identified as especially helpful. All three have their roots in the work done during and after the three future search events.

First, *power* was understood in terms of the resources (knowledge, skills, relationships, funding, etc.) required to achieve the shared goals. In this context power is inherently neutral. The greater the volume, variety, or complexity of the work required to achieve the goals, the more power may be needed by the system. The reason the partners needed to work together was that each could bring something unique to the table that was perceived as valuable in achieving the shared goals. They understood and trusted that this power would be shared equitably.

Second, the concept of *legitimate interdependence* helped frame conversations resulting from the fact that each partner has a larger mission

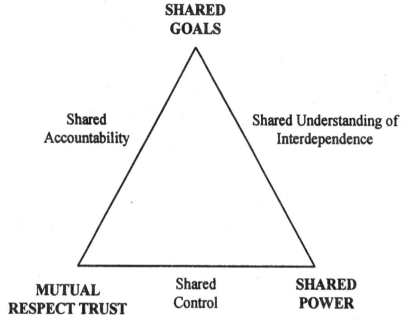

**SHARED
GOALS**

Shared
Accountability

Shared Understanding of
Interdependence

**MUTUAL
RESPECT TRUST**

Shared
Control

**SHARED
POWER**

Figure 14.2.   Working Together Benchmarks (Courtesy Chris Kloth)

than the project, has a board to which it is accountable, and, in several cases, is accountable to different regulatory bodies with different standards for the same function or activity. Meal planning provides an insight into two practical experiences of working in the context of legitimate interdependence.

All three partners provide meals to children and are committed to the principle that nutrition is essential to health, learning, and development. The partners are also committed to the idea that working together should reduce such overhead costs as food costs. In addition, they committed to making sure that, despite these differences and regardless of which agency enrolled each child, all children should feel they are part of one classroom and one school with one staff. Children enrolled by each agency should not experience meals as if they are from different programs. What was challenging was that food services are regulated by at least two local agencies, three state agencies and two federal agencies—each with its own standards and licensing or compliance procedures!

One of the HS organizations had food service capacity sufficient to provide all the meals for the new center and agreed to do so. This allowed considerable cost management for all the partners. However, HS meals, subsidized by the United States Department of Agriculture (USDA), are subject to a regulation about serving milk in pitchers that are left out on tables—supporting a family-style culture. On the other hand, the MR/DD board pays for meals with local tax levy generated funds and has a tradition of managing those funds frugally. This approach to serving milk seemed potentially very wasteful.

When the facility first opened, milk serving seemed like such a small issue that it was handled differently in each classroom. Then a regional HS administrative person visited the facility and noticed the lack of uniformity. The partners were advised that if a USDA inspector were to visit the site and see milk in any classroom being served any other way than in a pitcher, the agency providing the food service would not be reimbursed for any of the meals served. Regardless of what people thought about the regulation or the enforcement strategy, it became crystal clear that having common milk-serving practices was a matter of legitimate interdependence.

Finally, the above example also demonstrates how *trust and mutual respect* have grown out of the experiences that began with the future search process. Responsibility for serving milk is shared (controlled) by staff members and paid separately by each agency. If the MR/DD staff choose to serve milk the way they always have, there would be no regulatory sanction (accountability) for the board. However, the potential sanctions against the HS agency could have major consequences for that agency and for children served outside the partnership. HS has literally placed their ability to maintain their operating license in the hands of people over whom they have no direct control. Trust and mutual respect are built when all staff members agree to serve milk in a particular way in service of the shared goals, acknowledging explicitly what is at stake and sharing both control and accountability.

2003: WHAT HAS BEEN LEARNED?

"What is the long-term impact of this event going to be?" "Will the results of this event produce sustainable change?" These are questions that educational leaders have a right and responsibility to raise whenever someone, usually a consultant, promotes a particular planning strategy, especially if it includes pulling together a group of stakeholders for a two-and-a-half-day retreat and especially if it is intended to influence multiple subsystems as part of a larger system change process.

This story began with a future search focused on state-level policy. It moved to a future search focused on policies and practices at the local level. A third future search focused on the strategic plan of a single agency. Looking backward the developmental sequence seems logical and appropriate to having a long-term impact. The reality is that not one of us who was involved could have conceived such a story was about to unfold. Furthermore, if someone had tried to sell this storyline before it happened, imagine the litany of political posturing, "yes-butting" and other well-learned patterns of resistance that would have slowed the process dramatically or prevented it from starting at all.

One of the lessons of this story is that sustainable change often starts with an unanticipated opportunity. More important, it takes people who are disciplined optimists and strategic opportunists to link their own aspirations to those of others to achieve a common good. It also takes people willing to invest in building relationships based on trust and mutual respect despite past disappointments.

Virtually all the issues anticipated in any large, complex system existed in this one. While the governor could have proceeded to develop a strategic plan without investing the additional time and potential risk of including others, he and other champions in the system knew they needed to engage stakeholders in clarifying and articulating a shared vision and values if the plan was to have the desired impact. And, while some of the participants may have arrived at the first event with the intention of protecting turf instead of building common ground, the future search provided a setting in which they experienced an unprecedented sense of common ground in a very short period of time.

As the statewide plan unfolded there were people at the middle and line management levels of the system who embraced the opportunity and others who felt threatened by the proposed changes and big promises. At the service delivery level there was considerable mistrust of the wisdom and motives of public officials and bureaucrats who supported the plan. They wondered if children and families would experience any real benefits.

State government continues to frame its child-care and early education work in terms consistent with the results of the first conference. The local

FCF Councils still provide local leadership in adapting state policy to local conditions. A family cabinet made up of top-level officials of systems that affect the lives of children and families still meets to consider proactive opportunities and engage in problem solving.

Five years after the release of the county plan most of its goals had been achieved or significant progress was being made. Action For Children accomplished the goals of its three-year strategic plan in less than three years and developed a new three-year plan consistent with the values from all three future search events and committed to pushing the envelope even further. While the fact that these processes continue to operate more than 10 years after the first future search might be considered reasonable evidence of long-range, sustainable impact, one might wonder what the impact has been for children and families and the local public education system, as well as public and private human services that serve them.

At the school district level there is also evidence of sustainable change. In the spring of 2003 there was a long-anticipated opportunity to expand the services of the Family Partnership to the Columbus Public Schools. However, external pressures on the school system had made it difficult for this opportunity to get full attention. So few children were enrolled that there was a danger the program would not be able to operate. The partners quickly met with school officials. They learned that, while there had been three changes in the district's superintendent and senior administration, there were career educators in the system who remembered and invoked values, goals, and promises that had been articulated over the years with respect to CC/EE. The district renewed its commitment to the program and by the fall of 2003 it was fully enrolled.

Underlying every example of progress and success in this CC/EE story is the power of a shared vision rooted in institutional and individual relationships that have been developed over the years. These relationships are characterized by trust and mutual respect based on shared experiences of interdependence, including the experience of the vulnerability that comes with shared power, shared control, and shared accountability. In addition, these relationships are both strong enough and flexible enough to stand up to the complexity and volatility of changing economic, political, and social conditions in the broader community.

Future search conferences begin with the understanding that building sustainable futures requires bringing together diverse stakeholders and using the process of exploring the system's past, present, and future states to create the basis for a network of relationships. In addition, future search allows the stakeholders to begin to experience processes and build their skills at working together in new ways. This story of sustainable change and system resilience demonstrates that, with the help of disciplined optimists and strategic opportunists, a future search can be the critical first step in the journey of educational transformation.

15

Transforming a School of Education: Building System Coherence

Nancy Aronson, Rosemarie Barbeau, and
Karen Symms Gallagher

INTRODUCTION

This chapter is not about a future search in a school district. It is about a future search in a school of education, the Rossier School of Education (RSOE) at the University of Southern California (USC). We've included it because the experiences of this organization and the lessons learned are relevant and transferable to school districts. A school of education is an important partner in the overall education system. It shapes the future as it prepares leaders and researchers for the field. It faces similar challenges as school districts, for example, having large diverse constituencies; wrestling with issues of standards, relevance, and practical application; and wanting to impact the student experience in meaningful ways.

In addition to these factors, this case offers insights because the issues facing the organization were complex. RSOE was looking at systemic change, not tinkering around the edges of solving a particular problem. As you will see, the organization was highly fragmented. This is the story of its journey toward coherence.

In the four years since the future search conference, the Rossier School of Education has been able to show dramatic results that illustrate the power of future search to initiate systemic change. Products of this strategic planning methodology—the recommitment to the urban education mission, the consensus on four academic themes, and the development of a conceptual framework—have enabled the school to achieve a coherent, collective identity. Academic programs went from being a random collection of courses to four streamlined, coherent degree programs. For the first time in seven years RSOE had a balanced budget. It met summer tuition projections, thus starting fall semester without a revenue deficit. It improved its ranking in *U.S. News & World Report,* one indicator of how the school as a whole is gaining a more positive reputation and making significant strides in repositioning itself in the larger educational environment.

THEN AND NOW—JULY 2000 TO JUNE 2003

Table 15.1 provides a comparison of conditions and activities in the RSOE based upon the dean's entry impressions and as identified in the Academic Program Review (APR) Report in 2000 and as they were at the end of the academic year 2002–2003. This table is organized by the four broad areas addressed in the APR Report: academic programs, finances, infrastructure, and external perceptions. The examples of accomplishments demonstrate that the time and other resources invested in the future search and the subsequent activities did result in significant, measurable changes.

Core courses within the four academic degree programs support the conceptual framework. The doctorate in education (EdD), long the traditional trademark of the school, became the flagship, signature program. Faculty agreed to differentiate the EdD from the PhD and to focus on preparing educational leaders for practice. Core courses, organized around the four academic themes from the future search, and an integrated problem-based delivery replaced the old "It's my course and I'll do what I want" approach. In addition, by eliminating the typical discipline-based divisional structure, the EdD program no longer straddles two of the three divisions. EdD students now know that whatever their questions might be, they go to the EdD office for assistance.

The financial changes in the school are related directly to the restructuring of the school to program-based academic units. The school is experiencing its second year of balanced budgets and accurate tuition revenue projections. Faculty and staff understand the positive outcomes of reducing the number of courses, laying out a three-year plan of course sequences (EdD), and recruiting a targeted number of students who can only begin the EdD in the fall.

Table 15.1. Comparison of Conditions and Activities (Data from an Academic Program Review Report)

July 2000	*June 2003*
Academic Programs	
Discipline based and division centered (e.g., educational leadership, learning and instruction)	Program centered (e.g., PhD, EdD, master's)
	Some programs phased out, some programs enhanced, and new programs proposed
Collection of unconnected programs	Signature EdD program created and operational
Major overhaul needed: 23 degree programs and 35 full-time faculty	EdD is a practitioner-oriented degree for educational leaders
No distinguishing program differences between PhD and EdD	Core courses collaboratively developed and taught by full-time faculty
Individualistic and entrepreneurial: little faculty belief in the need to act collaboratively	Integrated content and problem-based approaches
	Areas of concentration have been collaboratively developed
	Critical standards about what is taught and how it is taught have been developed
Finances	
Roller-coaster budgets	Balanced budget in FY03
Had not correctly predicted revenue budget in five years	Enrollment targets for all programs
	Enrollment targets met for fall 2003
	First time in seven years RSOE met summer tuition projections, thus not starting fall semester with a revenue deficit
Infrastructure	
No consistency of recruitment or admission into the 23 degree programs	New roles for staff based on analysis of program needs; staff roles based on tasks to be accomplished for each program
Overlapping scheduling of required courses	
Faculty doing administrative roles because of lack of infrastructure	Executive director and four staff to administer EdD program
Low number of applications meant higher admission percentage	New schoolwide office of recruiting and admissions
Staff allocated based on faculty head count	New schoolwide office of accreditation and program quality
External Perceptions	
Individual accomplishment and reputation; faculty as a whole not highly regarded	Collective sense of direction
Few faculty involved in state or national educational organizations	Improved student test scores; larger applicant pool has led to greater selectivity of students
	Improved ranking in *U.S. News & World Report*
	Beginning to have a national presence (newsletters and journals)

Perhaps the most expensive aspect of the changes that have been made is the investment the school has made in infrastructure. All academic staff positions were redesigned to support the needs of EdD, PhD, master's, and BS degree programs in order to deliver the revised academic programs to the targeted student population. The commitment to world-class service by staff is matched by the organizational structures to support service delivery. For example, the EdD program has the largest number of academic staff, in part because it is the largest program and is in a two-year transition, implementing the new program while graduating the students who are in the old program. The school as a whole is gaining a more positive reputation and has made significant strides in repositioning itself in the larger educational environment, particularly on the campus and in professional education circles.

The key events, milestones, and principles that provided the track for this transformational journey are explained below.

IN THE BEGINNING—JULY 2000

Despite the fact that it's been three years since Karen Gallagher prepared to move to the University of Southern California (USC), she can vividly remember two strong images from her first visit to the Rossier School of Education (RSOE). To begin with, she was impressed with the leadership of the president and provost who had turned USC around in terms of student quality, curriculum coherence, and faculty reputation. Second, she was struck by how invisible the RSOE seemed—to the larger professional world of educators, to the internal stakeholders within the university, and to the faculty and staff within the school.

To be sure, the school has always had some strong, well-known faculty; excellent examples of men and women who have, through their scholarship and their teaching, made a difference in the lives of students and the directions of schools. Well-known graduates have made significant contributions to schools, school districts, colleges and universities, and state-level agencies. And yet the school as a whole had no reputation for meaningful contributions to education.

The school did have a particular image on campus. Although data were ambiguous, the school was known to have lower-quality students. It was also known as a good citizen, a place to put any and all projects which needed a home on campus but which did little to enhance the school's capacity for scholarship or professional practice. Like many other research universities, a few school of education faculty were highly regarded by faculty colleagues and university administrators alike, but they were viewed as exceptions to the general level of capability of faculty.

After a few weeks in her new role as dean, Karen realized that the faculty, staff, and, to a large extent, students had been acting as individual members of a loose confederation of programs. When she talked with faculty and staff individually, there was little direct knowledge of what others were doing. There was no belief in the need to act collectively, although most paid lip-service to ideas like "building a community of scholars." Most individuals confided that the best way to succeed at USC was to be an entrepreneur and to amass resources through grants, consulting, and/or students.

Contentious relationships between the faculty council and the dean's office, particularly during the previous two years, also had eroded any belief in the school's ability to move forward as a unit. To many outside the school, from alumni to senior university administrators, the school could not accomplish even seemingly simple tasks like offering required courses or showing up at statewide meetings.

The APR process at USC was revised in 1999, with the school of education in the first wave to undergo this extensive review. The University Committee on Academic Review (UCAR) recommended that the new dean develop a strategic plan and submit it to the university within a few months of the report's issuance. As the new dean, Karen agreed with the recommendation but not the time line. It would take more than a few months to develop a comprehensive plan. Having been a participant in a future search for the Lawrence Public Schools in Kansas (see chapter 1), she recognized the utility of this rigorous process as well as the importance to commit enough time to both the future search and follow-up activities.

THE JOURNEY FROM PLANNING THE FUTURE SEARCH TO APPROVAL OF THE CONCEPTUAL FRAMEWORK

From the future search in January 2001 to the approval of the conceptual framework that May, the faculty, staff, faculty council, and executive council had completed the tasks, made the decisions, and had the conversations necessary to make their ideas and aspirations a reality. Also, they had been able to do this in collaboration with their external partners. The activities leading up to the future search and concluding with the organization positioned for implementation are described below.

Planning the Future Search Conference

A planning group, formed in November 2000, brought the stakeholders around the table to begin this collaborative process. This in and of itself was a new way of operating. Group members included faculty representation across the discipline-based divisions of RSOE (with consideration of factors such as clinical and tenured faculty, ethnicity, and time at RSOE), K–12 administrators including a superintendent and a principal, an assistant dean, a staff member, a USC administrator from the provost's office, students, and the dean.

Stakes in the Future of RSOE

At the first meeting, participants were asked about their stake in the future of RSOE. What was their interest in being on this planning group? Answers to this question provided a way for the dean to gauge the energy and passion of others. She was able to get an initial read about how much interest and commitment was out there. This conversation was also an opportunity for the different stakeholders to hear what was important to each other. The comments listed below provide a glimpse into the dialogue that took place:

- The whole of the faculty is less than the sum of its parts. There is a need for an identity as a school—something that would enhance the whole.
- There is much individual talent and a need for coherence and collaboration.
- This is a teachable moment for us as a school.
- I want to be part of creating my future.
- There is a strong network (or potential network) out there just waiting to get behind something; RSOE has a rich tradition.

- I want the school to be nationally prominent, leading the dialogue on urban education, being relevant, doing research.

These ideas helped to shape the conference purpose and outcomes that were subsequently crafted by this group. They also began to set an intention. This is important, because when you consider the results, many of these interests have been addressed. It was not done by taking each of the underlying issues and problem solving. It was addressed by creating the desired future.

The Conference Theme and Purposes

The purpose, "Redesigning the RSOE Together: Leadership in Urban Education" emerged during the third planning meeting. The intent of "Redesigning" was to communicate that this was not just tweaking what they already had. "Together" was noted as a way to communicate the sense of community and desire for collaboration. "Leadership in Urban Education" reaffirmed the mission. The idea of a signature for the school began to take hold—an academic focus that would unify the RSOE as a whole. Academic themes would represent this type of focus. The desired outcomes created by the planning group follow:

- Determine academic themes which will serve as a framework for decision making;
- Begin to map implications of these themes for reviewing current degree programs and identifying new degree programs, identifying potential research priorities, developing nondegree programs, and promoting professional development opportunities;
- Organize for follow-up and action immediately after this conference; and
- Do this in a way that engages the faculty and reconnects the RSOE to the field.

Tensions Surface during the Planning

Certain tensions surfaced during the planning, stemming from issues that were highly charged and raised emotions. The discussion and subsequent clarity about each of them helped move the process forward to further shape the purpose and desired outcomes of the conference and people's commitment to them. These questions triggered important dialogues in the planning group.

What are the non-negotiables? One source of tension was the mission of the school, redefining excellence in urban education. The planning group did not have a shared meaning for this. Nor was there a shared commitment and enthusiasm for it within RSOE. A question was raised about whether the mission was up for discussion and perhaps even for a change at the future search. The dean was very clear that the mission was non-negotiable. Two other non-negotiables were the need for academic priorities and the university expectation that RSOE would be rated in the top 10 schools of education.

What do we mean by change? During the third meeting one of the veteran, tenured faculty members asked, "Are we creating something that everyone can just put what they already do under or is the intent to really narrow the focus of what we do? Could this lead to the elimination of some programs?" During the discussion, it became clear that the intent was to narrow the focus.

Are we really serious about making changes? Early in the planning there were serious questions about the capacity of this highly fragmented system to create a shared vision. Planning group members realized that the results of this conference were going to drive some critical decisions. This realization encouraged a large faculty turnout at the conference. Important business was going to be done.

Are a hundred people going to vote "yes" or "no" on my program? Tension rose about needing to make specific program decisions, that is, what courses will be offered versus creating a shared foundation for making those decisions. People kept bouncing from the big picture of the school to individual interests and "what's in it for me?" As people experienced the roller coaster of emotions—from excitement to anxiety, from hope to fear—it was hard for them to hold onto what was going to happen, when, and the interrelationships among the major areas of change needed.

The Future Search

The future search was held January 25–27, 2001. The participants included all RSOE faculty, USC administrators, representatives of the RSOE staff, alumni and current students, K–12 and higher education representatives, as well as community and foundation representatives. The common experiences, future scenarios for the school, and action plans provided the foundation for shaping the future direction of academic programs—RSOE's *signature*. The concrete outcome of the conference was the identification of four themes that would become the academic core: accountability, diversity, leadership, and learning. The intangible outcome was the momentum that launched the work of transforming the school.

Given the individualistic culture of RSOE and the high degree of fragmentation that existed in the organization, the identification of these themes represented a significant accomplishment. Much more collaborative work would need to occur over the next several months in order for faculty, in particular, to gain a much deeper level of shared meaning.

Implementation Planning Teams

The primary structure for continuing the work after the future search conference was the implementation planning teams (IPTs). Team leaders were selected based on interest, knowledge of the academic theme, and their ability to engage others in the process. The teams began work in mid-February 2001 and were open to any faculty and staff who wanted to join. Each team was responsible for clarifying and refining its academic theme and drafting a focus paper and presentation. Specifically, they were asked to produce a five-page white paper that would include the following information:

- A vision for the specific academic theme—including what the theme means for the RSOE;
- The link between the specific theme and the mission of RSOE; and
- The connection between the specific theme and the other academic themes.

The teams were also charged with working collaboratively, following the principles that had been experienced at the future search. They were asked to keep all meetings open and to encourage input from all stakeholder voices; suggested activities for the IPTs included focus groups, input forums, and faculty meetings.

The Challenge of Balancing Task and Process

The teams had a four-month time frame. The last all-faculty staff meeting, scheduled for May 10, 2001, was the deadline for teams to present their deliverables. The IPTs worked intensely to balance gathering ideas and feedback from others with developing their work product. It became very challenging for team members to manage their regular job responsibilities while working on the content of their theme and also paying attention to the engagement of others and the connections across the themes. This last issue, the connections across the themes, became increasingly important as the IPTs delved deeper into their specific areas. A natural tendency was to begin to lose sight of the whole. As a way of accommodating these multiple agendas, a one-day, large-group integration meeting was suggested.

The Integration Meeting

The integration meeting was held on March 30, 2001. This came at the halfway point in the IPTs' work. Once again it involved diverse stakeholders, many having attended the future search conference. Specific goals of this day-long meeting included 1) to more deeply understand the themes and see the connections and interrelationships between them, 2) to begin to weave the themes together to create RSOE's unique signature, and 3) to maintain the dialogue across all stakeholder groups.

In the opening, participants were told that the results of this meeting would be used to develop the conceptual framework—a more in-depth description of the interrelationships between these themes that comprise the signature of the school. The team leaders and the executive council, including the dean and the associate deans, would be guiding the next steps of the process based on the outputs of this meeting.

Acceptance of the Conceptual Framework

Outcomes of the integration meeting included common linkages, underlying constructs across the themes, and a recommendation to move into drafting an integration document. At this point, the team leaders and executive council determined that the major work of the IPTs had been completed, and it was time to move to creating the conceptual framework. One writer, with the help of others, created a draft. It was critiqued in April and unanimously approved by faculty on May 10. This two-page conceptual framework had the following sections: 1) "The Primary Educational Challenges of the 21st Century"; 2) "What Is Urban Education?"; 3) "Mission Statement"; 4) "Four Themes"; and 5) "The Future of the RSOE."

IMPLEMENTING THE CONCEPTUAL FRAMEWORK

From May 2001 until the writing of this chapter beginning in June 2003, the conceptual framework has served as a touchstone, a powerful reference point for the work of implementation. All work products and key decisions have been checked against the conceptual framework. Three major paths of work occurred: academic program review, curriculum development for the doctoral programs, and the development of the infrastructure to support the academic programs.

Academic Program Review

In the fall of 2001, criteria were developed and approved for academic program review. This enabled data-based decision making in evaluating current offerings and also provided guidance for future decisions. An external evaluation team undertook an independent program review (IPR) of the doctoral programs using these criteria. One result of this review was that six academic programs were phased out.

Curriculum Development for the Doctoral Programs

In the early winter of 2001, two curriculum teams were created to plan the EdD and PhD curriculum frameworks. Given that the EdD was to be the signature program of the school and a major source of revenue generation, tremendous focus was put on the development of this program. In December 2002, the faculty unanimously approved the new EdD curriculum. In February 2003, the new EdD program was approved by the university's Graduate and Professional Studies Committee (GPSC). Indeed, GPSC called the program submission a model. This was particularly notable because two years earlier, this same group had criticized the RSOE for having no curricular standards.

Infrastructure

In the fall of 2002, as the curriculum work on the EdD program was nearing completion, a restructuring steering task force was formed to develop recommendations for changing from divisions to a program-based structure. In April 2003, the university approved the RSOE plan to completely restructure the academic support staff. This represented a tremendous affirmation of the work that the RSOE had accomplished.

Impact on Students

How does all this translate to the student experience? Starting in the fall of 2003, 160 EdD students began their academic program. During their first year they will take core courses in accountability, diversity, leadership, and learning. In year two they can choose from one of four concentrations: 1) K–12 educational leadership (principals and superintendents), 2) community college leadership, 3) teacher education in a multicultural society, and 4) educational psychology and human performance. In year three, working in cohorts, they will begin their dissertations.

PRACTICES THAT SUPPORTED THE TRANSFORMATION

In addition to the work described in the previous section, certain leadership practices helped to create the path to transforming the school. These practices included orienting people to what was happening, clearly delineating how decisions would be made, and sharing information.

Orienting People

The dean paid attention to orienting people to the present situation. On a regular basis, she framed larger system issues such as where the school fits in the educational environment, both locally and nationally. She also developed a certain rhythm of orienting people to where the school was in the transformation process. Major meetings, whether large group, ad hoc, or faculty and staff, opened with a description of "where we've been, where we are, and what's next." This helped orient people to the dimension of time. It often involved the decision-making trail—reminding people of prior decisions and how they had built to the particular point in time. This practice is especially important in complex, identity-shifting change efforts because it helps reground people during times of high anxiety.

Decision Making

From the beginning of this effort, the dean was clear about the decision-making process. Some decisions were leader directed. For example, the mission was a non-negotiable. What was open for discussion and development were the academic themes and conceptual framework. Faculty groups, with input from other stakeholders, identified and added more depth to the themes and developed the conceptual framework. But only the faculty had final approval of the conceptual framework. Continually clarifying these roles helped create traction for the process to unfold. For the most part, groups did not spend time debating and spinning around issues that were not within their span of decision making.

Open Sharing of Information

Throughout the process, information was shared openly. For example, to provide a better understanding of current realities, faculty and other relevant stakeholders received the results from the various evaluations of the RSOE. As Richard Axelrod (2000) states, "Information lets the organization know what is happening in both the external and internal environments. Equipped with this information, the organization can make appropriate decisions" (pp. 148–49). Many of these reports, for example, the academic performance review (APR) and independent program review (IPR), pointed out some significant challenges and gaps between the school's intention and its impact. Jim Collins (2001) discusses the importance of confronting the harsh realities while creating a vision of possibility for the future: "Yes, leadership is about vision. But leadership is equally about creating a climate where the truth is heard and the brutal facts confronted" (p. 74). This occurred at the RSOE.

Another aspect of this practice is sharing information in its formative stage. As the IPTs were developing each of the four themes, they distributed their work for feedback and further shaping by others. The same was true as the conceptual framework was being crafted. This iterative process helped bring people along, so when it was time for a decision, more people had a deeper understanding and could support the work.

SYSTEM COHERENCE

Michael Fullan (2001) identifies five dimensions of leadership critical to effecting systemic change: providing moral purpose, understanding change, building relationships, creating and sharing knowledge, and making the system coherent. It is this last element, coherence making, which sparked our interest because of its relevance for so many situations in education today. Fullan (1999) also states:

> With change forces abounding, it is easy to experience overload, fragmentation and incoherence. In fact, in education this is the more typical state. Policies get passed independent of each other; innovations are introduced before previous ones are adequately implemented, the sheer presence of problems and multiple unconnected solutions are overwhelming (p. 27).

Does this sound familiar? It did to us, and it provided a stepping-off point for a deeper analysis of what had occurred at the RSOE.

System Coherence and Organizational Change

The key theme of this chapter is the RSOE's continuing journey from a fragmented system that was largely invisible to a coherent system with a collective identity. Our notion of system coherence emerged as we began to look at the organization change elements that could be found consistently across time in the change process of the school—from the work of the planning group through the future search conference and integration meeting and then on through the change work of the next two and a half years. These elements began to organize themselves into four key dimensions of system coherence: conceptual, contextual, relational, and task.

It became clear that each of the four dimensions was required for real organizational change to occur. Working all four dimensions continuously makes possible the shift from a fragmented collection of individuals to an organization that has a shared sense of direction, with sufficient clarity and momentum to enable people to take action in a coordinated way. When this type of action is sustained over time, fundamental change can occur. Each dimension is described in detail below, along with some concrete examples to help illustrate them.

Conceptual Coherence

Conceptual coherence relates to getting clarity and agreement on the big picture—who we are and where we're headed. People also refer to this as "getting on the same page." We saw three aspects of conceptual coherence as we looked across the change process at RSOE: the key building blocks of the school's collective identity, a collective sense of direction, and the change process itself.

Conceptual clarity and agreement on the key building blocks of identity involve the following types of questions: What is our mission and purpose as a school? Who are we as an organization, as distinct from a random collection of individuals? What do we care about? Where are our existing strengths?

Coming into the future search, the dean had identified as a non-negotiable that the mission of the school would continue to be urban education. At the conference participants, who previously had little cohesion or understanding about the mission, recommitted to it and developed initial conceptual clarity about its meaning.

The second aspect of conceptual coherence involves conceptual clarity and agreement on a collective sense of direction: Where are we headed as an academic institution? What are the academic themes that will form the basis for decision making about degree programs, curriculum, faculty hiring, student recruitment, organizational structure, etc.? What is our path forward?

In the future search, participants agreed on four academic themes around which the RSOE would reorganize itself. This shared set of themes was vital for RSOE, as it is an academic, research-oriented institution. A sufficient level of conceptual rigor was, therefore, required to establish the credibility of the change effort.

At the future search a path was established to develop the four themes into a robust, integrated conceptual framework or signature for the school. The immediate next step was to ask subgroups of faculty and other stakeholders to develop the themes more fully. This would be followed with reconvening the larger group to then begin to weave the themes into a conceptual framework, integrated and robust enough to serve as a driver for decision making for the school as it reorganized itself.

The third area of conceptual coherence involves working continually to develop conceptual clarity throughout the organization about the change process. This includes clarity about the key milestones and their timing, as well as a picture of the end state of the change process. One of the best examples of this was the roadmap for change that the dean created, refined with the planning group, and brought into the future search (see figure 15.1). The roadmap is a visual of the four trails (academic program, budget, infrastructure, and morale) and shows where the future search fit into the larger picture. The roadmap enabled people to quickly understand the various streams of change work that were underway, which elements of the work were included in the future search, and which were being dealt with elsewhere. It also gave a clear sense of the timing and sequencing of the work of the various streams.

Another practice for supporting conceptual clarity about the change process, as mentioned previously, involves telling and updating the story of "where we have been in this change process, where we are now, where we are going." Karen uses this practice whenever she is orienting a person or group for the first time to the change process, at key decision-making points with governance groups, and when working with task groups on the next phase of the work.

Contextual Coherence

Contextual coherence is about being connected to and aligned with our environment. It is about understanding clearly the broader context, or environment, in which the school operates, and then ensuring that the interests of the school are aligned with those of its external stakeholders.

Contextual coherence began with the representation of several key external stakeholder groups in the planning group: a member from the USC provost's office, a K–12 superintendent, and an urban principal. At the

Appendix 15.1: The Action Plan Road Map

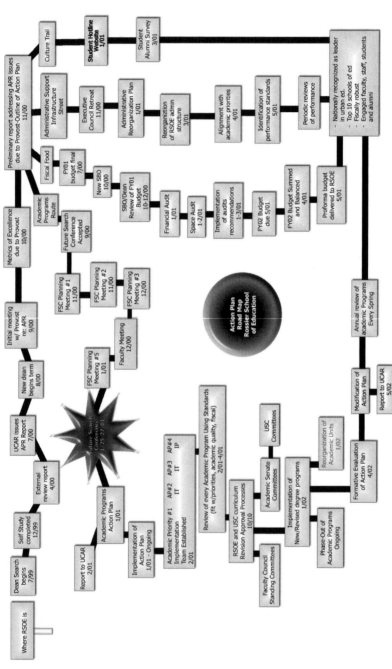

Figure 15.1. Action Plan Roadmap (Illustration by Nita St. Hilaire of AIM Strategies, Inc.)

future search, where 50 percent of the attendees were stakeholders from outside the school, the faculty was able to engage in dialogue and establish deeper relationships with them. Having these external representatives also provided the school with a "reality check" as it went about identifying the four academic themes. It was an opportunity to test whether the emerging direction of the school addressed the needs and expectations of those in the external context. As one principal attending the future search stated, her hope for the school was to "do somebody some good" or to focus the school in a way that made a concrete difference in the lives of students and their schools.

Early in the implementation of the conceptual framework, the dean and her executive council established criteria for academic program change, which included keeping in mind the interests of those outside the school.

After the future search, a highly focused communication plan was developed. This provided an opportunity to create messages for the broader university community and the large educational environment—California educators, other schools of education, and educational leaders on a national level.

Relational Coherence

There seem to be two interrelated aspects of relational coherence: shared ownership and clear decision-making roles. The first focuses on bringing people together and bringing people along—building a critical mass of ownership and commitment to action. The second focuses on governance and the relationship of different groups and entities to each other.

At the heart of shared ownership is building sufficient relationships to establish shared meaning and common ground—the basis for action. Relationships were built during the future search through the active engagement and involvement of each of the key stakeholder groups inside the school: faculty, staff, students, and the dean's office. People came to understand each other more deeply, saw the goals and aspirations they held in common, and as a result began to build trust across stakeholder groups. Relational coherence is a critical element of the *how* to the *what* of conceptual and contextual coherence.

Relational coherence also has to do with linking parts of the system with each other. The planning group meetings, the future search, and the integration meeting brought people together and created opportunities for connection (coherence) across organizational boundaries. For example, the planning group brought together people from across critical organizational boundaries: faculty council, each of the divisions, alumni, students, administration, and the field. The integration meeting brought people together across the academic themes. After the integration meeting, another method of building relational coherence evolved, with a senior faculty member serving in the role of organizational weaver, meeting with various task groups as they worked. He passed on information and planted seeds of the common ground he was hearing. By the time people came together for decision making, there were few surprises when recommendations were shared.

The second aspect of relational coherence relates to governance—the institutionalized roles and processes that make up the normal decision-making structure of the school. This governance structure, operating as designed, helps provide coherence to the change process. Decision rights are clear. For example, the faculty has a decision-making responsibility around areas like academic programs, concentrations, course offerings, and admission standards. The dean has a decision-making role in budget and scheduling.

Another example involved the creation of the four academic themes and the resulting conceptual framework. Although many stakeholders participated in the cocreation of the themes, according to the governance structure, the faculty in its role needed to approve the conceptual framework. Perhaps because most of them had been involved in the work getting to the conceptual framework, it was resoundingly approved.

Closely related to relational coherence is the final dimension, task coherence.

Task Coherence

Task coherence relates to action and accountability—who does what, in what time frame. Task coherence, in the context of the change process, refers to the support of ongoing action and task completion over time, which enables fundamental change to occur. At the core of task coherence is a set of functions that include identification of work to be done; sequencing of tasks—such that the right thing happens at the right time; selection of the right people to work on these tasks; bringing the completed work products in front of the appropriate governance groups for approval/ validation; and meeting deadlines.

The stewardship of task coherence at the RSOE was very much a leadership function. It began with the dean's establishment of the future search planning group, with the task in this case being the delivery of a conference. The task of the conference was the creation of the four academic themes. The next task was to explore each theme more deeply, hence the commissioning of the implementation planning teams. The integration meeting had as its task the integration of the four academic themes into the beginning of a conceptual framework.

Most of the concrete changes occurred after the implementation meeting. This work involved a focus on both task coherence and relational coherence. It involved a determination of what work needed to be done, what organizational commitment was required to support the results, and then who should do the work. Much of the work was done by ad hoc committees, established to complete a specific task and then disbanded when the task was complete. Some examples follow:

- Steering groups were formed to guide the redesign of the EdD and PhD programs. Every faculty member participated on the EdD steering group. Together the faculty made the ultimate decisions about areas of concentration and course offerings. The chairs of the EdD steering group were two professors—one representing the tenured faculty and one representing the clinical faculty. This was an example of relational coherence in service of task coherence, bringing together the thinking of two key groups inside the faculty (relational) to get the best results (task) that would also result in the most support for the outcomes (relational).
- Another committee reviews curriculum from a systemwide perspective versus the previous division-by-division determination of curriculum. The committee is made up of faculty from across the former divisional boundaries.
- A restructuring steering group was formed of faculty, staff, students, administration, and alumni. A subgroup of that committee, made up of staff, analyzed the work that the old academic staff was doing. This analysis formed the basis for a redesign of the academic support staff

structure that would be supporting the new program-centered organization.

The key theme here is the establishment of tasks, paired with a selection of people to work on these tasks, driven by whoever has the most information for the task as well as who needs to support the end-state work of the task group.

REFLECTIONS

In the writing of this chapter, the three of us have probably spent 100-plus hours in dialogue. This opportunity for reflection has deepened our own understanding of systemic change, particularly with respect to an organization's journey from fragmentation to coherence, the critical role of leadership, and the robustness of future search as a methodology.

During one of our conversations about this chapter Karen said to us, "We would not be where we are without the future search, and the future search alone would not have been enough." The future search planning gives the system what Barry Oshry (1996) calls a "time out of time." It creates an opening. Inside this opening, activities occur and new ways of being a system are experienced that create a readiness for the coherence dimensions (conceptual, contextual, relational, and task) to ripen and evolve. The future search shifts things long enough for bigger shifts to happen.

Many systems recognize that in order to be more effective they need to operate more coherently. They may not use this term. They may use phrases like "we're too siloed" or "we operate as independent contractors." Because the future search gives the system an experience in working in a more coherent, integrated way, continuing to operate in this way after the conference becomes more possible—not inevitable, but more possible.

The future search is robust because the coherence dimensions are embedded in the methodology—its set of principles, practices, and tools. As a result of a future search, people are clearer about where the organization is headed and are better connected to the larger environment. They have more understanding and trust for each other, and they know some steps to take to make things happen. The future search is so robust because it operationalizes the coherence dimensions as a way of working. It is both a pathway and a pivot point.

Following the conference, continuing work must occur across the four coherence dimensions to sustain commitment and action, achieve deeper levels of change, and produce results. In some organizations the work across the dimensions continues almost unconsciously because it's part of the way the organization does business. In many organizations, the work has to be more intentional. There seem to be three variables that bring about change in an organization:

- Where the organization is on the fragmentation–coherence continuum, that is, the current degree of fragmentation in how the organization operates.
- The level of change desired, that is, incremental or transformational.
- The level of leadership focus required (intentionality and follow through).

The more fragmented an organization is at the beginning of a change process and the more transformational the desired change, the greater the need for leadership focus. In the RSOE there was an extremely fragmented system in need of a huge transformational change called "redesigning the whole system." Given this starting point and level of desired results, this initiative required a very intensive leadership focus and attention to building coherence in each of the four dimensions over a long period of time.

The principles of future search support leaders to help bring about systemic change. They enabled the RSOE to focus on its urban education mission and how the mission would drive the program. The future search conference and the follow-up integration meeting enabled the faculty to gain conceptual coherence about the mission of excellence in urban education. The future search conference also helped focus the internal stakeholders (faculty) on the contextual realities. Thus the mission had to address the expectations of the greater university and its leadership and the needs of the educational profession in Los Angeles and the world. As the RSOE moved to shared meaning on these two dimensions of systemic coherence, the school's leadership, its faculty and staff, and the external stakeholders could deal with much more difficult aspects of building coherence; that is, changing the long-term relationships and work patterns. Indeed, a complex organization like the RSOE could not have moved developmentally from the conceptual and contextual agreement to aligning relationships and tasks without the common-ground vision for the future coming from the future search.

16

Kansas State Department of Education: Hope and a Sense of Possibility in a Time of Scarcity and Despair

Nancy Aronson, Rosemarie Barbeau, and Alexa Posny

INTRODUCTION

The goals gave us certainty and clarity. Because the goals were created with a broad mix of stakeholders, they resonated with others. When we shared them with people who had not been at the future search conference, they said, "Yes, these are right on target."

—Andy Tompkins, commissioner of education, Kansas

This quotation illuminates the core of the value of a future search—a process that enables a system to get clarity of direction and get people on board. While these results often occur in a future search, the economic and political realities surrounding the state of Kansas made the results of this case even more noteworthy.

This is a story about leadership. It is about leadership creating hope and a sense of possibility during a time of scarcity and despair. What may be surprising to some readers is that it is about a state department of education, an entity that is often perceived by others as an obstruction rather than as a meaningful, constructive partner in quality education. This is the story about the leadership journey of the Kansas State Department of Education (KSDE) and the pivotal role the future search played. This is a case of systemic change in an agency (often viewed as bureaucratic and intransigent) and how it led systemic educational change within a state.

Although this chapter is about a state department of education, it is very relevant to individual school districts because they share the same concerns and pressures. Both state and local levels must consider federal legislation and budget restrictions. Both often feel the pressure of high visibility and high stakes in today's educational environment. A high degree of collaboration among levels of the educational system (state department/districts/schools) is now required. Methods, such as future search, that facilitate the meeting of common goals are essential. This model of engaging levels of a system is transferable and effective regardless of which level initiates the engagement.

CONTEXT

The external pressures surrounding KSDE coupled with the internal realities in its own development created a rich leadership opportunity.

External Pressures

In 2001–2002 sweeping federal legislation impacted education across the country. The Elementary and Secondary Education Act (ESEA) was reauthorized under the title No Child Left Behind (NCLB). As a result of this legislation, states, local school districts, and specifically schools were being held more accountable for student performance than ever before in U.S. history. At that time, Kansas ranked high on educational measures, including nationally standardized tests. For example, Kansas has consistently ranked in the top 10 percent on the National Assessment of Educational Progress (NAEP). However, as in other states, the NCLB legislation meant devoting intensive work to developing systems for monitoring student growth based on increasingly higher expectations and more challenging standards.

At the same time economic circumstances in Kansas were dire. Budget shortfalls resulted in severe cuts for education. At the local level, districts were cutting staff at a time when they were being held to higher standards. Resources were scarce in many districts and feelings of vulnerability and despair prevailed.

KSDE Realities

A state department of education has a significant leadership role in the system of education (as do districts, schools, and classrooms). Under the leadership of the commissioner and his top leadership team, the role of KSDE had been moving away from one of compliance to one of leadership and support for learning in the schools. The highly prescriptive federal legislation was increasing the tension relating to the sustainability of this shift.

Even before the legislation was formalized, KSDE had made significant changes in its school accreditation process (QPA). Using the 12-year history of accrediting schools as well as QPA task force recommendations and results from a QPA survey, the accreditation process changed to a system that specified consistent criteria, added quality indicators, and clearly reflected federal accountability measures. Much of this change was congruent with the anticipated direction of the federal legislation.

The agency also had internal goals. It had been working on a continuous improvement process for the last several years. Customer satisfaction results from school districts and other stakeholders were generally positive. Yet the commissioner felt strongly that the agency could be even better. It needed to be reenergized, particularly about its role for the future. The commissioner had a clear sense that getting the right people in the room could help refocus and revitalize the agency and, at the same time, have a broader impact on education in the state. Alexa Posny, the assistant commissioner and one of the coauthors of this chapter, had been a parent at a future search conference in her child's school in 1994. She was familiar with the process and thought the principles of high engagement with a task focus could be effective here.

The core of the mission of KSDE was "to provide leadership, support and innovation to maximize results for all students." The leadership of KSDE believed it important to bring key stakeholders together to think through what this mission meant for the future strategic directions of the agency. The leadership also saw the potential for all levels of the educational system to be aligned. Convening a three-day future search conference to determine these strategic directions was a way to engage people deeply enough, and for a long enough period of time, to develop a shared picture of the future.

THE FUTURE SEARCH

Planning and Convening the Conference

Initial thinking and planning for the future search began within KSDE in the fall of 2001. The top agency leadership worked with its direct reports, the leadership team, to broaden support for engaging stakeholders in shaping the agency's future and getting clarity on the purposes it could serve. The ideas from the leadership team would be brought into the first planning group meeting scheduled for February 2002. During this time the consultants facilitated a leadership team orientation meeting and kept in regular contact with the three top leaders: Andy Tompkins, commissioner of education; Dale Dennis, deputy commissioner of the Division of Fiscal and Administrative Services; and Alexa Posny, assistant commissioner of the Learning Services Division. In January 2002 a pivotal conversation occurred between the top leadership of KSDE and the consultants. The realities and tensions of ESEA called into question whether or not to even have the conference. ESEA was having an enormous impact. The time deadlines were very tight and dramatic changes were called for. Compounding this was a $500 million state budget shortfall. Budgets were tight and potential participants might be concerned about the appearance of spending local money to attend a planning conference.

The commissioner, deputy commissioner, and assistant commissioner decided it was an opportunity. They believed leadership had a role in providing hope in a time of despair. By bringing the system together to collaborate on the future, KSDE was fulfilling that role. This was exemplified in how Andy Tompkins opened the conference on June 24, 2002. He asked the strategic partners of the Kansas State Department of Education (KSDE) not to get mired in the significant financial challenges being faced by the state and instead invited people to think and talk about the most meaningful role the agency could play in moving forward. One hundred stakeholders representing district-level administration, principals, teachers, students, parents, business and the community, legislators, chamber of commerce, higher education, KSDE staff, educational foundations, and the Kansas State Board of Education came together to shape the future of KSDE. The specific desired outcomes of the conference articulated by the planning group included 1) a shared vision of the role of

KSDE: what it would look like for KSDE to fulfill its role of leadership, support and innovation; 2) a set of strategic directions; and 3) an idea pool for members of KSDE to use as they planned to implement the strategic directions.

The planning and convening of the conference illustrated the two levels of leadership. One was the agency leadership of Andy Tompkins, Alexa Pochowski, and Dale Dennis. The other was the future leadership role of KSDE that was being collaboratively determined with other stakeholders in the conference.

As in all future search conferences, participants studied the past, reviewed the present, and envisioned their desired future. In this conference, in consultation with the leadership and the planning group, the consultants adapted some of the activities in order to create a rich context for the decision making about KSDE's strategic directions. These adaptations included

- Adding a fourth time line to the study of the past: personal, global, organization (KSDE), and education in Kansas.
- Having an activity called "State of the State" where participants used the Kansas State Board of Education goals to create a database about what is happening now (current best practices) and possibilities for the future.
- Designing a "Gallery Walk" so participants had a chance to walk around the conference room to look at and reflect on the above information.
- Taking the common-ground themes and drafting strategic directions after the conference close of day 2 and receiving feedback on day 3. This work by Andy Tompkins and Alexa Posny accelerated the development of a common picture of KSDE's future role.

Outcomes of the Conference

By the end of the 16 hours of work, conference participants had developed eight strategic directions. Each strategic direction was accompanied by a listing of ideas and possible initiatives. Following the conference, others became engaged in refining the strategic directions to make them meaningful and usable for the agency. Between August and October 2002, groups within KSDE refined the goals, identified outcomes, formulated an implementation plan, and developed measurement criteria. In early November, feedback was gathered from agency personnel and the original participants of the future search. The final version of the strategic directions was completed in December 2002:

- *Strategic Direction 1:* Provide leadership to ensure a quality workforce with KSDE and school districts.
- *Strategic Direction 2:* Become a recognized resource for best practices.
- *Strategic Direction 3:* Provide leadership for utilization of technology to enhance the educational system.
- *Strategic Direction 4:* Develop a coordinated and streamlined system for service delivery.
- *Strategic Direction 5:* Provide leadership for designing educational systems to meet the learning needs of all students.
- *Strategic Direction 6:* Create partnerships for advocacy of education for all students.

RESULTS

The results of the KDSE future search can be described in two ways: 1) broad impacts both internal and external to the KSDE and 2) accomplishments related to specific strategic directions following the conference.

Broad Impacts of the Future Search

When asked what she saw as the most important outcome of the future search, Alexa Posny pointed to the strides made inside KSDE: "It has changed the way we operate and think. We are breaking down the silos and barriers. We are having a common conversation about what is best for schools; there is true partnership and collaboration."

One example of this is the recent creation by agency staff of the school report card that was then used to measure the adequate yearly progress (AYP) of every school in Kansas, in support of the No Child Left Behind Act. The way in which it was developed within the agency represented a significant shift. It involved collaboration across programs, operations, technology, finance, and other roles within the agency. Alexa states, "That people were able to work so collaboratively was an amazing feat. In the past, communication and responsibility for tasks would have had to go through the silos." As a result of the high level of collaboration, more agency staff are more informed of the substance of the entire report card and are able to answer questions about it from the field.

According to Andy Tompkins, "The best outcome was the clarity of focus." He sees the agency staff continually working on five out of six of the strategic directions. Team leaders now develop their individual team goals to support these directions. The sixth, designing educational systems to meet the learning needs of all students, clearly cuts across the other strategic directions and will be worked on continuously over time.

In addition, the new strategic directions provided an increased focus as a total agency. In the past, team leaders would have been exclusively focused on their own team and their own day-to-day operations. Now there is more thinking in terms of the whole agency—looking at the big picture. A unifying phrase used throughout the organization to describe their shared role as an agency is "instructional leadership with a relentless focus on student results."

Integrated, cross-functional databases are being developed. As Dale Dennis, deputy commissioner summarizes, "Internally, it caused a lot of us to rethink where we are going and how to get there—and to work more together as a team."

External to the KSDE, important strides have also been made as a result of the future search. As Dale Dennis says, "It helped create a vision and focus for the state. It became more state-wide, rather than just being for us." It resulted, he says, in many more educators focusing on academic achievement for all kids. Rather than having conversations about blame, people are asking, "How can we solve the problem?" Rather than "How well are our buses running?" people are focused on "How well are our students doing?"

At one point, we summarized what we had heard from Alexa Posny by saying to her, "It sounds like people are much more on the same page and aligned." She pointed out that that was far too conceptual a way of stating the outcome, "There was more emotion involved, there was buy-in, everyone focused on the same thing." In fact, a network was created at the future search, a greater bonding and connection among people. When the NCLB legislation hit, instead of fragmentation and people pulling apart, the bonds got deeper. Even more focus occurred across levels. It was the dialogue at the future search that was the beginning of a common understanding and the recognition that "We need to work with each other."

The primary role of the agency has shifted. The question within the agency has changed from "How do we get schools to comply?" to "What is best for schools?" In spite of the increased demands of NCLB, the schools and districts see the shift at KSDE away from simply a compliance role. The requests from the field reflect this shift. Questions have more depth; they go way beyond asking for clarification about paperwork details. Alexa Posny points out, "They call us about all sorts of things now." Andy Tompkins adds, "If the field comes to us now with a problem, they believe we will help solve the problem."

Alexa Posny sees an increasing need in education for models of successful processes for collaboration in meeting common goals across all levels of the system, especially in today's context of financial constraints and the level of challenge that comes with the No Child Left Behind legislation. "No one of us is unaffected by what may or may not be happening at other levels of the system."

Accomplishments by Strategic Direction

The discussion that follows and table 16.1 delineate KSDE's accomplishments since the future search. The focus of Strategic Direction 1 was to ensure a quality workforce, both within the agency as well as in the field. The emphasis was always on quality—quality KSDE staff and quality educators. One of the most notable accomplishments in this area has been the shift in how positions are advertised, resulting in more highly qualified and experienced people applying for positions within KSDE. Changes have been made to the electronic educator employment board, resulting in over 2 million hits, 22,000 registered users, and 1,850 teachers hired last year. Two new recognition programs were established. The Horizon Award, in conjunction with the Kansas Confidence in Public Education Task Force and the Kansas Education Association, now recognizes those first-year teachers who are "up and comers" in the profession. The Challenge Award, in conjunction with Kansas National Education Association (KNEA) and KASB (Kansas Association of School Boards), now recognizes schools that have overcome significant

Table 16.1. Accomplishments for Six Strategic Directions

Then	Now
#1: Ensure a quality work force	
Recruitment difficult	Recruitment wide-ranging
Settled for what was available	Keep looking until the right person is found
Sought applicants via newspaper ads	Enhanced advertising strategies including electronic
Emphasized content expertise	Emphasize leadership capabilities
	Provide interview training for all staff
Ad-hoc leadership training	Focused leadership training
Collected data on educator supply	Advocate for specific components in educator supply
#2: Become a recognized resource for best practices	
Provided information requested from schools	Department proactively assists schools through a variety of tools with greater access
Provided data on achievement to schools	Provides assistance to help schools use data effectively to make decisions
Focused on legal interpretations and compliance monitoring	Provides focused technical assistance resulting in what works for students/schools
#3: Use technology to enhance the educational system	
Paper reports from schools	Web-based reports from schools
A variety of technology hardware, software, and programs	A standard technology system with integrated software
Text-based school report card	User-friendly data charts and graphic-based school and district report card
#4: Develop a coordinated and streamlined system for service delivery	
Technical assistance specific to each agency team	Technical assistance collaboratively provided by integrated support teams (ISTs)
Focused on compliance and completion of paperwork	Focused on technical assistance and solving problems
"Do things right"	"Do the right things"
#5: Design educational systems to meet the learning needs of all students	
Focus on improvements in the current structure	Focus on ensuring the system meets the needs of all students and is based on seven core principles of system redesign
Change in practice based on interest	Change in practice based on research and focused on student learning
#6: Create partnerships for advocacy of education for all students	
Communicated with the field via paper and mail	Communicate electronically with the field via e-mail
Each team communicated separately	Coordinate communication through the use of listserves
Infrequent	Timely and more frequent
Little formal or informal contact with federal congressional delegation	Purposeful formal contact with all federal delegations, leading to informal contact via e-mails with ongoing input actively sought; developed results-based legislative recommendations

(*continued*)

Table 16.1. Accomplishments for Six Strategic Directions (*continued*)

Then	Now
Nationally recognized teacher recognition program	Expanded the teacher of the year program to include recognizing first-year teachers (Horizon Awards) and developed the Challenge Awards to recognize schools making progress with a large proportion of disadvantaged students

obstacles and positively impacted the academic achievement of disadvantaged students.

Strategic Direction 2, to become a resource for best practices, arose from the need to view and use KSDE as a repository for best practices. The field felt strongly that KSDE should identify and collect current information on best practices; disseminate this information; provide linkages between and among partners, organizations, and other stakeholders; and create online professional development. Of significant note is the development of a web-based best practices instructional tool that links the state curricular standards with instructional lesson plans, current research, and other instructional resources. At quarterly meetings held by KSDE, all 120 state curriculum leaders share what they are doing to meet the needs of all students. Information shared at the meetings becomes web-based and is offered online, making it available to any and all staff in the state.

Part of the intent of the Strategic Direction 3 was to create the technological tools to provide schools and districts with an interactive database that would eliminate redundancy of information and lead to a qualitative and quantitative data management system to assist in decision making and classroom instruction. Nearly all of the reports that schools must now submit to the agency are web-based. It is expected that the entire system will be integrated within the next year. Then, schools will only have to enter demographic data once each year. KSDE now has the ability to develop reports that the schools may have had to generate in the past. In addition, districts and schools will have ready access to their own integrated data.

Specific to Strategic Direction 4 was the need from the field for decentralized and regionalized assistance to constituents, including working with other related agencies to provide technical assistance. Of greatest significance was the operationalization of cross-team work in response to NCLB. An important aspect of KSDE's leadership role is that of providing professional development for other service providers. KSDE has implemented monthly in-house training for regional service center personnel to coordinate the work of their professional development providers who assist schools and districts in bringing best practices and providing information and support to meet the requirements of state and federal requirements.

KSDE has also formed integrated district support teams (DSTs) that represent special education, Title I, and school accreditation team members. These teams are assigned regionally in the state to assist schools to improve. These DSTs consistently meet to review data, develop needs assessments, plan services, and provide technical assistance for these schools. Never before have program personnel representing specific funding streams (e.g., special education, Title I, or school accreditation) worked collaboratively to assist schools in making curricular and instructional changes based on student results.

Additionally, a teachers' listserv has been developed and a specific plan to support school improvement has been implemented.

Of special note, in the past, each program area would develop its own content-specific presentations and workshops to deliver across the state. The impact on the field was twofold:

• Overload: more and more information, mandates, and compliance details to be managed.
• Fragmentation: both duplication of information being required by different program areas and "disconnects" across programs with little sense of the whole or how the pieces fit.

Now, three program areas—special education, school improvement, and state and federal programs—have developed a joint workshop on No Child Left Behind, quality performance assessment (statewide school improvement), and CIM (special education continuous improvement monitoring). They integrated the information and multiple teams with cross-program representation conducted over 50 workshops across the state. The workshops were very well received.

In partnership with stakeholders, Strategic Direction 5 focused on removing real or perceived barriers to redesigning education as we now know it. It also looked at developing a single accountability system for all schools. This system would ensure that students met high standards, leading to high academic achievement for all. The most significant progress made in reaching this strategic direction was the state board's formulation of seven core principles of school redesign: 1) focus on challenging standards, 2) appropriate instruction, 3) a flexible system, 4) data- and research-based decision making, 5) professional development, 6) engaged parents, and 7) community involvement.

As a result of the board's focus on these principles, the agency has provided quality professional development for effective practices and effective school and classroom models. Specifically, the annual statewide conference, entitled "Closing the Gap," was the largest ever and was attended by over 1,100 educators, as compared to 400 in the past. KSDE also offered ongoing summer academies in core content areas, especially in the areas of reading and mathematics (required by NCLB). Highlighted at these academies were the redesigned state standards in reading and mathematics, both of which were completed this past year.

Strategic Direction 6 emphasized the continued need to form ongoing partnerships with congressional legislators, organizations, businesses, parents, and other stakeholders. The purpose is to ensure public confidence in Kansas education and to make everyone in the state collectively responsible for all children. One of the major accomplishments was meeting with the members of the federal congressional delegation on NCLB and IDEA (Individuals with Disabilities Education Act). Numerous media briefings have been held to inform the media about Kansas's results in relationship to NCLB. This upfront sharing has resulted in positive news articles about school improvement. A major stakeholder group of 25 was convened to develop a communication plan related to NCLB. A compact disc (CD) of parent-friendly materials has been disseminated to the field. Of greatest impact was the community conversation held in September 2003. Over 800 people representing teams from almost every district in the state and including parents, board members, teachers, and administrators engaged in a daylong conversation on how to ensure Kansas schools are not just good but great. The governor of Kansas kicked off the conversation, followed by Andy

Tompkins and Alexa Pochowski sharing the state of the state of education. Districts across the state are now replicating these community conversations.

ENABLING AND SUSTAINING CHANGE

The strategic directions aligned the education system in Kansas from top to bottom—from the state board of education to KSDE to the field, including districts, schools, statewide educational organizations (e.g., PTA), institutions of higher education, and regional educational service centers. Underneath the strategic directions was an important value: what will be best for students and what will be best for the schools. The strategic directions provide a frame of reference for decision making and responding to external trends. The directions focus the work within KSDE and are used as a basis for reporting results to the Kansas State Board of Education and communicating with the field.

Frame of Reference for Decision Making and Responding to External Trends

The strategic directions provided a powerful anchor during turbulent times. They were a resonant frame of reference for responding to the pressures in the educational environment. For example, the commissioner and assistant commissioner presented the strategic directions to stakeholders in the compelling context of NCLB and changes in the school accreditation process (QPA). As Alexa Posny points out, "The strategic directions regrounded people in what's important. When people are negative about NCLB, we can use the strategic directions to ask the questions about what's good for kids."

Focus for the Work within KSDE

The strategic directions are used at multiple levels of concreteness to impact the work within the agency. The following examples show how the leadership has embedded the strategic directions in the everyday life of the agency.

- Members of the leadership team reference agenda items to the strategic directions at their meetings. The meeting agendas literally have the directions listed, and topics are cross-referenced to show the connection.
- The strategic directions are posted on the main, first-floor bulletin board. They are very visible to employees and visitors to KSDE. Apparently this represents quite a coup!
- The strategic directions show up in conversations. As ideas are presented for consideration, the question is routinely asked, "Where is this taking us in terms of our strategic directions?"
- The education system in Kansas represents interlocking levels; a change to one level ripples through the others. As an example, program consultants in the areas of special education (SPED), state and federal programs, and school improvement are now working as an integrated team. When this team makes site visits to the field, the district personnel with responsibility for SPED, state and federal programs, and school improvement all must be in the room together—looking at a school's data in their entirety as well as their own piece—increasing the likelihood of a more coordinated effort on behalf of principals, teachers, and students.

Reporting Results and Communicating with the Field

The strategic directions are meaningful to the Kansas State Board of Education, the members of KSDE, and the field. After the future search, the assistant commissioner showed how the strategic directions were fulfilling the board's goals and principles.

Twice a year KSDE reports to the Kansas State Board of Education on the progress staff have made toward reaching the strategic directions. In talking with the public and other stakeholders, members of KSDE frame the topics formally and informally with the strategic directions. For example, at a recent statewide curriculum meeting, conversation was about highly qualified personnel and best practices, two of the strategic directions.

In summary, the strategic directions have three strong attributes: They provide certainty about where the agency is headed, there is a great deal of buy-in within KSDE and the field, and they are worded in a way that is meaningful and easily accessible. These attributes make the directions relevant and usable for the system. At the future search the group was asked, "What is the right role for KSDE?" Now KSDE is *being* that role.

LEADERSHIP ADVICE

At a follow-up meeting with Andy Tompkins approximately a year after the future search, we asked what advice he had for others who might consider this methodology when faced with the need to do futures planning:

- If you work hard to get the right people in the room, the results of the meeting will be validated in the larger system.
- The real leadership part of this is using the results—*doing it*. Be relentless in keeping the focus.
- Keep people thinking about things larger than themselves, or else what is on their plates will consume them.

CONSULTANT REFLECTIONS

In reflecting on our work with KSDE, the following stood out to us regarding leadership, conference purposes, and adapting conference activities.

Leadership: Holding a Future Focus in a Disturbing Present

As mentioned earlier, the purpose of the future search was to redefine the role, particularly the leadership role, of KSDE. By choosing to go forward with this conference in the face of severe financial conditions and significant regulatory pressures, the top leadership team of KSDE was already demonstrating a new level of leadership. It was leading with a future focus, even while it and its stakeholders were reeling from disturbing developments in the present.

Every future search can be seen as an act of courage on the part of leaders who convene a large group of external stakeholders to create a future together. Leaders publicly face the current reality in all of its glory—both in terms of what works about what they have been doing and what really doesn't.

When the question arose, "How can we do a future search at a time like this?" The leadership answer was, "How can we *not* go through with our future search at a time like this?"

On the first day of the future search, Andy Tompkins challenged participants to acknowledge the difficulties of the present while also focusing on a better future that would happen only if they worked together. The courage and focus of Andy Tompkins and his top leadership team inspired us and reminded us that to convene a future search is always a bold act of leadership.

What Kind of Help Do You Want?

In designing the future search conference agenda, we worked with the planning group to determine the level and types of input they wanted from future search participants. While the agency was genuinely seeking guidance from the various stakeholder groups on their future role, it was not starting with a blank slate. The planning group decided to ask for two things from participants: to help cocreate the strategic directions (shaping the future role) for KSDE and to help generate a list of options for realizing those directions—the idea pool. Into this pool went a number of ideas that had been floating around throughout the conference, as well as other ideas specifically focused on how to generate this information. Following the future search, the agency staff took the time to thoughtfully integrate its current commitments into the strategic directions and began to select ideas from the idea pool that would move them forward.

In each of the future searches we have supported as consultants, there is always a question about the level of detail that planning group members are considering. The learning from this case is to frame this design question for the planning group even more clearly. There is a continuum of the kinds of help participants in a future search can provide—from simply helping to generate goals or directional statements to providing potential ideas or strategies for getting to those goals, all the way to cocreating goals, strategies, and actual tasks moving forward.

What we saw again is that there is no one right answer about how far to go in the planning process. What is right depends on the realities and needs of the organization convening the future search.

The State of the State Activity

As mentioned earlier, included in this conference was an activity called State of the State. The activity used the Kansas State Board of Education goals to create a shared picture of what was currently happening across the state and possibilities for the future. This activity served four important purposes:

- By using the board's goals as a frame of reference, the ultimate outcomes—the strategic directions for KSDE—were more likely to be aligned.
- The current best practices and future possibilities provided a rich information base for shaping the role of KSDE.
- The activity affirmed current efforts and sparked positive thoughts about the future.
- The information helped people think wisely, build on strengths, and dream of the future.

CONCLUSION

On September 4, 2001, we had our first conversation with Andy Tompkins about a future search. During the course of the discussion we asked a number of questions, including, "How will you know if you have been successful in this work? What will be different as a result of having done this?" In a follow-up memo, we summarized his responses:

- It will help us get at the deeper questions: What is our role in anticipating what is needed in the field?
- The ultimate leadership: We can help our multiple constituencies work with us to see a preferred future and help us move from compliance to meaningful assistance.
- The outcomes would be a reference point for improvement efforts: We would first visualize a picture of what we want in the future and then back into a solution or approach. This would enable us to move from a reactive, problem-solving mode to a more proactive, future-oriented, and integrated approach to our improvement efforts.

- People would have pictures of the future and be able to walk toward them together. It would not only be my role to keep the focus, but rather it would be a shared responsibility.

Because of the future search conference, these deeper aspirations were realized in the form of the strategic directions and the subsequent results and broader impacts. These outcomes are now shaping the next phase of KSDE's leadership journey.

Epilogue: Engaging the System by Changing Conversations in School Districts

Kim Martens, Nancy Aronson, and Rita Schweitz

If we keep doing what we've always done, we'll always get what we've already got.

—Anonymous

FUTURE SEARCH: THE NEXT GENERATION IN STRATEGIC PLANNING

Future search represents an opportunity to "walk the talk" of effective teaching and learning. Every day, educators are working to apply the next generation of what is known about this. Teachers are going beyond rote memorization and engaging students in higher-level thinking and knowledge construction. They are emphasizing self-management of learning where students work independently to meet standards rather than fostering dependency on authority for the right answer. The work of cooperative learning is also evolving as students refine their capabilities as team players and contributors to the learning of others. Building administrators and teachers are working to apply these principles to themselves and their students as they aspire to create learning communities in their schools by actively engaging in meaningful dialogue, sharing what works, and discovering possibilities for the future. This modeling at the school level impacts what happens at the classroom level. What does this have to do with future search?

Future search models these principles of effective teaching and learn-ing on a system level. It goes well beyond members of the system pro-viding input. It is a real-time experience for the educational community in sharing information, analyzing what it means, and drawing conclusions. People have their perspectives broadened by interacting with others with different views. Mapping the larger environment in all of its glorious com-plexity helps to heighten the collective confusion that can lead to new pos-sibilities. Future search offers your community a real-time experience of working in groups, engaging in dialogue, discovering common ground, and crafting a vision for the future.

As leaders of change in a classroom, a school, or a district, you pay at-tention to the process as well as the results. Yes, you want the results of higher test scores as a measure of student achievement. *And*, you want the critical by-products of efficacy, stronger relationships, and a sense of community because these are at the heart of sustainability and making other things possible over time. They are also at the heart of our human-ity. Future search offers a method that seamlessly combines a focus on process and results.

Additionally, the principles and practices of future search address some of the limitations of previous planning models, particularly those involv-ing outside stakeholders. Future search addresses administrators' fear of opening up "their" systems by clearly delineating the boundaries and re-sponsibilities of all stakeholders. Community stakeholders play a vital role in shaping and implementing the future direction of the district. How-ever, they do not write action plans for other groups, nor do they tell them what to do. As described in many of the cases in this book, new relation-ships are developed and nurtured in this process as information and ex-pectations are openly shared. The trust that's developed as people work to-gether and appreciate their similarities and differences is the basis for positive change.

In previous planning models, plans were very detailed, leaving little room for input and creativity by those who would actually be implement-ing the action. This level of detail made adapting to rapidly changing ex-ternal realities much more challenging. People in the district saw imple-menting the action plans as separate from their day-to-day planning and action, contributing to overload and fragmentation. In contrast, the out-comes of the future searches in this book provided both stability and focus. The level of detail did not restrict further development of new ideas or cause burn out.

RESULTS YOU CAN EXPECT FROM A FUTURE SEARCH

From the 16 case studies in this book and from other work with which we have been involved and are familiar, we know that school districts face many of the same issues. A review of the cases in this book highlights the following shared themes:

- Meeting the needs of all children—leaving no child behind.
- Student-centered curriculum—whole child through whole curriculum.
- Abundant resources—locating additional funding.
- Expansion and integration of technology.
- High-quality staff—"leaderful" organization.
- Safe schools.
- Schools as centers or hubs—partnering with community services.
- Readiness to learn—access to early childhood education.

The uniqueness in each case also demonstrates the flexibility of future search to address specific and emergent issues. We never know what solutions and actions future search will create. We do know that by the end of the future search conference, participants will have a shared understanding of the school district's past and present; a shared vision of the district's future; initial individual, group, and stakeholder commitments to action; and the voice of all other points of view in everyone's head.

In sharing information from all perspectives, everyone gains a new understanding of their interrelatedness and realizes that they are all in the "same boat" and can move forward only when they are all "rowing together in the same direction." They will have been immersed inside the whole system and will find it difficult to "unlearn" its importance.

COSTS

Costs are always a concern in the tight budgets of school systems. The costs of future search include facilities, food, supplies, printing, mailing, facilitator fees, and expenses. Administrators have found different ways to fund their future search and planning efforts. Some have used monies in their existing budgets that have been allotted for strategic planning, especially when state departments of education have mandated such efforts. Some have requested monies in their upcoming budgets. Some have looked to local, state, and national grantors for funding. Some have partnered with their communities for in-kind and donated services, such as space, food, preparation, printing, and administrative assistance.

Administrators must consider not only the costs involved in sponsoring a future search but also the costs involved in *not* sponsoring one. The value of getting the community's support for school system improvement is immeasurable. The progress recounted in our 16 chapters far exceeds the initial costs of the future searches. Administrators must ask themselves how much the future is worth to them and then creatively find ways to fund their efforts. As one administrator explained, he was convinced when he examined the potential "return on expectations." His goals justified the costs and he found a way to pay for them.

ADMINISTRATIVE EXPERIENCE

Many of the authors in this book are school district administrators who relate their successes and challenges in using future search for districtwide change. Their stories highlight their direct experiences. Leaders and participants do not need to become proficient in our methodology to be able to plan with it. Future search is based on the assumption that we do not need to teach people anything for them to be able to participate. They need only to show up and use the skills, experience, and motivation they already have. For some, participating in a future search before leading one has helped to reassure them that it works. For others, taking the three-day training workshop in managing a future search reinforced this assumption. Many simply engaged in the process and trusted that it was just what they needed to do.

We have found that school leaders embrace future search principles because they are congruent with their leadership philosophies and styles. The principles of "bringing the whole system in the room, exploring the whole elephant before seeking to fix any part, keeping common ground and future focus front and center, and encouraging self-management and responsibility for action" make sense to them. Leaders who have been willing to adopt these principles have made significant system break-throughs. No personality changes are required. No additional training is required.

A word of caution: Future search does not make up for weak leadership and should not be used by leaders afraid of losing control or by those who believe that solutions must come from outside experts.

SUPPORT, FOLLOW-UP, AND SUSTAINABILITY AFTER A FUTURE SEARCH CONFERENCE

Sustaining the momentum and implementing action after the future search conference is critical. We know that even without support, action happens. We also know that with intentional support, the likelihood of sustained action is much greater. We highly recommend that while planning the future search, there be a thoughtful effort for follow-up—one that models the planning and the future search conference. Supporting follow-up meetings and creating structures to help turn plans into action go a long way to sustaining the momentum for change initiated in the conference. The following methods have been used to sustain the implementation effort:

- Incorporating results into a district's regular operational planning process.
- Including goals from the future search conference in budget processes.
- Creating a steering group composed of the chairpersons of all the action groups.
- Connecting goals and results to other initiatives.
- Sponsoring additional future searches.
- Further developing action plans and implementation strategies.
- Informing the community about progress, highlighting synergy, discovering where further collaboration is needed and which emerging areas need to be addressed because of unanticipated changes in the environment. This can occur at regular district meetings, at regular

review meetings, at a one-day follow-up meeting nine months to a year after the future search conference, in newsletters, on listservs, and in local newspapers.

Frequently new relationships formed during the future search can result in actions that are not declared as part of the action plans. These actions are aligned with the common ground and initiated to achieve shared goals. Coordinating actions and communication among the diverse stakeholder groups improves the impact of the action.

The future search conference is not a substitute for rational planning processes—it is an umbrella for building commitment and a forum for working through the dynamic issues that are barriers to action. Strategic directions set in the conference are almost always reduced or combined afterwards as well as sequenced and prioritized. The conference is only the beginning of action.

REPLICABILITY OF FUTURE SEARCH

This book is the result of a call for stories to Future Search Network members about future searches in school districts. We are aware of well over 100 future searches in the education sector, many of which can be found at the Future Search Network web page (http://futuresearch.net/method/applications/index.cfm).

Future search is a flexible "tool" based on a set of principles and activities. These 16 diverse case studies illustrate many uses of future search in education. In some cases it was used for visioning and determining strategic futures; in other cases it was used to address critical issues, such as racism and health.

Future search has also been used at the building level within a school district; teachers have applied the principles to classrooms. It has been used for implementing school safety plans and for facilities planning. As illustrated in one case, the principles were applied to scheduling decisions, in another to launching a new program in biotechnology.

Future search can be an effective tool for curriculum development, particularly across the pre-K–12 or pre-K–16 continuum. It can be used for complex issues that involve "cross-boundary" or cross-stakeholder work where it is important for people to be on the same page to move forward. The possibilities are plentiful!

As successful as future search can be, there are certain conditions under which we would not recommend its use. We would not run a future search if:

- The leader is the only one who has energy and commitment.
- Leadership is not committed to using the results.
- There is a predetermined answer (e.g., set of goals) and leadership is hoping the conference participants come up with the same ones.
- There are no compelling reasons for bringing people together to discover common ground and take action other than a state mandate.

NEXT STEPS

If you are intrigued with the possibility of future search for your system, we would like to suggest some of the following steps:

- Contact any of our contributors (see the contributor contact information at the end of the book).
- Check the Future Search Network web page: www.futuresearch.net.
- Become a member of the Future Search Network, with access to the *Future Search Newsletter*, the listserv, and the conference database.
- Read books about future search.

CLOSING THOUGHT

In *Change Forces: The Sequel* (1999), Michael Fullan eloquently describes how easy it is for educators to experience overload and fragmentation. And it is also possible for them to experience energy, commitment. and coherence! Educational leaders want others deeply and constructively engaged in helping the next generation to have the best education possible. Leaders can encourage the kind of engagement that leads to ownership and action by shifting the conversation from "What's wrong?"

to "What's possible?" and from "Who do we blame?" to "How can we partner together to create a better future?" These ideas are simple but not easy. Future search, by its structure and principles, can help. As demonstrated by the cases in this book, future searches are rich, informing learning opportunities that energize and renew a school district and its community.

References

Axelrod, R. H. (2000). *Terms of engagement: Changing the way we change organizations.* San Francisco: Berrett-Koehler.

Barth, R. S. (1990). *Improving schools from within: Teachers, parents and principals can make the difference.* San Francisco: Jossey-Bass.

Bennis, W., & Mische, M. (1995). *The 21st Century Organization: Reinventing through reengineering.* San Diego: Pfeiffer.

Bohm, D. (1996). *On dialogue.* New York: Rutledge.

Bridges, W. (1991). *Managing transitions.* Reading, MA: Addison-Wesley.

Bridges, W. (1992). *The character of organizations: Using Jungian type in organizational development.* Palo Alto, CA: CPP Books.

Bunker, B. B., & Alban, B. T. (Eds.). (1992). Special issue: Large group interventions. *The Journal of Applied Behavioral Science, 28,* 471–591.

Bunker, B. B., & Alban, B. T. (1997). *Large group interventions: Engaging the whole system for rapid change.* San Francisco, CA: Jossey-Bass.

Charan, R., & Colvin, G. (1999, June 21). Why CEO's fail. *Fortune Magazine,* 68–78.

Collins, J. (2001). *Good to great: Why some companies make the leap . . . and others don't.* New York: Harper Business.

Cooperrider, D., & Whitney, D. (1999). *Appreciative inquiry.* San Francisco: Berrett-Koehler.

Dannemiller, K., & McNeil, J. (1998). *Beginning to develop whole-scale change competencies.* Unpublished manuscript.

Edwards, C., Gandini, L., & Forman, G. (Eds.). (1993). *The hundred languages of children: The Reggio Emilia approach to early childhood education.* Norwood, NJ: Ablex.

Ellinor, L., & Gerard, G. (1998). *Dialogue: Discovering the transforming power of conversation.* New York: John Wiley & Sons.

Eoyang, G. H. (2002). *Conditions for self-organizing in human systems.* Unpublished doctoral dissertation, Union Institute and University.

Evans, R. (1996). *The human side of school change: Reform, resistance, and the real-life problems of innovation.* San Francisco: Jossey-Bass.

Falk, I. (2003). *Social capital and the family support field.* Chicago: Family Support America.

Federal Register. (1999). *Assistance to states for the education of children with disabilities,* at www.ed.gov/legislation/FedRegister/finrule/1999–2/062499a.html (accessed June 24, 1999).

Fullan, M. (1999). *Change forces: The sequel.* New York: RoutledgeFalmer.

Fullan, M. (2001). *Leadership in a culture of change.* San Francisco: Jossey-Bass.

Fullan, M. (2003). *Change forces with a vengeance.* New York: RoutledgeFalmer.

Future Search Network website. (2003). www.futuresearch.net/method/success/index.cfm (accessed August 17, 2003).

Gladwell, M. (2000, 2002). *The tipping point: How little things can make a big difference.* Boston: Little, Brown and Bay Back Books.

Goldsmith, M. (1996). Ask, learn, follow up and grow. In F. Hesselbein, M. Goldsmith, & R. Beckhard (Eds.), *The leader of the future: New visions, strategies, and practices for the next era.* San Francisco: Jossey-Bass.

Goleman, D., Boyatzis, R., & McKee, A. (2002). *Primal leadership: Realizing the power of emotional intelligence.* Boston: Harvard Business School Press.

Greenleaf, R. (1977). *Servant leadership.* Mahwah, NJ: Paulist Press.

Hamel, G., & Prahalad, C. K. (1994). *Competing for the future.* Boston: Harvard Business School Press.

Healthy bodies, minds, and buildings. (March 2000). *Educational Leadership, 57,* (6).

Healthy Learners Board. (2002) *Healthy learners board: Improving student achievement by improving student health in Minneapolis public schools.* [Brochure]. Minneapolis, MN: Author.

Healthy learners board website. www.healthylearner.org (accessed July 1, 2003).

Hesselbein, F. (Ed.). (1996). *The leader of the future.* San Francisco: Jossey-Bass.

Isaacs, W. (1999). *Dialogue and the art of thinking together.* New York: Doubleday.

Jacobs, R. (1994). *Real time strategic change: How to involve an entire organization in fast and far-reaching change.* San Francisco: Berrett-Koehler.

Jaworski, J. (1996). *Synchronicity: The inner path of leadership.* San Francisco: Berrett-Koehler.

Johnson, S. (2001). *Emergence: The connected lives of ants, brains, cities and software.* New York: Touchstone.

Kloth, C. (2000). *Working together: A new look at the old news.* Columbus, OH: ChangeWorks of the Heartland.

Koestenbaum, P. (2000). *The Leadership Diamond®2000,* at www.pib.net/model .htm (accessed February 5, 2003).

McDaniels, Gene (1969). *Compared to what.* Recorded by Les McCann and Eddie Harris, Atlantic Jazz 1537-2.

Meyer, C. (1994, May–June). Measuring corporate performance: How the right measures help teams excel. *Harvard Business Review, 94,* 305.

Mintzberg, H., Ahlstrand, B., & Lampel, J. (1998). *Strategy safari.* New York: The Free Press.

Nation's Cities Weekly: Official Publication of the National League of Cities, 22 (45). (1999, November 8). Washington, DC, p. 10.

Nelson, J., Essien, J., Loudermilk, R., & Cohen, D. (2002). *The public health competency handbook: Optimizing individual and organizational performance for the public's health.* Atlanta, GA: Affiliated Graphics, Inc./KITS.

New, R. (1990). Excellent early education: A city in Italy has it. *Young Children, 45* (6), 4–10.

Office of the Governor of the State of Ohio (1992, August 21). *Head Start—State of Ohio collaboration project search conference summary: A shared vision of collaborative service delivery.* Columbus: State of Ohio.

Olson, E., & Eoyang, G. (2001). *Facilitating organization change: Lessons from complexity science.* San Francisco: Jossey-Bass/Pfeiffer.

Pearce, T. (2003). *Leading out loud.* San Francisco: Jossey-Bass.

Oshry, B. (1996). *Seeing systems.* San Francisco: Berrett-Koehler.

Pascale, R. T., Millemann, M., & Gioja, L. (2000). *Surfing the edge of chaos: The laws of nature and the new laws of business.* New York: Crown Business.

Perley, W. (2003, January 8). Major reforms empower students at Lester B. Pearson School Board. *The Gazette,* (Montreal, Canada), pp. A10–11.

Perme, C. M. (1998). Whole system change: A case study in the use of large group interventions and OD methodologies to effect change in a local school district. *OD Practitioner: The Journal of the Organization Development Network, 30* (2), 12–17.

Public Education Network. (2002, October 31). *Position paper, Schools as centers of community life,* at www.publiceducation.org/papersopeds-schoolcenters .asp (accessed August 26, 2003).

Putnam, R. D. (2000). *Bowling alone.* New York: Simon & Schuster.

Reina, D., & Reina, M. (1999). *Trust and betrayal in the workplace.* San Francisco: Berret-Koehler.

Schlechty, P. (1991). *Schools for the 21st century: Leadership imperatives for educational reform.* San Francisco: Jossey-Bass.

Search Institute website. www.search-institute.org/assets (accessed October 23, 2003).

Senge, P. M. (1990). *The fifth discipline: The art and practice of the learning organization.* New York: Doubleday/Currency.

Senge, P. M., Kleiner, A., Roberts, C., Ross, R. B., & Smith, B. J. (1994). *The fifth discipline fieldbook.* New York: Doubleday/Currency.

Siedman, K. (2002, October 24). Students begin to make voices heard at school boards. *The Gazette* (Montreal, Canada), p. A6.

Solomon, P. (2001). Healthy start operational grant proposal.

Splett & Associates. (2002, October). *Evaluation of the healthy learners asthma initiative.* St. Paul, MN: Patricia L. Splett.

Svendsen, A., & Laberge, M. (2003, May). *Co-creating power: Engaging stakeholder networks for learning & innovation.* Collective Wisdom Initiative Seed Paper, at www.collectivewisdominitiative.org/social_application.htm (accessed September 4, 2003).

Weisbord, M. (1987). *Productive workplaces: Organizing and managing for dignity, meaning, and community.* San Francisco: Jossey-Bass, Inc.

Weisbord, M. (1992). *Discovering common ground.* San Francisco: Berrett-Kohler.

Weisbord, M., & Janoff, S. (1995). *Future search: An action guide to finding common ground in organizations and communities.* San Francisco: Berrett-Kohler.

Welch, M. (2001). *Knitting together fragmented services: Full service and community schools.* Harvard Graduate School of Education, at www.gse.harvard.edu/news/features/welch05172001.html (accessed August 21, 2003).

Wenger, E., McDermott, R., & Snyder, W. M. (2002). *Cultivating communities of practice.* Boston: Harvard Business School Press.

Wheatley, M. J. (1992). *Leadership and the new science.* San Francisco: Berrett-Koehler.

Wheatley, M. J. (2002). *Turning to one another: Simple conversations to restore hope to the future.* San Francisco: Berrett-Koehler.

Vogelsang, J. (2003, February 26). *Fostering sustainable and resilient nonprofits.* New York: Support Center for Nonprofit Management.

Yankelovich, D. (1999). *The magic of dialogue: Transforming conflict into cooperation.* New York: Simon & Schuster.

Index

Essien, Joyce, 145
equality, *xv*, xviii, 159, 161, 165,
170–73
equity, 159, 161, 165, 170–73, 188
Equity Action Plan, 187–89, 191

Falk, Ian, 93
Families and Children First Initiative,
227–28, 230
food programs, 92, 103, 131–32,
239–40
follow up. *See* accomplishments
Forty Developmental Assets Program.
See Search Institute
foundations. *See* grants
fragmentation, 5, 71–72, 83, 89, 252,
257, 264, 274, 277
fragmentation–coherence continuum,
265
Franklin County (OH) Board of
Mental Retardation &
Developmental Disabilities,
234–36, 240
Fullan, Michael, 35, 76, 84, 121, 257,
291
funding: blended, 81, 233–34, 236;
collaborative (*see* funding,
blended); constraints, xx, 3–4, 98,
161, 165, 168–69, 174, 287–88;
equalization, 57; formula, 21, 24,
58, 67; government, 21, 67–68,
227; private, 81, 129, 135, 149,
155; shared (*see* funding, blended)
future search: adaptations, 271; costs,
55, 287–88; dilemmas and
challenges around planning for,
22–24; network, xiv, xx, xxiii, 43,
55, 179, 290–91, 294; parallel
conferences xxiii, 22, 24, 43;

principles, xxi; replicability, 291;
roots, xxii; variation, 186

Gantt chart, 43, 49–50, *52*
Gioja, Linda, 206
goals: institutionalized, 3–6; purpose
vs. goals, 82
Goethe, 177
Goleman, Daniel, 114
governance, 121, 152, 156, 195, 236,
259, 261–66
grants, 93, 141, 147, 150, 235; 21st
Century Grant, 101, 134–35; Allina
Foundation, 141, 147; California
Community Foundation, 135;
Center for Disease Control through
the Lung Association of
Minnesota, 150; Children's
Defense Fund through the Robert
Woods Johnson Foundation, 147;
Colorado Foundation for Families
and Children, 96; The Educational
Foundation of the Los Angeles
County Office of Education, 135;
Federal Substance Abuse and
Mental Health Administration
Grant, 134; Healthy Families
Grant, 134; Healthy Learners
Board, 150; Healthy Start Grant,
123, 125, 128–29, 134; Los
Angeles Care Grant, 131, 134;
Naperville (IL) Education
Foundation, 113; Nebraska
Foundation for Families and
Children Grant, 98, 113; Peter
Kiewit Foundation Grant, 101;
Safe Schools, Healthy Students,
14; San Gabriel (CA) Foundation,
126–27, 135; San Gabriel (CA)

About the Editors

Kim Martens has over 20 years of facilitation, training, and community development experience. She has worked both in Canada and internationally and has extensive experience working in cross-cultural settings with diverse groups. Her work has focused mainly on participatory planning, issue-based stakeholder meetings, children's rights, program design and evaluation, and organizational analysis. She has managed over 30 future searches in Canada, Africa, and Asia. Kim has acted as a mentor to over a dozen facilitators. She has cofacilitated five "Managing a Future Search" workshops. She is a columnist for *FutureSearching* and is one of the founding members of the Southern Ontario Future Search Network.

Kim Martens, Facilitation and Training Consultant
8 Balfour Court
Guelph, ON N1L 1A9
Canada
tel: 519-837-9566 / e-mail: martenskim@rogers.com / website: www
    .martensconsulting.ca

Rita Schweitz specializes in planning and facilitating meetings and conferences that produce desired results. With over 20 years of national and international experience, she specializes in bringing the whole system together to establish collaborations, find common ground, and move quickly to action. Her work often includes diverse stakeholders and emphasizes

303

client ownership of the process and implementation of the results. Rita has managed over 35 future searches, including 10 in education. Rita is a founding member of Future Search Network, a certified member of Associated Consultants International, and a Certified Professional Facilitator™ by the International Association of Facilitators. She has published numerous articles in professional journals and books.

Rita Schweitz, Rita Schweitz Facilitating & Consulting
International Association of Facilitators—Certified Professional Facilitator™
3574 South Poplar Street
Denver, CO 80237
tel: 303-300-2200 / fax: 303-756-0307 / e-mail: rita@schweitzfacilitating .com; website: schweitzfacilitating.com

Contributor Contact Information

Nancy Aronson
Arsht/Aronson: Organization and Community Change Consultants
2150 Diamond Rock Hill Rd., Malvern, PA 19355, U.S.A.
tel: 610-296-7533; fax: 610-296-7354; e-mail: naronson1@cs.com

Beverly Kamens Arsht
Arsht/Aronson: Organization and Community Change Consultants
285 Highview Dr., Radnor, PA 19087, U.S.A.
tel: 610-687-5571; fax: 610-687-4461; e-mail: barsht1@comcast.net

Emily Moore Axelrod
Vice President, Axelrod Group
723 Laurel Ave., Wilmette, IL 60091, U.S.A.
tel: 847-251-7361; fax: 847-251-7370; e-mail: emily@
    axelrodgroup.com

Rosemarie M. Barbeau
Organization Development Consultant
18715 Vasquez Ct., Salinas, CA 93908, U.S.A.
tel: 831-455-1386; fax: 831-455-1382; e-mail: rbarbeau1@aol.com

Mary Ann (Meyer) Bobosky
President and CEO, Advocates Building Communities, Inc.
50 West Chicago Ave.
Naperville, IL 60540, U.S.A.
tel: 630-997-3420; fax: 630-357-3114; e-mail: maryann@
  advocatesbc.com

Claudia Chowaniec
Business and Strategic Planning Consultant
285 Clemow Ave., Ottawa, Ontario, K1S 2B7, Canada
tel: 613-233-9378; fax: 613-233-6033; e-mail: precept@sympatico.ca

Sandra Joy Garvey Crowther
Executive Director, Planning and Program Improvement
Lawrence Public School System
110 McDonald Dr., Lawrence, KS 66044, U.S.A.
tel: 785-832-5000; fax: 785-832-5016; e-mail: scrowthe@usd497.org

Pat Deans
Director of Community Services, Lester B. Pearson School Board
1925 Brookdale Ave., Dorval, Quebec, H9P 2Y7, Canada
tel: 514-422-3000; e-mail: pdeans@lbpsb.qc.ca

Michael George Erwin
Administrative Director, Middle Bucks Institute of Technology
Jamison, PA 18929, U.S.A.
tel: 215-343-2480; fax: 215-343-8628; e-mail: mgerwin@comcast.net

Karen Symms Gallagher, Emery Stoops, and Joyce King-Stoops Dean
Rossier School of Education, University of Southern California.
Waite Phillips Hall, Suite 1100, Los Angeles, CA 90089-0031, U.S.A.
tel: 213-740-5756; fax: 213-821-2158; e-mail: rsoedean@usc.edu

Ray Gordezky
Organizational Learning Consultant
26A Westwood Ln., Richmond Hill, Ontario, L4C 6X9, Canada
tel: 905-771-0162; fax: 905-771-1142; e-mail: Ray-g@rogers.com

Jim Grieve
Director of Education
Peel District School Board, HJA Brown Education Centre
5056 Hurontario St., Mississauga, Ontario, L5R 1C6, Canada
tel: 905-890-1010, ext. 2005; fax: 905-890-6698; e-mail:
  jim.grieve@peelsb.com

Sally H. Hilderbrand
Assistant to the Superintendent for Curriculum, Instruction, and
  Assessment
Perkiomen Valley School District
3 Iron Bridge Dr., Collegeville, PA 19426, U.S.A.
tel: 610-489-8506, ext. 1104; fax: 610-489-2974; e-mail:
  shilderbrand@pvsd.org

Sandra Janoff
Codirector, Future Search Network
9 Arthurs Round Table, Wynnewood, PA 19096, U.S.A.
tel: 610-896-7034; fax: 610-658-0991; e-mail: sjanoff@futuresearch.net

Vera Jashni
Management and Leadership Consultant
P.O. Box 3620, Thousand Oaks, CA 91359, U.S.A.
tel: 805-492-9358; fax: 805-492-9378; e-mail: jashni91360@msn.com

Jean Y. Katz
Jean Katz Consulting
10383 Rochester Ave., Los Angeles, CA 90024, U.S.A.
tel: 310-276-7941; fax: 310-205-0539; e-mail: jeankatz@earthlink.net

Chris Kloth
Senior Partner, ChangeWorks of the Heartland
250 South Virginialee Rd., Columbus, OH 43209-2052, U.S.A.
tel: 614-239-1336, ext.1; fax: 614-237-2347; e-mail:
  chris@got2change.com

Rebecca Love
Director, Early Childhood Education
Franklin County Board of Mental Retardation and Developmental
   Disabilities
2879 Johnstown Rd., Columbus, OH 43219, U.S.A.
tel: 614-475-0564, ext. 449; fax: 614-475-5702; e-mail:
   BLovefcbmr@aol.com

James Gordon Merritt
Retired Superintendent of Schools, North Platte, NE
   2307 Hardison Dr., Norfolk, NE 68701, U.S.A.

Sara E. Stoltzfus Mullett
Director, Health-Related Services
Minneapolis Public Schools
2225 E. Lake St., Minneapolis, MN 55407, U.S.A.
tel: 612 668-0851; fax: 612 668-0855; e-mail: Smullett@
   mpls.k12.mn.us

Kenoli Oleari
Senior Partner, Horizons of Change
Organization and Community Change Consultants
1801 Fairview St., Berkeley, CA 94703, U.S.A.
tel: 510-601-8217; fax: 510-595-8369; e-mail: kenoli@igc.org

James Edward Parry
Retired Superintendent of Schools
Principal and Owner, Organizational Consulting Ltd.
P.O. Box 743, Carson City, NV 89702, U.S.A.
tel and fax: 775-841-0770; e-mail: jparry@sbcglobal.net

Catherine M. Perme
Human Systems Dynamics Institute
50 East Golden Lake Rd., Circle Pines, MN 55014, U.S.A.
toll-free tel: 866-HSDINST; direct tel: 952-831-4131;
   e-mail: cperme@hsdinstitute.org; website: www.hsdinstitute.org

Alexa Posny
Assistant Commissioner, Kansas State Department of Education
120 SE 10th Ave., Topeka, KS 66612, U.S.A.
tel: 785-296-2303; fax: 782-296-1413; e-mail: aposny@ksde.org

Susan M. Rowan
Director of Programs, The Learning Partnership
90 Eglinton Ave. East, Suite 603
Toronto, ON M4P 2Y3, Canada
tel: 416-481-0799; fax: 416-482-5311
srowan@thelearningpartnership.ca

Ken Seeley
President and CEO, Colorado Foundation for Families and Children
303 East 17th Ave., Denver, CO 80203, U.S.A.
tel: 303-837-8466; fax: 303-837-8496; e-mail: kens@
   coloradofoundation.org

Shelley Sweet
President, Intercept Management Consulting
659 Ashton Ave., Palo Alto, CA 94306, U.S.A.
tel: 650-493-1300; fax: 650-494-0955; e-mail: shelleysweet@
   sbcglobal.net

Marvin R. Weisbord
Codirector, Future Search Network
530 Wynlyn Rd., Wynnewood, PA 19096-1317, U.S.A.
tel: 610-896-7035; fax: 610-658-0991; e-mail: mweisbord@
   futuresearch.net